for Skill Book 3

Long Vowel Sounds

Frank C. Laubach
Elizabeth Mooney Kirk
Robert S. Laubach

ISBN 0-88336-913-3

New Readers Press
Publishing Division of Laubach Literacy International
Box 131, Syracuse, New York 13210

Printed in the United States of America

Edited by Caroline Blakely and Kay Koschnick
Cover design by Chris Steenwerth
9 8 7 6 5 4 3 2 1

Table of Contents

SB indicates the page in *Skill Book 3.*

TM indicates the page in this teacher's manual.

The Laubach Way to Reading

The Laubach Way to Reading is a basic reading and writing series developed primarily for adults with little or no reading ability. The series consists of four skill books and correlated readers for student use. The teacher's manual for each skill book gives detailed instructions and lesson plans.

The series provides a systematic development of basic reading and writing skills. Each lesson includes vocabulary development, phonic or structural analysis of words, the reading of a short story, comprehension checks, and writing practice. The lessons progress from the sounds and regular spellings of basic consonants to those of the short vowels, the long vowels, and finally to irregular spellings and more difficult reading, writing, and grammar skills.

The skill books and correlated readers may be used with both speakers of English and those who are learning English. A separate series of manuals, the Laubach Way to English, provides complete instructions for teaching the skills of listening, speaking, reading, and writing English to the non-English-speaking student.

Although designed primarily for adults, the Laubach Way to Reading may also be used successfully with high school dropouts or students in intermediate grades who need remedial work in basic reading, writing, or spelling. Classroom teachers, teacher aides, and volunteer tutors may all use the books effectively.

Skill Book 1: Sounds and Names of Letters

Beginning on a zero level, *Skill Book 1* lays an essential foundation in word attack and comprehension skills. The names and one sound for each letter of the alphabet and the digraphs *ch, sh,* and *th* are introduced. Simple sentence patterns encourage fluency in reading. Blending of sounds, punctuation, silent reading, and manuscript writing are introduced. A total of 132 words is used.

Skill Book 2: Short Vowel Sounds

Lessons are structured around the short vowel sounds, *y* as a vowel as in *city,* and the *r*-controlled vowel sounds for *er, ir, ur,* and *ar.* The digraphs *ng* and *wh* are introduced, as are beginning and ending consonant blends. Simple skills of punctuation, structural analysis, comprehension, and sentence writing are introduced. A total of 192 new words is introduced.

Skill Book 3: Long Vowel Sounds

This book presents the long sounds for *a, e, i,* and *o* with their regular spellings, one regular spelling for long *u,* and the sound for *or* as in *York.* Comprehension skills include finding main ideas, summarizing content, recognizing implied meaning, developing opinions, and predicting outcome. Lessons include functional materials like ads, bills, menus, letters, and checks. A total of 399 new words is used. Cursive writing is taught at this level. For this, the student needs the separate cursive writing workbook, and the teacher the instruction book.

Skill Book 4: Other Vowel Sounds and Consonant Spellings

This book continues with the regular spellings for the long *u* sound and goes on to the letter combinations *oo, ou, aw, oi,* and their variant spellings. The book also covers different sounds represented by the same consonant symbol, such as the *s* in *see* and *please,* and regular spellings for consonant sounds that may be spelled in more than one way, such as the /k/ sound in *keep* and *can.*

Word analysis skills are strengthened by more work with contractions and compound words and by the student's becoming familiar with the most common prefixes and suffixes. Practice is given to increase reading speed.

Comprehension skills emphasized include making inferences, identifying cause and effect, drawing conclusions, and understanding the mood and atmosphere of a story. Also, students are helped to interpret the authors' opinion and to evaluate their own reactions to what they read.

Correlated Readers

The correlated reader for each skill book is a collection of stories or articles using much of the same vocabulary as the skill book. The correlated readers are an intrinsic part of the series as they provide opportunity for the student to gain confidence and independent reading habits.

About the Authors

More than 50 years of continuous experience in literacy education lie behind the Laubach Way to Reading. In 1930 in the Philippines, the late Frank C. Laubach (1884-1970) originated a method of teaching adults to read and write in their own language. After Laubach lessons had been used in some 300 languages, the method was applied to teaching in English. *Streamlined English* was published in 1946. In the 1960s, a complete revision and expansion, the New Streamlined English series, was published. The current Laubach Way to Reading series thus represents the third generation of Laubach curricula in English.

Author Elizabeth Mooney Kirk started working with Frank Laubach in 1945, developing *Streamlined English.* Her background includes master's degrees in education and journalism, developing adult literacy programs in India and Kenya, teaching adults and children, and training tutors and writers. Mrs. Kirk was co-author with Frank C. Laubach and Robert S. Laubach of the New Streamlined English series.

Co-author Robert S. Laubach is chairman of the board of Laubach Literacy International and founder of its New Readers Press division. He started his literacy work as a teenager in the Philippines and then assisted his father in literacy campaigns in some 50 countries. He has a doctorate in reading education and taught literacy journalism at the university level for 30 years.

REGULAR SPELLING OF VOWEL SOUNDS

	Sound	Examples	Regular Spelling
Short Vowels	i	in	i
	y	lily	y
	u	up	u
	e	egg	e
	a	apple	a
	o	olive	o
	er	fern, burn, bird	er, ur, ir
	ar	arms	ar
Long Vowels	ā	paper, day, paint, cake	a, ay, ai, a-e
	ē	we, tree, eat, key, Pete	e, ee, ea, ey, e-e
	ī, ȳ	I, my, tie, night, time	i, y, ie, igh, i-e
	ō, or	go, boat, snow, York, home	o, oa, ow, or, o-e
	ū	music, argue, few, cure	u, ue, ew, u-e
Other Vowels	ū *or* oo	news, due, tuition	ew, ue, u
	oo	moon	oo
	uu	book	oo
	ou	cloud, town	ou, ow
	aw	auto, paw, all, walk	au, aw, a(ll), a(lk)
		bought	ough(t)
	oi	oil, boy	oi, oy

This chart shows the regular spelling of vowel sounds taught in the Laubach Way to Reading. Generally, the vowel sounds are taught in the order of frequency of their use. When vowel sounds are spelled in more than one way, the spellings that occur most frequently are taught first.

Principles on Which Laubach Lessons are Based

Establishing letter-sound relationships. The letters of the alphabet and the sounds they stand for are taught in a systematic manner. This series uses existing phonetic regularities, emphasizes regular spellings, and provides aids to irregular spellings.

Learning through association. Letters and sounds are presented through key words with picture associations.

Moving from the known to the unknown. The student starts with the spoken word, which he knows, and moves in short steps to the written word, which he does not know.

Familiar vocabulary. Words used are in the spoken vocabulary of the adult. Vocabulary is controlled, with a limited number of new words in each lesson.

Use of repetition to strengthen the visual image. Each word and sentence pattern is repeated several times soon after it is taught.

Use of meaningful content. From the beginning, reading for meaning is stressed.

Something new in each lesson. Each lesson teaches something new in a familiar lesson pattern.

Independence in learning. Visual aids, phonic skills, consistent lesson patterns, and uniformity of format make it easy for the student to help himself.

Lessons are easy to teach. The lessons are planned for maximum self-help and minimum teacher help. The detailed manuals for teachers make it possible for inexperienced teachers to use the materials successfully.

Books in the Laubach Way to Reading series will be available as they are developed. If you need a book not yet published, use one on the same level in the New Streamlined English series.

Introduction to Skill Book 3

Lessons in *Skill Book 3* present the long sounds for *a, e, i,* and *o* with their regular spellings, the long sound for *u* with one spelling (as in *music),* and the sound for *or* as in *York.*

The main new concept for the student is that a long vowel sound may be spelled in several ways. Each of these ways is presented in a chart with a formula to help the student read the words for himself. Systematic presentation of regular spelling patterns and simple rules help the student determine whether a vowel sound in a word is long or short.

More word recognition, comprehension, writing, and spelling skills are introduced. These are listed in detail in the chart called Skills Introduced or Reinforced in Skill Book 3 on pages 12-15. You may use this chart as a guide to your student's progress.

Materials Needed for This Level

Skill Book 3 has 24 lessons. Each chart that presents a vowel sound has a format similar to that in *Skill Book 2.* The first chart introduces all of the vowel sounds that are taught in this book.

As in previous skill books, the chart is followed by a story. The stories in this book are longer, with longer sentences and more variation in sentence patterns. Paragraphs are indented. Each story is followed by a written checkup. Comprehension is further developed as the student progresses from noting simple facts to finding main ideas, summarizing content, recognizing implied meaning, predicting outcome, and relating what he reads to his own experience and values.

Each lesson has a section called Reading for Living with a short functional reading selection and a related written exercise. Selections include menus, letters, ads, bills, and other practical materials.

The student does the writing lesson in a separate notebook. Instructions for the writing lesson are given in each lesson of this manual.

After each group of lessons on a particular vowel sound comes a lesson called More Reading. This lesson serves both as a review and as an opportunity for independent reading. There are four such lessons.

Skill Book 3 introduces 426 words and three symbols, not counting variants formed by adding known endings.

The correlated reader *Changes* is introduced in Lesson 22. (Replicas are not included in this manual.) *Changes* has two fictional stories and two factual stories. It introduces 117 additional new words.

Cursive writing is to be taught after Lesson 22 in the skill book is completed. The student uses a separate workbook, *Laubach Way to Cursive Writing;* instructions for teaching this workbook are found in the *Cursive Writing Teacher's Guide.* In Lesson 23-24 of *Skill Book 3,* cursive writing takes the place of dictation exercises. Alternative writing exercises are provided for students who have already learned cursive writing.

For an outline of how the first five cursive writing lessons mesh with the skill book and correlated reader, see page 125. While finishing the last four cursive writing lessons, teachers should follow the suggestions for using supplementary reading activities given in the section called Completing Level 3 on page 139.

Checkups for Skill Book 3, a separate booklet, should be given after the student completes *Skill Book 3* to help evaluate his progress in reading and writing. Directions for administering and scoring the *Checkups* follow the lesson plans in this manual.

Supplementary Materials

Focus on Phonics-3 and the *Workbook for Skill Book 3* of the Laubach Way to English series may be used as supplements to meet individual needs. Suggestions for their use are in the lesson plans.

Schedule

In most cases, a student can cover a lesson in a session of one to one-and-a-half hours. He will probably need an additional half hour for the homework. A student who has two or more sessions a week should be able to complete the skill book, correlated reader, and checkups in 12 to 15 weeks. Completing the cursive writing course will take an additional two or three weeks. It is important that the student cover each lesson and not skip through the skill book. The lessons are systematically organized to give him a foundation of independent reading skills.

General Plan for the Lessons

The sequence for the presentation of most lessons in *Skill Book 3* is as follows:

I. Reading	II. Skills Practice	III. Writing
Chart Story Story Checkup Reading for Living	Practice on phonics and word recognition skills	Check homework from previous lesson Writing lesson in separate notebook Practice exercise in skill book Homework assignment in skill book

The review lessons follow the same sequence but have no written exercises in the skill book. Supplementary practical materials are suggested for you to make or collect for the Reading for Living section. A worksheet called Review Practice is suggested for each review lesson. The Review Practices are given in the appendix on pages 140-143 in a form suitable for photocopying.

Each lesson plan suggests ways of checking the student's progress and reinforcing skills in which he needs more practice. The student should not be slowed down unnecessarily, however, in order to cover supplementary material.

RESPELLINGS

The self-help device of respelling new words continues in *Skill Book 3* in accordance with these policies:

- In Lesson 1, words are respelled in the same way as in *Skill Book 2*. That is, they are not divided into syllables, and double consonants are retained.

- Beginning in Lesson 1, a macron is used over a vowel letter to indicate the long vowel sound for that letter, as: *ā, ē, ī, (ȳ), ō, ū.*

- Beginning in Lesson 2, new words are divided into syllables.

- In *Skill Book 3,* a new word is respelled for one or more of these reasons:

1. The word contains a regular spelling that has not yet been taught. When a new word contains a two- or three-letter regular spelling for a long vowel sound, and that spelling has not yet been taught, the vowel letter is marked with a macron. For example, *say* is introduced before *ay* is taught, so it is respelled *sā.*

2. The word contains an irregular spelling. The irregular part of the word is respelled with the most similar regular spelling pattern that has been taught. For example, *ice* is respelled *ise* when the spelling *i-e (i*-consonant-silent *e)* has been taught for the long *i* sound, but the *c* needs to be respelled.

If, however, respelling the word with a regular pattern would result in another real word, the vowel letter is simply marked with a macron, as in *eight (āt), great (grāt),* and *peace (pēs).*

Only the part of the word that is irregular is respelled; any part that has already been taught is left as it is. For example, when *agree* is shown as *u gree,* the beginning sound needs to be respelled, but *ee* has already been taught as a spelling for long *e.*

3. The word contains a spelling that is regular for more than one sound. In the case of a long vowel sound spelled with the single letter *a, e, i, o,* or *u,* a macron is placed over the vowel letter to indicate that it stands for the long sound, not the short sound. Examples of this are *both (bōth), union (ūn yun),* and *even (ē ven).*

When *ow* stands for the long o sound, the *o* will always be marked with a macron, as in *own (ōwn),* to make sure that *ow* is not given the pronunciation it has in *down* (which will be taught in *Skill Book 4).*

4. The word contains a schwa sound that needs respelling to prevent a wrong pronunciation. The schwa sound, which can be represented by any of the vowel letters, occurs often in unstressed syllables. It is not respelled when the short sound for the vowel is not very different from the schwa sound, as in *eaten (eat en)* and *limit (lim it).* When it is necessary to respell the schwa sound, the letter *u* is used because the short sound for *u* is nearly the same as the schwa sound. Examples are *again (u gen)* and *Carla (Car lu).*

5. The word has more than one syllable and is divided into syllables to make it easier to read. In some cases, no other change is needed, as in *yesterday (yes ter day).*

A double consonant is respelled with one consonant as in *application (ap li cā shun)* and *arrive (u rive).* If these words were respelled with their double consonants as *ap pli cā shun* and *u rrive,* the student might try to pronounce two distinct sounds for *p* in *application* and might be confused by a syllable beginning with a double consonant *(rrive).*

6. The word is a compound word, made up of two smaller words. In the respelling, a compound word made up of two known words is simply divided between the known words for easier recognition. The known words are not respelled in any way nor divided further into syllables. An example is *timetable (time table).*

NOTES ON STYLE

Slash marks. Slash marks around a letter or letters indicate the sound for which they stand. Thus, you say /b/ like the beginning consonant sound in *bird* and /a/ like the beginning vowel sound in *apple.*

Italics. Letters in italic are read by their letter names, as *a, b, c.*

Abbreviations. Many of the instructions for teaching the lessons are given in dialog form. To save space, the letter *T* indicates *Teacher* and *S* indicates *Student.*

Brackets [ ] and parentheses ( ). Brackets are used to enclose the expected student response. Within dialog, parentheses are used to enclose what the teacher is expected to *do* but not to *say.*

Pronouns referring to *teacher* and *student*. Although the authors recognize that there are teachers and students of both sexes, they have chosen for the sake of brevity to use the pronoun *she* to refer to the teacher and *he* to refer to the student. In the skill book, stories and illustrations show both sexes in a variety of roles and activities.

SKILLS INTRODUCED OR REINFORCED IN SKILL BOOK 3

Phonics skills	Lesson	1	2	3	4	5	6	7	8	9	10	11	12	13	14	15	16	17	18	19	20	21	22	23 A	23 B	24 A	24 B
1. Recognize the long vowel sound /ā/ and its regular spellings:	*a* as in *paper*	•	•				•				•					•						•				•	
	ay as in *day*			•			•				•					•						•					
	ai as in *paint*				•		•				•					•						•					
	a-e as in *cake*					•	•				•					•						•					
2. Recognize the long vowel sound /ē/ and its regular spellings:	*e* as in *we*	•						•			•					•						•				•	
	ee as in *see*							•			•					•						•					
	ea as in *meat*								•		•					•						•					
	e-e as in *Pete*									•	•					•						•					
	ey as in *key*									•	•					•						•					
3. Recognize the long vowel sound /ī/ and its regular spellings:	*i* as in *I*	•										•			•	•						•				•	
	i-e as in *time*											•	•		•	•						•					
	ie as in *tie*													•	•	•						•					
	y as in *my*	•												•	•	•						•					
	igh as in *night*														•	•						•					
	i + nd as in *find*														•	•											
	i + ld as in *child*														•	•											
4. Recognize the long vowel sound /ō/ and its regular spellings:	*o* as in *go*	•															•					•				•	
	o-e as in *home*																	•		•		•					
	oa as in *boat*																		•	•		•					
	ow as in *snow*																			•		•					
	o + ld as in *old*																•			•							
5. Recognize the long vowel sound /ū/ and one regular spelling:	*u* as in *music*	•																					•			•	
6. Recognize the sound /or/ and its regular spellings:	*or* as in *York*	•																			•	•				•	
	ore as in *store*																				•	•					
7. Review *er, ir, ur* as spellings for the sound /er/					•								•														
8. Review digraphs *th* and *wh*								•																			
9. Recognize these new beginning consonant blends:	*sn* as in *snack*	•											•														
	sp as in *spent*			•			•				•																
	cr as in *cry*													•		•											
	fl as in *fly*													•		•											
	str as in *street*	•	•				•				•	•		•													
	thr as in *three*							•						•													
10. Review other beginning consonant blends		•	•	•	•	•	•	•			•	•	•	•	•	•											
11. Recognize these new ending consonant blends:	*lk* as in *milk*	•					•																				
	ld as in *child*														•	•	•					•					
	mp as in *camp*																			•		•					
12. Review other ending consonant blends		•		•			•					•	•		•	•				•	•	•					
13. Recognize sound for *le* in final syllable, as in *table*			•																								
14. Recognize sound for *ce* at end of word, as in *nice*													•			•											
15. Recognize rhyming words					•	•	•	•			•		•					•	•		•						

Word recognition skills / Lesson	1	2	3	4	5	6	7	8	9	10	11	12	13	14	15	16	17	18	19	20	21	22	23 A	23 B	24 A	24 B
1. Recognize words by blending sounds	•	•	•	•	•	•	•	•	•	•	•	•	•	•	•	•	•	•	•	•	•	•	•	•	•	•
2. Recognize same words by sight in context	•	•	•	•	•	•	•	•	•	•	•	•	•	•	•	•	•	•	•	•	•	•	•	•	•	•
3. Recognize the number of syllables in a word		•	•	•	•	•	•	•	•	•	•	•			•	•	•				•	•				
4. Recognize contractions	•						•			•				•	•	•	•		•	•	•	•		•		
5. Recognize compound words			•	•	•			•				•		•	•	•	•	•		•		•			•	
6. Recognize words joined by a hyphen, as *baby-sitter*		•																					•			•
7. Review endings, recognizing variants of root words:																										
— with *-s* or *-es*	•	•				•																				•
— with *-ing*			•			•				•	•		•				•									•
— with *-ed*				•		•				•							•									•
8. Recognize variants of root words:																										
— with noun ending *-er*								•		•	•													•		•
— with adjective ending *-er*												•			•					•	•	•		•		
— with adjective ending *-est*																				•	•	•		•		
— with adjective ending *-y*																		•	•		•					
— with adverb ending *-ly*																			•		•			•		
— with noun ending *-ness*																									•	
9. Recognize variants with final *y* changed to *i* before:																										
— verb or noun ending *-es (-ies)*													•	•	•							•				•
— verb ending *-ed (-ied)*													•	•	•											•
— adjective endings *-er* and *-est (-ier, -iest)*																										•
10. Recognize variants with *ie* changed to *y* before *-ing,* as in *die, dying.*															•											
11. Recognize root words in words with endings	•					•			•	•	•	•	•	•	•				•			•				
12. Recognize that verb forms ending in *en* are related to known verb forms, as in *eat, eaten*								•			•				•		•									
13. Recognize that prefixes *in-* and *non-* mean *not* in the words *injustice* and *non-violent*																										•
14. Recognize the symbols $ and ¢	•		•	•		•		•	•							•										
15. Recognize the symbol & (and)																				•						
16. Read times written with numbers and colon, as 1:30													•	•												
17. Recognize *a.m.* and *p.m.* and their meanings													•	•		•			•							
18. Recognize a few other simple abbreviations						•					•	•			•					•		•				•

Comprehension skills / Lesson	1	2	3	4	5	6	7	8	9	10	11	12	13	14	15	16	17	18	19	20	21	22	23 A	23 B	24 A	24 B
1. Recognize main idea of a paragraph	•	•	•	•	•	•	•	•	•	•	•	•	•		•		•		•							
2. Summarize the main ideas of a story	•	•		•	•	•	•	•	•	•	•		•	•	•	•	•	•	•						•	•
3. Read factual material to obtain information											•	•	•				•	•				•			•	•
4. Scan story or paragraph to find specific information	•	•	•	•	•	•				•	•	•										•	•	•	•	•
5. Recall important facts or details	•	•	•	•	•	•	•	•	•	•	•	•	•	•	•	•	•	•	•		•	•	•	•		
6. Read dialog and identify the speakers	•		•	•	•	•		•									•	•		•						
7. Identify the characters in the story	•	•			•	•						•	•					•				•				
8. Interpret the feelings of the characters							•			•			•	•	•						•		•	•	•	•
9. Interpret facts and draw inferences	•	•	•	•	•	•	•	•	•	•			•	•	•	•	•	•	•		•	•	•	•	•	•
10. Recall sequence of events									•				•		•	•	•	•	•	•						
11. Recognize cause and effect																	•		•	•	•		•	•	•	•
12. Predict outcomes																	•		•	•			•	•	•	•
13. Distinguish between fact and fiction											•	•										•			•	•
14. Understand figurative language in story																									•	•
15. Relate story to own experience, knowledge, values		•	•	•	•		•	•			•					•	•	•	•	•	•	•	•	•	•	•
16. Read orally with expression						•	•			•			•	•	•	•					•	•	•	•	•	•
17. Read and understand these practical everyday materials:																										
menu and prices	•					•																				
package directions with chart		•				•																				
checks			•			•																				
prices and quantities				•		•																				
personal letters					•										•									•		
numbers and number words							•	•		•																
grocery ad								•																		
repair bill									•																	
applications											•	•			•											
news item (obituary)													•													
air line timetable														•												
want ads for home furnishings																•					•					
instructions in case of fire																	•									
road map																		•								
traffic signs																			•		•					
store directory																				•						
map of North America																						•				
supplementary materials										•					•						•					

Note: In regard to the writing skills listed below, note that cursive writing begins immediately after Lesson 22 and continues over approximately nine lesson periods. Instruction is given in a separate workbook, the *Laubach Way to Cursive Writing*. In Lessons 23-24, cursive writing takes the place of dictation exercises. Alternative writing exercises are provided here for students who already know cursive writing. Neither cursive writing skills nor alternative exercises are listed below.

Writing and spelling skills — Lesson	1	2	3	4	5	6	7	8	9	10	11	12	13	14	15	16	17	18	19	20	21	22	23 A	23 B	24 A	24 B
1. Write words and sentences from dictation	•	•	•	•	•	•	•	•	•	•	•	•	•	•	•	•	•	•	•	•	•	•				
2. Write a paragraph from dictation																			•	•						
3. Fill in missing words or numbers in sentences	•	•	•	•	•	•	•	•		•	•	•	•	•	•	•		•	•	•				•		
4. Write short answers to questions	•	•	•	•	•			•	•		•	•	•			•	•	•	•	•	•	•	•	•	•	•
5. Write sentence answers to questions				•	•		•	•	•					•		•										
6. Write questions based on reading material						•				•				•												
7. Write original sentences						•									•						•					
8. Write a short summary of a story										•						•		•	•							
9. Use capital letters on names of days and months		•	•		•	•			•		•	•	•	•		•		•								
10. Use capital letters on place names											•	•	•	•		•		•				•				
11. Write prices and money amounts, using $ and ¢	•	•	•	•		•		•	•	•						•										
12. Write number words							•	•		•																
13. Write contractions, using apostrophe							•			•						•	•		•		•			•		
14. Write dates, spelling out month and using comma											•	•	•		•											
15. Write dates, using numerals for month, day, and year												•														
16. Write times with numerals, colon, and *a.m.* or *p.m.*													•	•	•	•										
17. Write a check			•																							
18. Write a short thank you letter					•																					
19. Fill in simple application forms												•			•											
20. Form new words by adding these endings: *-s* or *-es*	•	•				•																				•
-ing			•		•	•				•	•	•	•				•			•						•
-d or *-ed*				•		•				•		•					•			•						•
-r or *-er*								•			•	•			•					•	•	•		•		•
-est																				•	•	•		•		
-y																		•	•	•	•					
-ly																			•	•	•			•		
-ies (change *y* to *i*)													•	•	•							•				•
-ied (change *y* to *i*)													•		•											•
-ier, iest (change *y* to *i*)																										•
21. Know when to double final consonant before endings			•					•		•					•		•	•			•	•		•		•
22. Know when to drop final silent *e* before endings			•		•	•				•	•	•					•		•		•					•
23. Know when to use *k* or *ck* at end of word					•							•														

Study skills — Lesson	1	2	3	4	5	6	7	8	9	10	11	12	13	14	15	16	17	18	19	20	21	22	23 A	23 B	24 A	24 B
1. Follow written instructions	•	•	•	•	•	•	•	•	•	•	•	•	•	•	•	•	•	•	•	•	•	•	•	•	•	•
2. Keep a notebook for dictation and some homework	•	•	•	•	•	•	•	•	•	•	•	•	•	•	•	•	•	•	•	•	•	•				
3. Organize notebook page following oral instructions	•	•	•	•	•	•	•	•	•	•	•	•	•	•	•	•	•	•	•	•	•	•				
4. Alphabetize words																				•	•	•	•			
5. Locate words in an alphabetical list																							•	•	•	•
6. Use a table of contents																							•	•	•	•

LESSON 1 Skill Book 3 Pages 2-7

OBJECTIVES

To help your student:

- become acquainted with the long vowel sounds /ā/, /ē/, /ī/, /ō/, /ū/, and the vowel sound /or/.
- recognize that *y* sometimes stands for the sound /ī/.
- recognize the macron over a vowel letter (as in ā) as an aid in pronouncing long vowel sounds.
- recognize the vowels sounds in the following chart words, which were previously taught as sight words: *I, my, go, York.*
- read the new chart words *paper, we, music,* and identify the long vowel sound in each.
- read the new words in the lesson by applying phonics skills.
- recognize that the contraction *I'll* means *I will.*
- recognize the use of indentation for the beginning of a paragraph.
- summarize a story and identify characters.
- scan a story to find a certain paragraph.
- recognize the symbols $ and ¢.
- read and copy some prices.
- find and read some items on a simple menu.
- identify the long vowel sounds and the sound /or/ in spoken words.
- recognize the beginning consonant blends *sn* as in *snack* and *str* as in *street.*
- review the beginning blends *sm, st, dr, fr, cl, gl.*
- recognize the ending blend *lk* as in *milk*, and review the ending blends *nk, nt, sk, st.*
- review the endings *-s* and *-es.*
- write words and sentences from dictation.

INTRODUCTION

T: In *Skill Book 2*, you learned the short sound for each vowel. In *Skill Book 3*, you will learn the long sound for each vowel. (On title page, point to and read the full title, *Skill Book 3: Long Vowel Sounds.*)

I. Reading

CHART: Page 2

Title and vowel letters

T: The title in the top left-hand corner tells the lesson number. Please read it. [S. Lesson 1.]

T: Across the top of the page, you see the five vowel letters and one other letter that is sometimes a vowel. Please read the names of the five vowels. [S: *a, e, i, o, u.*]

T: When you read the names of the vowels, you also gave the long sounds /ā/, /ē/, /ī/, /ō/, /ū/. The long sound of the vowel is the same as its name.

T: (Point to *y (ī).*) But the long vowel sound for *y* is /ī/, not *y.*

T: What do you see over each letter? [S: A straight mark.] This mark tells you that the sound for the vowel is long. The vowel is not usually written with a line over it. But in this lesson it is written that way to help you know that the vowel sound is long. Soon you will learn some rules to help you know when the vowel sound is long. Then you won't need the mark.

T: This chart is arranged like the charts in *Skill Book 2.* In Lesson 1, the chart introduces all of the vowel sounds you will learn in this book. In the following lessons, each chart will help you study one vowel sound at a time.

Line 1

T: Look at the first picture and the word next to it. The third column will help you pronounce the word. What is the word? [S: paper.] How many sounds are there in the word *paper?* [S: Four.]

T: Say each sound as I point to the letter or letters for the sound. [S: /p/.../ā/.../p/.../er/.] How many vowel sounds are in the word? [S: Two.] Which vowel is long? [S: *a.*] How do you know it is long? [S: There is a mark over it.]

T: Under the word *paper*, you see the vowel *a.* What sound does *a* stand for in *paper?* [S: /ā/.] Good. Look at the last column, and read the word again. [S: paper.]

Line 2

T: Look at the next picture and word. If you need help in pronouncing the word, look at the third column. What is the word? [S: we.]

T: Look at the third column. How many sounds are in *we?* [S: Two.] What is the vowel letter? [S: *e.*] What does *e* stand for in the word *we*? [S: /ē/.] Look at the last column, and read the word again. [S: we.]

Line 3

T: Look at the next picture and word. This is a word you have had before. What is the word [S: I.] Look at the third column. What sound does the letter *i* stand for in the word *I?* [S: /ī/.] Is this a long vowel sound or a short vowel sound? [S: Long.] Look at the last column, and read the word again. [S: I.]

Line 4

T: Look at the next picture and word. What is the word? [S: go.] What is the name of the vowel? [S: *o.*] What sound does *o* stand for in the word *go?* [S: /ō/.] Look at the last column, and read the word again. [S: go.]

Lesson 1

ā, ē, ī, ō, ū, ȳ, (ī)

	paper	p ā p er ā	paper
	we	w ē ē	we
	I	Ī ī	I
	go	g ō ō	go
	music	m ū z ī c ū	music
	my	m ȳ ȳ (ī)	my

or

YORK ST.	York	Y or k or	York

My Class

Jason (Jāson)	Carla (Carlu)	class	listen	(lisen)
David (Dāvid)	Lopez (Lōpez)	snack	write	(rīt)
		study	sentence	(sentens)

I am Jason Hunt. I work at a market on River Street. I go to class after work. I have some paper. The paper is for my class.

After work, I will pick up my friend David Miller. He works at a factory on York Street. I will pick up David at the factory. We will go to class in my car.

Carla Lopez works at a music shop on York Street. We will pick up Carla at the music shop. She will go to class with us.

We will study hard in class. We will study the lesson. We will write on the paper. We will write sentences. We will write letters to friends. Ms. Smith will help us write sentences. She will help us write letters.

After class, Carla, David, and I will go for a snack. We will go to Fran's Snack Shop. It is on York Street. We can get a quick snack at Fran's. We can listen to music. We can have a snack and listen to music.

From the snack shop, we will go to Garden Street. Carla lives on Garden Street. Then David and I will go to First Street. David lives at 917 First Street. I live at 942 First Street.

I work hard. I study hard. But I have fun.

Line 5

T: Look at the next picture and word. The third column will help you pronounce the word. What is it? [S: music.] How many vowel letters are in the word *music?* [S: Two.] What are they? [S: *u* and *i*.] Which one is long? [S: *u*.] How do you know? [S: There is a mark over it.] What sound does *u* stand for in the word *music?* [S: /ū/.] Good. Look at the last column, and read the word again. [S: music.]

Line 6

T: Look at the next picture and word. What is the word? [S: my.] What is the name of the vowel in *my?* [S: *y*.] What sound does *y* stand for in *my?* [S: /ī/.] Good. The long vowel sound for *y* is the same as the long sound for *i*. Read the word again. [S: my.]

Line 7

T: (Point to *or* above the line.) Here is another sound that you will study in this book. You hear this sound in a street name that you had in *Skill Book 1*. (Point to *York*.) Read the word. [S: York.]

T: Look at the third column. How many sounds are in *York?* [S: Three.] The letters *or* are together to show that they stand for one sound. What is the sound? [S: /or/.] Read the word again. [S: York.]

Note: The sound for *or* has regional variations. Let S. make the sound the way he normally pronounces it in words like *York*. If your pronounciation is different, explain that people from different parts of the country pronounce *or* in different ways.

Review

T: Look at the letters at the top of the page. Give the long sound for each. [S: /ā/, /ē/, /ī/, /ō/, /ū/, /ī/.] What letter is sometimes a vowel? [S: *y*.] What is the long vowel sound for *y?* [S: /ī/.]

T: (Point to *or* above the last line.) What is this sound? [S: /or/.] Good. Now please read the words again.

Have S. read each word in the chart again as you point to it, going down the last column.

STORY: Page 3 (My Class)

Title and new story words. Ask S. to read the story title. Help him sound out the new word *class* if he needs help. Have him read the other new words listed at the top of the page. Have him look at the respelling of the word for help in sounding it out. Call attention to the long vowels and the consonant blend *sn* in *snack*. If the name *Lopez* is unfamiliar to S., help him pronounce it and point out that it is a family name.

Note: The sound /u/ in an unstressed syllable, as in *Carla,* is often referred to as the *schwa* (shwah) sound. The schwa sound is made in the same way as the sound /u/ but with less force. The schwa sound may be represented by any of the vowel letters. In this book, the schwa sound is respelled—with a *u*—only where most needed to avoid wrong pronunciation.

Explanation of paragraphs

T: The story is divided into paragraphs. In this book, the paragraphs are *indented.* Look at the first sentence. Notice that the first word begins a little way in from the margin. We say that it is indented. This tells us that it is the first word in the paragraph. Look over the page, and find each word that is indented. How many are there? [S: Seven.] This means that there are seven paragraphs.

Explanation of the word *I* in the story

T: In this story, a man is telling about himself. The word *I* in the story refers to the person who is *telling* the story, not the person who is reading it. Read the first sentence, and find out the name of the person telling this story. [S: Jason Hunt.]

Directed silent reading. Ask S. to read the whole story to find out what Jason tells about his class. Then have S. summarize the story by telling the important things. Have him summarize in the third person, as below. The summary might be like the following:

[Jason will go to class after work. He will pick up his friends, David and Carla, and take them to class in his car. They will study hard in class. After class, they will go to the snack shop. Then Jason will take his friends home.]

Scanning and oral reading. Have S. scan the page to find the paragraph that tells about each of the following ideas. Have him read the paragraph aloud.

Ask S. to find and read the paragraph that tells:

1. where Carla Lopez works [par. 3].
2. where David Miller works [par. 2].
3. what they will do in class [par. 4].
4. where Jason Hunt lives [par. 1].
5. what they will do at Fran's Snack Shop [par. 5].
6. where they will go from the snack shop [par. 6].
7. how Jason sums up the way he lives [par. 7].

STORY CHECKUP: Page 4

Title and new words

T: This is a checkup on the story that you just read. We have talked about some of the important things in the story. This checkup will give you practice in finding details in the story.

Have S. read the new words *story* and *missing* at the top of the page. Then have him read the title *Story Checkup.*

First exercise

T: (Point to the introduction.) This part gives you some information that will help you do the exercise. Read it, please. [S: The names in this story are: Jason Hunt, David Miller, Carla Lopez, Ms. Smith.]

T: (Point to first direction in bold type.) This sentence tells you what to do. Read it. [S: Write the name.] You are to write a name from the list above to answer each question. You may remember the answer, or you may need to look back in the story to find it.

Have S. read the first question aloud and either tell the answer or look it up. Have him write the name on the line. Let him answer the other questions by himself. Tell him he may look back in the story if he doesn't remember the answer. When he has finished, have him read each question and answer aloud. Help him find the correct answer in the story for any items he has wrong.

Second exercise. Have S. read the second direction in bold type, *Write the missing word.*

T: In front of each sentence, there are two forms of an action word—with and without the ending *-s.* Look at the sentence, and decide which form you should use.

Do the first item with S. Have him read aloud both forms of the word (*live, lives*) and decide which form to use in the sentence. Then have him do the others by himself. When he finishes, have him read each sentence aloud. Help him correct any errors. Make a note of any errors so you can give extra practice at the end of the lesson.

Note: If S. answers the first one or two items incorrectly and if he does not ordinarily pronounce the *-s* ending on verbs, help him do the exercise in this way. Read the complete sentence aloud to S. with the correct form of the verb. Have him tell which form he heard and then write it in the blank.

READING FOR LIVING: Page 5

Title and new words. Have S. read the new word *read* at the top of the page Then have him read the title *Reading for Living.*

T: This is a new section. You will have one like it in most of the lessons in this book. This section will help you use your reading and writing skills in everyday life. The Reading for Living section in this lesson will help you read and write some words and prices that you might find on a menu.

Have S. read the new words. Explain that *I'll* means *I will.* If S. pronounces the *o* in *coffee* as /aw/, let him do so. Explain that in some parts of the country, it is pronounced /o/.

Story Checkup

story, missing

The names in this story are:

Jason Hunt David Miller Carla Lopez Ms. Smith

Write the name.

1. Who works at the market? ______
2. Who works at the factory? ______
3. Who works at the music shop? ______
4. Who has a car? ______
5. Who lives on Garden Street? ______
6. Who lives on First Street?

   ______ and ______
7. Who will go to class with Jason?

   ______ and ______
8. Who will help them write? ______

Write the missing word.

live lives	1. David and Jason ______ on First Street.
work works	2. I ______ at the market.
work works	3. Carla ______ at a music shop.
write writes	4. We ______ on the paper.

Reading for Living

read (rēd)

ham	milk	I'll (īll)	salad (salud)
hamburger	drink	sandwich	coffee (coffē)

Jason, Carla, and David were in Fran's Snack Shop. Fran hurried to them.

Fran asked, "What will you have?"

Jason said, "I'll have a ham sandwich."
Carla said, "I'll have an egg salad sandwich."
David said, "I'll have a hamburger."

Fran asked Jason, "What will you have to drink?"
Jason said, "I'll have a glass of milk."

Fran asked Carla, "What will you have to drink?"
Carla said, "I'll have a cup of coffee."

Fran asked David, "What will you have to drink?"
David said, "I'll have a glass of milk."

Directed silent reading. Ask S. to read the page silently to find out who was in the snack shop and what they ordered. When he finishes, ask these questions:

Par. 1. Who was in the snack shop?
Par. 2. What did Fran ask them?
Par. 3. Who wanted a hamburger?
What did the others want?
Par. 4. What did Jason want to drink?
Par. 5. What did Carla want to drink?
Par. 6. What did David want to drink?

Then ask the following questions that do not have direct answers in the reading section:

1. Who is Fran? [Probably the owner.] What makes you think so? [Because it's called Fran's Snack Shop.]
2. What size snack shop do you think it is? Why? [Small. Fran herself waits on them.]

Oral reading. Have S. read the page aloud. If you have several students, each one might read the part of one of the characters. Otherwise, you might read the questions and have S. read the responses. Then switch roles.

bill	¢ (cent)	70¢	(seventy cents)
cost	$ (dollar)	$1.00	(one dollar)
		$1.70	(one dollar and seventy cents)

Sandwiches

Ham sandwich.........$2.00
Egg salad sandwich.....$1.00
Hamburger............$1.70

Drinks

Milk....................70¢
Coffee..................50¢

Write the missing numbers with $ or ¢.

Jason got a ham sandwich.
The ham sandwich cost ________.
Jason got a glass of milk.
The milk cost ________.
His bill was $2.70.

Carla got an egg salad sandwich.
The egg salad sandwich cost ________.
Carla got a cup of coffee.
The coffee cost ________.
Her bill was $1.50.

David got a hamburger.
The hamburger cost ________.
David got a glass of milk.
The milk cost ________.
His bill was $2.40.

Copy the word. Add -s or -es. What is the word?

egg eggs dish dishes

1. glass ________ 6. paper ________
2. car ________ 7. salad ________
3. drink ________ 8. box ________
4. class ________ 9. friend ________
5. dress ________ 10. sandwich ________

Drop -s or -es. Write the word.

friends friend dishes dish

1. cups ________ 6. sentences ________
2. bills ________ 7. names ________
3. classes ________ 8. kisses ________
4. words ________ 9. sandwiches ________
5. glasses ________ 10. shops ________

READING FOR LIVING: Page 6

T: This is another part of the Reading for Living section. Read the title. [S: Reading for Living.] On this page, you will read the menu and write the prices of the things Jason and his friends ordered.

New words and symbols. Have S. read the new words *bill* and *cost* at the top of the page. If he pronounces *cost* with the vowel sound /aw/, let him do so. Explain that it is pronounced /o/ in some parts of the country.

T: You have read prices written in words. In this section you will read prices written in numbers with the dollar sign or the cent sign.

T: (Point to ¢.) This is the cent sign. It looks like a *c* with a line through it.

T: (Point to $.) This is the dollar sign. It looks like an *S* with a line through it.

T: (Point to 70¢.) Look at this price written in numbers. Then look at it written in words. Read the price. [S: Seventy cents.] When the price is just cents and no dollars, it is often written this way. The cent sign comes after the number.

T: (Point to $1.00.) Look at this price written in numbers. Then look at it written in words. Read the price. [S: One dollar.] When the price is a dollar or more, it is written like this. First comes the dollar sign. Next comes the number that tells how many dollars there are. What is it? [S: One.] After the number 1, what mark do you see? [S: A period.] The period separates the dollars from the cents. What comes after the period? [S: Two zeros.] That means there are no cents. The price is exactly one dollar.

T: (Point to $1.70.) Read the next price. [S: One dollar and seventy cents.] What number is written after the period in this price? [S: 70.]

Note: If S. already knows how to read prices, omit the detailed explanation of how they are written.

Menu and prices. Have S. read the menu aloud. Call attention to the *-es* ending in *sandwiches.*

Write the missing number with $ or ¢. Have S. read this direction himself. Have him read the first two sentences aloud and tell what price goes in the blank by looking at the menu. Have him write the price. Show him how to make the dollar sign if he needs help. Then, have him read the next two sentences aloud, tell the price of the milk, and fill in the blank. Finally, have him read the last sentence of the paragraph aloud. Complete each paragraph the same way.

Note: If there is a sales tax on restaurant meals in your area, discuss this with S. Explain that the sales tax has not yet been added to each person's bill on page 6.

II. Skills Practice

T: Please close your book. We will have a few practice exercises on some sounds and endings in this lesson.

Practice 1: Recognizing Long Vowel Sounds

T: Listen as I say two words.
Which word has a long vowel sound:

back, bake?	*met, meat?*	*bite, bit?*
hop, hope?	*goat, got?*	*us, use?*
ate, at?	*cut, cute?*	*note, not?*
bed, bead?	*pill, pile?*	*up, you?*

T: I will say two words. Which word has the sound /or/:

shirt, short?	*yard, York?*	*four, fur?*
born, burn?	*farm, form?*	*mark, more?*

Practice 2: Identifying Long Vowel Sounds

T: I will say three words. All three words will have the same vowel sound. Listen carefully. What vowel sound do you hear:

make, late, came?	[S: /ā/.]	*no, old, so?*	[S: /ō/.]
write, by, fine?	[S: /ī/.]	*use, you, few?*	[S: /ū/.]
he, me, see?	[S: /ē/.]	*for, or, fork?*	[S: /or/.]

Practice 3: Beginning Blends *sn* and *str*

T: Listen to this word, and tell me what two consonant sounds you hear at the beginning: *snack*. [S: /sn/.] (Write *sn* on the board.) We call this the *sn* blend.

T: I will say two words. Listen carefully.
Which word begins with the consonant blend *sn:*

snake, shake?	*stale, snail?*	*smash, snow?*
slap, snap?	*speak, sneak?*	*snore, smoke?*

T: Sometimes a consonant blend has more than two sounds. Listen to this word, and tell me how many consonant sounds you hear before the vowel: *street*. [S: Three.] What are the sounds? [S: /s/, /t/, /r/.] Very good. (Write the word *street*.) Read the word. [S: street.] The word *street* has a blend made up of three letters. What are they? [S: *str*.] Good. (Draw a line under *str*.) We call this the *str* blend.

T: Which word begins with the consonant blend *str:*

strip, rip?	*stuck, struck?*	*string, sting?*
trap, strap?	*stand, strand?*	*state, straight?*

Practice 4: Beginning Blends *sm, st, dr, fr, cl, gl*

T: (Write the blends *sm, st, dr, fr, cl, gl* on the board.) Here are some beginning consonant blends you had in *Skill Book 2*. Please read them. [S: *sm, st, dr, fr, cl. gl.*]

T: I will say a word from this lesson. Which consonant blend do you hear at the beginning of the word:

class?	*Smith?*	*drink?*	*friends?*
glass?	*Fran?*	*study?*	*story?*

Practice 5: Ending Blends *lk, nk, nt, sk, st*

T: Listen to this word, and tell me what two consonant sounds you hear at the end: *milk*. [S: /lk/.] This is a new ending blend. (Write *milk*, and underline *lk*.)

T: Which word ends with the consonant blend *lk*:

sill, silk?	*elk, elm?*	*hulk, hull?*	*sick, sulk?*

T: Listen to this word, and tell me what two consonant sounds you hear at the end: *drink*. [S: /ngk/.] That is the same ending blend you had in *thank* and *think*. (Write *drink*, and underline *nk*.)

Follow the same procedure for the ending blends in *cent, cost, ask*. Underline the ending blend in each. Then say each of the following words, and have S. tell which blend the word ends with.

desk	*hunt*	*risk*	*rest*
dust	*sink*	*ant*	*blank*

Practice 6: Endings *-s* and *-es*

Write the word *letters* on the board. Have S. read the word and then tell what it would be without the *-s* ending. Then write these words: *friend, paper, shop, word, name, sentence*. Have S. read each word and then tell what it would be with the *-s* ending.

Write the word *class* on the board. Ask S. what ending to add to make it mean more than one class [*-es*]. Then write these words: *pass, kiss, watch, dish*. Have S. read each word and tell what it would be with the *-es* ending.

III. Writing

CHECK HOMEWORK

Find out if S. has completed *City Living*. Talk about the stories he has read, and ask what parts he liked best. If he hasn't finished the book, encourage him to do so.

Check the homework on page 78 of *Skill Book 2*, and help S. correct any errors. If S. didn't bring *Skill Book 2*, have him bring it next time and check the homework then.

WRITING LESSON (In Notebook)

> In *Skill Book 3*, the student will need his own notebook for the Writing Lesson section of each lesson. A wide-ruled, 8½-by-11-inch, spiral-bound notebook is recomended. It does not need to have more than 50 pages. Be sure that your student has a notebook before you begin Lesson 1.
>
> You will need a few sheets of similar notebook paper to use for demonstration.

Have S. write his name on the cover of his notebook. Then have him open it to the first page.

Page arrangement

Note: As you explain to S. how to set up this page, demonstrate by writing the titles and numbers on your own notebook paper. A sample page is shown here.

T: In the upper left-hand corner, write *Lesson 1.* (Write this on your own paper, and have S. copy it.)

T: Your writing lesson will have three sections. The first section is called *Words.* Watch as I write the title *Words.* Your paper has lines that you can use as top and bottom guidelines, but there is no dotted middle guideline. The title *Words* begins with a capital *W.* So I will start at the top guideline and go down to the next guideline. (Demonstrate writing *W.*) Small *o* is a short letter, so I will start the top of the letter halfway between the two lines. (Demonstrate writing the rest of the title *Words,* and let S. copy it.)

Have S. write the numbers 1 through 5 in one column and the numbers 6 through 10 in another column. Have him skip a space under the title *Words* and between numbers.

Words

T: Look at the guidelines at the top and bottom of your number 1. Tall letters go from the top guideline down to the bottom guideline. Start the top of short letters halfway between those two lines.

Dictate the following words for S. to write. Keep checking to be sure he writes them in the correct places.

1. we	6. he
2. go	7. she
3. my	8. class
4. paper	9. snack
5. I	10. ham

Check the words for the correct spelling. Circle the number of any word S. misspelled. Have S. erase the whole word and write it again correctly.

Sentences

T: The next section is called *Sentences.* Skip a space and write this title. Watch where I write *Sentences.* (Demonstrate and have S. copy.)

Have S. skip a space and number from 1 through 4, also skipping a space between numbers. Dictate these sentences:

1. I am in class.
2. She is in my class.
3. We will go in my car.
4. He is my friend.

Check what S. has written. Circle any words in which there is an error.

Study

T: The third section of your writing lesson is called *Study.* Skip a space after your last sentence, and write the title *Study.*

Lesson 1
Words
1. 6.
2. 7.
3. 8.
4. 9.
5. 10.
Sentences
1.
2.
3.
4.
Study

Demonstrate where to write *Study,* and have S. copy it. Have S. write any words he missed in the word and sentence dictation. Ask him to study these words at home.

If S. didn't miss any words, have him write the title *Study* anyway. Explain that this part of the lesson is for practicing words he missed, but since he didn't make any mistakes, he doesn't have to do this part.

HOMEWORK: Page 7

Have S. read the title. For each exercise, follow these steps: Have S. read the directions aloud. Go over the sample items with him. Have him do number 1, and check to see that he understood what to do. Then ask S. to finish the page at home.

CHECKING PROGRESS

Checkups for Skill Book 2. Go over the results of these *Checkups* with S. if you have not already done so. Be sure that he understands anything that he did not do correctly.

Review of short vowel sounds and consonant blends. If the results of the *Checkups for Skill Book 2* indicated that S. needed supplementary review lessons, it is assumed that you have given these before starting *Skill Book 3.*

But, if the results indicated that S. needs to review only a few skills, plan some practice exercises directly related to the lesson in *Skill Book 3.* For example, if S. needs practice on any consonant blends that are in the words for this lesson, such as *fr* in *friend* or *cl* in *class,* plan additional exercises to help him master them. The workbook *Focus on*

Phonics-2B: Consonant Blends has exercises on beginning and ending blends and on *r*- controlled vowels which you may find useful. Let S. know what sounds and blends he needs to study most.

Word recognition. Keep a list of old words that S. may not have been sure of when he was reading this lesson. Make flash cards for these words. You can use these by themselves to practice recognition. Or, you can have S. put words together to make sentences.

MEETING INDIVIDUAL NEEDS

Some students may need to move at a slower pace and may need additional practice on certain skills. Or, your student may be one who can sight-read at a higher level than that of the skill book, but who is weak in phonics skills. The suggestions in this section will be helpful for both kinds of students. They may also be used when you have some extra time at the end of a lesson period.

Using flash cards. Make a flash card for each chart word in Lesson 1. In the top left-hand corner of each card, write the number 1. Then write the word. On the back side, write the word as it is written in column 3 (the respelling column) of the chart.

Show S. the side of the card with the word written correctly. Turn the card over only if he needs help in sounding out the word. If he studies these cards at home, tell him to look first at the side with the number 1 on it.

Spread out the cards, and ask S. to point to the word that has a certain vowel sound studied in this lesson. For example, ask him which has the sound /ō/.

Make a separate flash card for the name of each person in the story. Put the person's first and last names on separate cards. Put the person's street address on a different card. If the house number is given, put it on a different card. Mix up the cards. First, have S. match the first and last names for each person in the story. Then, have him put the correct street address by each name. (Let S. look back at the story as he does this.)

Practice with verb ending *-s*. If S. had trouble with the second part of the Story Checkup, give more practice on when to use the ending *-s* on action words. Review this rule: We use the *-s* ending on an action word after *he, she,* or *it*, or any other word that can take the place of *he, she* or *it* in the sentence. Otherwise, we can use the form without *-s*.

Write these examples, underlining the words in italic:

He works hard.	*David* works hard.
She works hard.	*Carla* works hard.
It works.	*The clock* works.
They work hard.	*David and Carla* work hard.
I work hard.	
You work hard.	
We work hard.	

Use the exercise below, which is similar to the one in the Story Checkup. Let S. look at the examples as he does the exercise. If he has difficulty, ask him if he can substitute *he* or *she* for the words that tell *who*.

(listen, listens)	We ______ to music.
(help, helps)	Ms. Smith ______ us in class.
(work, works)	David and I ______ hard.
(write, writes)	Carla ______ letters.
(live, lives)	You ______ on my street.
(pick, picks)	Jason ______ up his friends.
(live, lives)	She ______ on Garden Street.
(get, gets)	They ______ a quick snack at Fran's.

Using *Focus on Phonics*. The workbook *Focus on Phonics-3: Long Vowel Sounds* uses a word-family approach (rhyming words) to help students learn many new long vowel words. It should be used only under your direction, with the help of the teacher's edition. This workbook is correlated to *Skill Book 3*. The numbered practices in the workbook may be used after the skill book lesson of the same number. For example, after Lesson 1, you may use Practice 1, which contrasts the short and long vowel sounds for each vowel.

Using the *Workbook for Skill Book 3*. Although this workbook was developed for ESOL students in the Laubach Way to English program, it can be helpful for native speakers of English, too. Many lessons contain a cloze exercise based on the story in the skill book lesson. In a cloze exercise, every 5th, 6th, 7th, 8th, or 9th word in the reading passage is left blank for the student to fill in. (The answer may be any appropriate word, not just the same word that was used in the story.) Cloze exercises integrate word recognition skills with the skills of using context and grammatical clues in the reading material. Among the writing skills developed in the *Workbook for Skill Book 3* are using the correct forms of nouns and verbs, completing sentences, and combining sentences.

Be sensitive to the amount and timing of any extra work you give your student to be sure that it is appropriate for him. Use the supplementary materials that will best reinforce the skills he needs, but don't burden him with so much extra practice that he loses a sense of progress.

On the other hand, as the student becomes a more independent reader, he will want to read more material for enjoyment. Several local literacy councils have developed a variety of reading materials correlated to this level of the reading series.

LESSON 2 — Skill Book 3, Pages 8-13

OBJECTIVES

To help your student:

- recognize the long sound for *a* as in *paper.*
- read words in which the sound /ā/ is represented by the letter *a* at the end of a syllable.
- become acquainted with the meaning of *syllables* and how to tell the number of syllables in a word.
- recognize a final syllable formed by a consonant plus *le*, as in *table*, and its sound.
- distinguish between the long and short sounds for *a*.
- summarize the main ideas of a story.
- recognize the main idea of a paragraph.
- recall or locate details in the story.
- read package directions for preparing instant food, using a simple chart.
- review the beginning consonant blend *str*.
- write words and sentences from dictation.

INTRODUCTION

T: In your last lesson you learned what the long vowel sounds are. Please say them. [S: /ā/, /ē/, /ī/, /ō/, /ū/.] This lesson is about one of those sounds. Open your book to Lesson 2 on page 8, and find out what it is.

I. Reading

CHART: Page 8

Title and key word. Have S. read the title *Lesson 2*.

T: Please point to the vowel in the top right-hand corner. What is the name of this vowel? [S: *a*.] What is the long sound for *a?* [S: /ā/.]

T: (Point to *paper*.) What is the key word? [S: paper.] (Point to *a*.) What is the sound for *a* in *paper?* [S: /ā/.]

Line 1

T: Look at the first picture and the word next to it. (Point to them.) This name was in the last lesson. What is it? [S: David.]

T: (Point to column 3.) What is the first vowel sound in *David?* [S: /ā/.] How can you tell that the letter *a* stands for the sound /ā/ in this word? [S: There is a mark over it.]

T: (Still pointing to column 3.) In this column, the word is divided into two parts. We call these parts *syllables.* Each syllable has one vowel sound. We can tell how many syllables are in a word by the number of vowel sounds we hear. Listen to the word *David*. What is the first vowel sound? [S: /ā/.] What is the second vowel sound? [S: /i/.] So how many syllables are there in the word *David?* [S: Two.]

T: Listen to the word *Dan*. How many vowel sounds do you hear? [S: One.] Right. *Dan* is a one-syllable word because it only has one vowel sound. Some words have many syllables. You will have some new three-syllable words in this lesson.

Lines 2-6. Go over the rest of the chart in the same way, calling attention to the sound /ā/ in each word and to the number of syllables in each word.

Review. Have S. read each word in the chart again as you point to it, going down the last column.

T: What is the first vowel sound in each of these words? [S: /ā/.] What letter stands for the sound /ā/? [S: *a*.]

T: How many syllables do most of these words have? [S: Two.] Does any word in the chart have only one syllable? [S: No.] Which word has more than two syllables? [S: *radio*.] Notice that, in each of these words, the vowel sound /ā/ comes at the end of the first syllable.

Have S. cover the picture column and read the words in the chart again, going down the last column.

STORY: Page 9 (Carla's Story)

Have S. read the story title and new words. Call attention to the number of syllables in each word. If a word has a long vowel sound, have S. tell what the sound is. Tell S. that the mark in *baby-sitter* is called a hyphen. Explain that a hyphen is sometimes used to join two words that are used together as one word.

Note: Starting in Lesson 2, where we begin dividing words into syllables, a double consonant such as *tt* will be respelled with only one consonant, as in dictionary respellings. The reason for this is to avoid confusing the student. He has already learned in *Skill Book 2* that a double consonant has just one sound. But he might try to say two sounds if he saw the same consonant in two different syllables, as *sit ter.*

Also, when one part of a compound word has already been taught (such as *baby* in *baby-sitter*), the known part will not be respelled. This is true whether the compound word is written with a hyphen or as one word (such as *landlady* in Lesson 4).

Directed silent reading

T: Carla was one of the three friends that went to class together in the last story. In this story, Carla is telling about herself. Who will the word *I* mean in this story? [S: Carla.] Read the whole page to yourself, and find out five things about Carla.

After S. finishes reading, have him tell five things about Carla. List these on the board or on paper. Encourage S. to tell the main points rather than details. Main points should include:

Lesson 2

ā

paper

ā

	David	Dā vid	David
April 1 2 3 4 5 6 7 8 9 10 11 12 13 14 15 16 17 18 19 20 21 22 23 24 25 26 27 28 29 30	April	Ā pril	April
	baby	bā by	baby
	lady	lā dy	lady
	table	tā bul	table
	radio	rā dē ō	radio

8 Lesson 2

Carla's Story

love (luv)	me (mē)	apartment (u part ment)
month (munth)	Rosa (Rō su)	baby-sitter (baby sit er)

My name is Carla Lopez. I live in an apartment on Garden Street. I have lived in this apartment for ten months.

I work at a music shop. I started work in April. I have worked at the music shop for six months.

After work, I go to class. I started the class in April. April was not a bad month! David was at the first class. David has helped me a lot in class. He and I are friends. David helps me with Rosa. He loves Rosa.

Rosa is my baby. She is two. My baby cannot go to work with me. She cannot go to class with me. A baby-sitter must look after her. Mrs. King is my baby-sitter. Mrs. King is a lady in my apartment building. This lady loves my baby. My baby loves her. I am happy that this lady is my baby-sitter.

It is after work. I have picked up Rosa from Mrs. King's apartment. Rosa is with me in the kitchen. Rosa is sitting at the table. She is singing. I am working at the table. I am starting dinner.

A radio is on the table. I am listening to the radio. The radio says that it is half past six. I must hurry. My friend David is coming to dinner.

Lesson 2 9

1. Carla lives in an apartment.
2. She works in a music shop.
3. After work, Carla goes to class.
4. Carla has a baby named Rosa.
5. A baby-sitter looks after Rosa while Carla is at work and at class.
6. David is Carla's friend.

T: How many paragraphs are in the story? [S: Six.] How can you tell where a paragraph begins? [S: The first word is indented.]

Scanning and oral reading. Have S. scan the page to find the paragraph that tells the most about each of the following topics. Have him read the paragraph aloud.

1. The baby-sitter [par. 4]
2. Carla's work [par. 2]
3. Where Carla lives [par. 1]
4. Carla's friend David [par. 3]
5. The radio [par. 6]
6. What Carla and Rosa are doing in the kitchen [par. 5]

Reading between the lines. In this section, S. will relate facts in the story to each other or draw inferences from clues in the story. In some cases, he will be asked to tell when certain information is not in the story (that is, it is neither stated nor implied). More general discussion questions will ask S. to use his own experience and powers of reasoning to relate topics in the story to everyday life.

You should ask all of the questions that relate to the story. But you may skip any general discussion questions that would be too sensitive or would not be of interest.

Suggested answers are given here for questions related to the story. But be flexible about accepting other answers if S. can make a reasonable case for his answer.

Questions for this story are listed below.

1. The story shows that Carla is raising her child alone. But can you tell from the story whether Carla is a widow, divorced or never married? [No.]
2. Do you think the baby-sitter is about the same age as Carla or much older? Why? [Much older. Carla calls her *Mrs.* instead of using her first name.]
3. Do you think Carla is in love with David, or are they just good friends? [She *says* they are friends.]
4. Tell why you agree or disagree with each statement:
   a. Carla is trying to make a good life for herself and her child.
   b. Carla works so hard that she has no time for herself or her child.
5. What are some of the problems that a single parent with young children—like Carla—faces?

Story Checkup

answer (an ser)

Answer with one or two words. Write the answer.

1. Who has worked at the gift shop for six months?

____

2. Who has helped Carla in class? ______________________
3. When did Carla start the class? ______________________
4. Who is the baby-sitter? ______________________
5. What is the baby's name? ______________________
6. Who is coming to dinner? ______________________

Answer with *yes* or *no*. Write the answer.

1. Does Carla Lopez live on Garden Street? ______________________
2. Is David Carla's brother? ______________________
3. Can Rosa go to class with Carla? ______________________
4. Does Rosa love the baby-sitter? ______________________
5. Did Carla pick up Rosa after work? ______________________
6. Is Carla listening to the radio? ______________________

Reading for Living

instant (in stant) potatoes (pu tā tōz) pat water (wot er)

Carla is getting dinner. She and David will have ham, salad, and potatoes for dinner. The potatoes are instant potatoes. This is on the box of instant potatoes.

	Water	Butter	Milk	Instant Potatoes
For 1 person	1 half cup	1 pat	1 quarter cup	1 half cup
For 2 persons	1 cup	2 pats	1 half cup	1 cup
For 4 persons	2 cups	4 pats	1 cup	2 cups

Put water, butter, and milk in a pan.
When the water gets hot, add instant potatoes.
Cover and let stand.

Fill in the numbers and words.

1. Carla is getting dinner for two persons.
   She puts ______________ of water in a pan.
   She puts in ______________ of butter.
   She puts in ______________ of milk.
   When the water gets hot, she adds ______________ of instant potatoes.

2. I have four persons in my family. For four persons,
   I will put ______________ of water in a pan.
   I will put in ______________ of butter.
   I will put in ______________ of milk.
   When the water gets hot, I will add ______________ of instant potatoes.

STORY CHECKUP: Page 10

Have S. read the title *Story Checkup* and the new word *answer*. Ask him to read the first direction silently and then aloud. Have him read the first question to himself and then write the answer. Tell him that he may look back at the story if he doesn't remember how to spell a word. Check what he has written. If he has an error, refer him to the story and have him write the answer correctly.

Let S. complete the exercise, and then check his answers. Have him correct any errors by referring to the story.

Proceed in the same way for the second exercise.

READING FOR LIVING: Page 11

Have S. read the title and the new words. Call attention to the number of syllables in each word and the long vowel sounds in *potatoes*. For *potatoes*, also point out that the ending is *-es* and the root word is *potato*. Tell S. that we add *-es* instead of just *-s* to some words that end with *o*. For *water*, explain that the sound /er/ is a syllable by itself.

T: The paragraph at the top of the page tells what Carla is making for dinner. Read it to yourself and then name the things. [S: Ham, salad, and potatoes.] What kind of potatoes is Carla making? [S: Instant.]

T: The directions here are like the ones on the box of instant potatoes. Going across the top line of the chart are the names of the things you need to prepare the potatoes. Read these items as I point to them. [S: Water, butter, milk, instant potatoes.]

T: (Point to the column at the far left.) This column tells how many persons to prepare for. Read the first line. [S: For 1 person.] If you want to prepare potatoes for just one person, how much water would you need? [S: 1 half cup.] How much butter? [S: 1 pat.] A pat of butter is about a tablespoon. How much milk? [S: 1 quarter cup.] How much of the instant potatoes? [S: 1 half cup.]

In the same way, go over the amounts needed for two persons and four persons. Then tell S. that the directions at the bottom of the chart tell how to put the things together. Have him read these directions silently and then aloud.

Have S. read the direction for the exercise to himself. Then follow these steps:

1. Have S. read all of the sentences in number 1 to himself.
2. Ask him *how many persons* is Carla making potatoes for.
3. Have him find the correct line in the chart for this number of persons.
4. Have S. read aloud the first sentence with a blank. Then have him find the answer in the chart and write it in the blank.
5. Let him complete the sentences in number 1.

Follow the same steps for the sentences in number 2. If S. needs help in either part, do the sentences with him, one at a time, helping him find the answer in the chart.

II. Skills Practice

T: Please close your book. We will have some listening exercises on some of the new things in this lesson.

PRACTICE 1: Identifying the Long Sound for *a*

T: I will say two words. Which word has the long sound for *a* as in *paper*:

apple, table?	*ate, at?*	*Dan, David?*
lady, happy?	*navy, flag?*	*little, table?*

PRACTICE 2: Identifying the Number of Syllables

T: In this lesson, you learned several longer words. Longer words have two or more parts. We call these parts *syllables*. The syllables are the beats or parts you hear when you say the word.

T: Some words have only one beat when you say them. Listen to these words. Each of them has only one syllable. (Tap your fingers on the table once as you say each word.) *I, go, class, write, we, York, drink.*

T: These words have two beats when you say them. (Tap twice as you say each word.) *Baby, sandwich, music, kitchen, paper, garden, apple.* Each of these words has two syllables.

T: A word has a syllable for every vowel sound you hear. But if it's hard for you to hear the number of vowel sounds, listen to the number of beats it has.

T: Now I will say some words you've had in your reading. Listen, and tell me whether the word has one syllable or two. You can say the word after me and tap the number of beats if you want to.

love	[1]	*David*	[2]	*water*	[2]
lady	[2]	*Carla*	[2]	*me*	[1]
snack	[1]	*Jason*	[2]	*coffee*	[2]
story	[2]	*month*	[1]	*paper*	[2]

If S. makes a mistake, repeat the word slowly and tap as you say it.

T: Some words have more than two syllables. Listen as I say some words with three syllables. (Tap three times as you say each word.)

telephone	*Indian*	*potato*	*vacation*
grandmother	*radio*	*October*	*umbrella*

T: Now I'll say some more words you've had in your reading. Listen to each word, and tell me whether it has two syllables or three.

sandwich	[2]	*hamburger*	[3]	*answer*	[2]
potato	[3]	*sentence*	[2]	*study*	[2]
salad	[2]	*April*	[2]	*seventy*	[3]
radio	[3]	*apartment*	[3]	*another*	[3]

PRACTICE 3: Recognizing *le* at the End of a Word

T: (Write *table*, and have S. read it.) How many syllables are there in *table?* [S: Two.] The first syllable is /tā/. What letters are in the second syllable? [S: *ble*.] How are they pronounced? [S: /bul/.] What is the sound for *le*? [S: /ul/.]

T: (Write *uncle, apple, little, whistle* in a column under *table*, and have S. read them.) How many syllables are in each of these words? [S: Two.] What comes before the *le* in each of these words, a vowel or a consonant? [S: A consonant.] How is the *le* pronounced? [S: /ul/.]

PRACTICE 4: Consonant Blends *st* and *str*

Write the words *stand* and *street*. Have S. read each word aloud and tell what blend it begins with. As he answers, write *st* and *str* under the correct words.

T: Listen to each word I say. Point to the consonant blend it begins with, *st* or *str*.

string	*stuck*	*straight*	*steam*
sting	*struck*	*state*	*stream*
strap	*study*	*strip*	*stay*

III. Writing

CHECK HOMEWORK: Page 7

Check this page with S. Help him correct any errors. Make note of the type of errors so you can give further practice. If S. didn't do the assignment at home, give him some time to do it in class.

WRITING LESSON (In Notebook)

Have S. arrange the page as he did in the first lesson, writing the titles *Lesson 2* and *Words* and then numbering from 1 to 10 in two columns.

Words. Use the chart on page 8 and the story words at the top of page 9 to help S. study the following words before he writes them. Call attention to these points:

baby, lady—end with the short vowel sound for *y*.

David, April—begin with a capital letter because they are names.

table—ends with the sound /ul/ written with *le*.

radio—the sound /ē/ is written with *i*.

Carla, Rosa—begin with a capital letter because they are names; end with the sound /u/ written with *a*.

month—the vowel sound /u/ is written with *o*.

As S. studies each word, have him look at it carefully as you call attention to any special points. Then have him close his eyes, spell the word to himself, and then look at the word again to see if he was right.

Dictate these words for S. to write.

1. baby	6. radio
2. lady	7. Carla
3. David	8. Rosa
4. April	9. month
5. table	10. me

Have S. check his work by looking back at the chart and story words. Have him circle the number in front of any word he missed. Then have him erase the whole word and write it again correctly.

Sentences. Have S. write the title *Sentences* and number from 1 to 4. Then dictate these sentences.

1. Rosa is Carla's baby.
2. That lady is Mrs. King.
3. David helped me in class.
4. The radio is on the table.

Check what S. has written. Circle any word with an error. Have S. erase it and write it correctly. Have him correct any errors in punctuation and capitalization.

Study. At the bottom of the page, have S. write the title *Study* and any words he missed in the first two parts. Encourage him to study these words at home.

Writing prices with the dollar and cent signs. On a new page, have S. write the heading *Dollars and Cents*. Say a price, such as $3.25. Have S. tell you how to write it, and then copy it on his own paper. Be sure he knows that the dollar sign comes first and that the period comes between the number of dollars and the number of cents. Dictate the following prices for S. to write. When he has finished, check his work and give any help needed.

$3.00	$1.00	$4.75
$2.50	$6.25	$7.10

Follow the same procedure to help S. write prices with the cent sign, such as 50¢, 25¢, 60¢. Dictate a few of these for him to write.

PRACTICE: Page 12

Have S. read the title *Practice*, using the respelling in the new words section to sound it out. Then have him read the other new words. Tell him the sight word *sound*.

T: You have just done some practice exercises orally. The exercises on this page are similar. But to do them, you must read the words and the directions. Then you will mark or write the answers.

Have S. read the first direction silently and then aloud. Go over the sample with him. Then have him do number 1. Check to see that he has it right, and then let him complete this exercise. Check his answers. If he has any errors, have him read the words aloud and listen for the /ā/ sound.

Have S. read the directions for the second exercise. Go over the sample with him. Have him say each word aloud before he writes the number of syllables. Check his answers. If he made an error, have him read the word again. Or, you may say the word slowly, emphasizing the syllables.

HOMEWORK: Page 13

Go over the directions and the first item in each exercise with S. Ask him to complete this page at home. Also, encourage him to read the story and the Reading for Living section again.

CHECKING PROGRESS

The Practice section of this lesson will tell you if S. is beginning to be able to distinguish the short and long vowel sounds for *a* and to recognize the number of syllables in a word that he hears. There will be more practice on these skills in the following lessons.

MEETING INDIVIDUAL NEEDS

If S. needs more practice in word recognition, make flash cards for the chart words in Lesson 2, similar to those described in Lesson 1. Also make flash cards for *Rosa, baby-sitter,* and *Mrs. King*.

Show S. the side of the card with the word written correctly. Turn the card over to the respelling only if he needs help in sounding out the word. Mix up the cards and have him read them again.

Add the flash card for *Carla* from Lesson 1. Spread out the cards on the table, and have S. point to the card that answers each of these questions:

1. In what month did Carla start class?
2. What is the baby's name?
3. Who is Mrs. King?
4. Who is Carla's friend?
5. What is on the table?
6. Who is telling the story in Lesson 2?

Practice practice (prac tis), say (sā), sound, syllable (sil u bul)

Say the words. Which word has the sound ā? Circle that word.

snack (snake)

1. baby happy
2. apple table
3. paper faster
4. name man
5. after April
6. Jason happen
7. Dan David
8. radio traffic

Look at the picture, and say the word.
Under the picture, write the number of syllables in the word.

1. ______ 2. ______ 3. ______ 4. ______

5. ______ 6. ______ 7. ______ 8. ______

12 Lesson 2

Homework

Write the word.

baby mother	1. Rosa is Carla's ______.
man woman	2. The baby-sitter is a ______.
six ten	3. The radio says it is half past ______.
David Jason	4. ______ is coming to dinner.
ham fish	5. They will have ______ for dinner.

Say the word. Write the number of syllables.

1. lady 2
2. hat ______
3. April ______
4. potato ______
5. that ______
6. baby ______
7. has ______
8. radio ______
9. paper ______
10. apartment ______
11. man ______
12. hamburger ______

Lesson 2 13

In *Focus on Phonics-3*, Practice 2 may be used after Lesson 2. It gives more practice in distinguishing the short and long vowel sounds for *a*.

In the *Workbook for Skill Book 3*, the exercises for Lesson 2 may also be used.

LESSON 3 — Skill Book 3, Pages 14-19

OBJECTIVES

To help your student:

- recognize that the letters *ay* usually stand for the sound /ā/ as in the key word *day*.
- read words in which the sound /ā/ is written with *ay*.
- understand that the sound /ā/ at the end of a word is usually written *ay*.
- distinguish between the short and long vowel sounds for *a*.
- identify the beginning consonant blend *sp* as in *spent* and review the beginning blend *pl* as in *play*.
- review the ending consonant blends *nk* as in *bank*, *nt* as in *rent*, and *st* as in *last*.
- read a paragraph to find details.
- read dialog and identify the speakers.
- interpret facts and draw inferences from clues in the story.
- write short answers to Yes/No questions about the story.
- read and write a check.
- recognize the number of syllables in a word.
- review the ending *-ing*.
- write words and sentences from dictation.

INTRODUCTION

T: In the last lesson, you learned that sometimes the letter *a* stands for the sound /ā/ as in *paper*. In this lesson, you will learn that in some words another letter is used with *a* for the sound /ā/.

I. Reading

CHART: Page 14

Title and key word. Have S. read the title *Lesson 3*.

T: Look at the letters in the top right-hand corner. What two letters are together? [S: *ay*.] After *ay* there are two little marks. These marks stand for the word *equals*. I'm sure you have heard the expression "two and two equals four" or "five and five equals ten." Here it is written *ay* = *ā*. This means that when *a* and *y* are together in a word, they usually stand for the sound /ā/. (Point to *ay* = *ā*.) Read this part aloud. [S: *ay* equals *ā*.]

T: (Point to *day*.) Look at this picture and word. After the word, you see the equal sign. (Point to =.) Then you see the word written with a long mark over the *a*. What is the word? [S: day.] Under the word, you see the two letters together that stand for the sound /ā/. (Point to *ay*.) What are they? [S: *ay*.] Read this line. [S: *ay* equals *ā*.] From now on, when you see *ay* together in a word, you will say /ā/. That part of the word will not be rewritten for you.

Lines 1-6

T: Look at the other words in the chart. In each of these words, the sound /ā/ is written with the letters *ay*. Study each line. Notice the number of syllables in each word. Notice if any part of the word is written in a different way than it sounds.

After S. has studied the chart silently, have him read each word aloud, going down column 2. Then ask these questions:

1. What letters stand for the sound /ā/ in these words? [S: *ay*.]
2. How many syllables are there in each of the first five words? [S: One.]
3. What consonant blend does *play* start with? [S: *pl*.]
4. What part of the word *away* is written in a different way than it sounds? [S: The first sound.] What is the sound for the first *a* in *away?* [S: /u/] How many vowel sounds are there in *away?* [S: Two.] How many syllables are there in *away?* [S: Two.]
5. Where does the sound /ā/ come in each of these words? [S: At the end of the word.]

Explain that when the sound /ā/ comes at the end of a word, it is usually written *ay*.

Review. Have S. read each word in the chart again, including the key word. Go down the last column.

STORY: Page 15 (After Payday)

Ask S. to read the story title. Help him sound out the new words. Call attention to the number of syllables in each word. Ask S. what long vowel sound is in *Mason*, and then point out that the long vowel sound comes at the end of the first syllable. For *today, yesterday* and *payday*, have S. tell what the long vowel sound is. Point out that *payday* is one word made up of two small words. Also, point out that the sound /ā/ written with *ay* comes at the end of these words. In *payday*, it comes at the end of each of the small words.

Directed silent reading. Ask S. to read the first three paragraphs silently to find out who the story is about and what they have to do after payday. After he tells this, have him read paragraph 3 again to himself and name four bills the Masons have to pay. Then have him read paragraph 4 to find out who is writing the checks.

T: The rest of the story is written as conversation between Ray and Kay. Read it to yourself, and find out some of the things they talked about.

After S. has finished reading the story silently, have him tell the main things the Masons talked about. These things may include how much they spent, how much they have left, what they can do for fun, what they can do after the next payday, when they can go away.

Lesson 3

ay = ā

day = dā

ay = ā

pay	pay	pay
May	May	May
Kay	Kay	Kay
Ray	Ray	Ray
play	play	play
away	u way	away

After Payday

rent	next	card	Mason (Mā son)	today (to day)
spent	last	check	hundred (hun dred)	yesterday (yes ter day)
had				payday (pay day)

Today is the first day of May. Yesterday was payday. Yesterday was payday for Kay and Ray Mason. Their payday is the last day of the month. They got five hundred dollars.

The Masons are paying their bills today. Ray is looking at the bills. Kay is writing checks.

The Masons have to pay a lot of bills in May. They have to pay their rent today. The rent is for May. They have to pay the telephone bill for April. They have to pay the water bill for three months. They have to pay Kay's doctor bill. They have to pay some other bills.

Kay writes a check for the rent. She writes checks for the other bills.

Ray asks, "Have we spent the last cent?"

Kay laughs, "No, we have not spent the last cent. But we have spent a lot. Yesterday, we had five-hundred twenty-five dollars. Today, we have seventy-five dollars left."

"We can live on that," Ray says. "The next payday is May 15. But can we have any fun?"

Kay says, "Yes, we can play cards. Carla and David can come and play cards with us. It is fun to play cards."

Ray says, "We can have a little fun. But we can have a lot of fun after the next payday. We will have five hundred dollars. And we will not have many bills then. We can go away after the next payday. Let's go away the last three days in May."

"Yes, let's go away then," says Kay.

Oral reading. Starting with paragraph 5, have S. read the part that one of the characters says while you read what the other one says. Then reverse roles.

Reading between the lines. Discuss these questions.

1. The story tells us that the Masons together got $500 on their payday. But can we tell how much of this was Ray's pay and how much was Kay's? [No.]
2. When was the payday that the story is about—the first day in May or the last day in April? [Last day in April.] When will the Mason's next payday be? [May 15.] How often are they paid? [Twice a month.]
3. Which of these statements do you think best describes how well off the Masons are? Why?
   a. They are so rich they can do anything they want.
   b. They make enough money to live on, but they don't have a lot left over.
   c. They have a very hard time living on the money they make.

Relating the story to everyday life. You may want to discuss one or more of these topics with S. if time allows.

1. The Masons talked about going away at the end of May. What holiday at the end of May were they probably talking about? [Memorial Day.] What are some things people do on this holiday?
2. The Masons are paid twice a month—on the 15th and on the last day of the month. What are some other common pay periods people have? [Weekly, once a month.]
3. What common household expenses that people have are mentioned in the story? What are some other common household expenses the Masons might have that are not mentioned?

Story Checkup

short

Write a short *yes* or *no* answer.

Was yesterday the Mason's payday? Yes, it was.

1. Do the Masons have to pay a lot of bills? ____________
2. Does Ray write the checks? ____________
3. Have the Masons spent a lot? ____________
4. Have they spent their last cent? ____________
5. Is their next payday April 15? ____________
6. Can the Masons play cards? ____________
7. Do the Masons plan to go away in May? ____________

16 Lesson 3

Reading for Living

bank your

On April 29, the Masons had $25.00 in the bank. On April 30, they put $500.00 in the bank. Then they had $525.00 in the bank. They had to pay their bills with that $525.00.

Today is May 1. Kay writes a check for the rent. This is the check.

Ray Mason
Kay Mason
301
May 1 1986
Pay to Ellen Smith $ 225.00
Two hundred twenty-five and 00/100 DOLLARS
First City Bank
Garden City, CA
Kay Mason

Today is May 15. You are paying your bills. You have a bill from Dr. John Black. The bill is for $25.00. Write the check to pay your bill. Write your name on the check.

1264
______ 19__
Pay to ______ $ ______
______ DOLLARS
______

Lesson 3 17

STORY CHECKUP: Page 16

Have S. read the title, new word, and directions. Go over the sample question with him. Then let him complete the exercise by himself. Tell him that he may look back at the story if he doesn't remember an answer. Check his work. If he has an error, refer him to the story and have him write the answer correctly.

READING FOR LIVING: Page 17

Have S. read the title and new words. Then have him read the first two paragraphs silently and then aloud.

Reading the check

T: This is a check from the Masons' checkbook. Some things were printed on the checks by the bank before the Masons got their checkbook. Some things on this check have been filled in by Kay.

T: Let's look at the printed parts first. Whose names are printed in the top left-hand corner? [S: Ray Mason, Kay Mason.] This means that either Ray or Kay can sign the check.

T: In the lower left-hand corner are the name and address of the bank. In the address, the letters *CA* stand for California. Read the name and address of the bank. [S: First City Bank, Garden City, California.]

T: In the top right-hand corner is the number of the check. In a checkbook, each check is printed with its own number. What is the number? [S: 301.]

T: Now let's look at the parts Kay filled in. On the first line, she filled in the date. What is it? [S: May 1, 1986.]

T: The next line begins with the words *Pay to*. On this line, Kay wrote the name of the person the bank is to pay. Read the whole line. [S: Pay to Ellen Smith.]

T: After the dollar sign, Kay filled in the amount to pay. Look at the amount written in numbers. How many dollars? [S: 225.] Are there any cents? [S: No.]

T: On a check, the amount is written once in numbers. Then it is written again in words. This makes it harder for someone else to change the amount.

T: On the next line, you will see the amount in words. How many dollars? [S: Two hundred twenty-five.] The word *and* is used to separate the dollars from the cents. (Point to 00/100.) The cents amount is written in numbers over the number 100. This is because there are 100 cents in a dollar. When there are no cents, we write two zeros over 100. After we finish writing the amount, we draw a line so that no one can add anything. Now look at the whole line. It is read as *Two hundred twenty-five dollars and no cents.*

T: At the bottom of the check, Kay signed her name. We call this a signature. Your signature is always on file at the bank. When you open a checking account, the bank has you sign your name on a signature card. You must always sign your name the same way as on the signature card.

Writing a check. Have S. read the paragraph that tells what to do. Then help him fill out the blank check using Kay's check as an example. After he has finished, show him how to write in numbers and in words some amounts that contain both dollars and cents, such as these:

$5.35 Five and $\frac{35}{100}$

$76.29 Seventy-six and $\frac{29}{100}$

II. Skills Practice

T: Please close your book. We will have some practice on some of the new things in this lesson.

PRACTICE 1: Distinguishing the Long Sound for *a*

T: Which word has the long sound for *a*:

play, plan?	*pan, pay?*	*man, May?*
Dan, day?	*say, sad?*	*Ray, ran?*

PRACTICE 2: Identifying the Number of Syllables

T: Listen to each word I say, and tell me how many syllables it has. Remember, the number of vowel sounds will tell you how many syllables.

Mason	[2]	*hundred*	[2]	*play*	[1]
today	[2]	*yesterday*	[3]	*playing*	[2]
spent	[1]	*check*	[1]	*radio*	[3]

PRACTICE 3: Beginning Consonant Blend *sp*

Write *spent* on the board. Have S. read it and tell what blend it begins with. As he answers, underline *sp.*

T: Which word begins with the consonant blend *sp*:

pot, spot?	*sell, spell?*	*spoke, smoke?*
spin, pin?	*seed, speed?*	*sneak, speak?*
park, spark?	*spend, send?*	*spill, still?*

PRACTICE 4: Beginning Consonant Blend *pl*

Write *play* on the board. Have S. read it and tell what blend it begins with. As he answers, underline *pl.*

T: Which word begins with the consonant blend *pl:*

pay, play?	*late, plate?*	*please, class?*
plan, pan?	*place, lace?*	*black, plant?*
pain, plain?	*lot, plot?*	*glad, plug?*

PRACTICE 5: Ending Blends *st, nt, nk*

On the board, write these words in three columns: *last, rent, bank.* Have S. read each word and tell what consonant blend it ends with. As he answers, write the blends *st, nt, nk* as headings over the three columns.

Read the words listed below. Have S. tell which blend each word ends with. As he answers, write the word in the correct column. Finally, have S. read all of the words in each column.

fast	*tent*	*must*	*pink*	*list*	*spent*	*cost*
thank	*just*	*went*	*cent*	*think*	*drink*	

PRACTICE 6: Ending *-ing*

Write the following words in two columns. Have S. read each root word and its *-ing* form.

say	*saying*
pay	*paying*
play	*playing*

Write these words in two columns. Have S. read both forms of each word. Ask him what change is made in the root word before *-ing* is added. Remind him that we drop final silent *e* before adding *-ing.*

write	*writing*
love	*loving*
live	*living*

Write these words in two columns. Have S. read both forms of each word. Ask him what change is made in the root word before *-ing* is added. Remind him that, when the root word is one syllable, we double the final consonant after the short vowel sound.

run	*running*
get	*getting*
plan	*planning*

Have S. read each root word and its *-ing* form again, telling how many syllables each has. Point out that the *-ing* ending adds a syllable.

III. Writing

CHECK HOMEWORK: Page 13

Check this page with S. Have him correct any errors. Make note of the type of errors for further practice. If S. didn't do the assignment at home, give him some time to do it in class.

WRITING LESSON (In Notebook)

Have S. arrange his page as he did in the previous lessons, writing the titles *Lesson 3* and *Words* and then numbering from 1 to 10 in two columns.

Words

T: The chart words in this lesson are easy to spell if you remember how the sound /ā/ is spelled at the end of a word. What two letters stand for the sound /ā/ in words like *day?* [S: *ay*.] I will say the chart words and three words from the story. You can spell the story words by listening carefully to the sounds.

Dictate these words to S. to write.

1. day	6. play
2. pay	7. away
3. May	8. payday
4. Kay	9. hundred
5. Ray	10. checks

Have S. check his work by looking back at the chart and story words. Have him circle the number in front of any word he missed. Then have him erase the whole word and write it again correctly.

Also, have S. write the word *they*, and have him study it. Explain that *ey* for /ā/ is an exception and that he will need to remember it.

Sentences. Have S. write the title *Sentences* and number from 1 to 4. Dictate these sentences.

1. Today is the first day of May.
2. Yesterday was payday.
3. They have to pay the rent.
4. Do the Masons plan to go away?

Check what S. has written. Circle any word with an error. Have S. erase it and write it correctly. Have him correct any errors in punctuation and capitalization.

Study. At the bottom of the page, have S. write this title and any words he missed in the first two parts. Encourage him to study these words at home.

Writing checks. On a new page, have S. write the heading *Writing Checks.* Have S. look again at the sample check on page 17 of the skill book. Review how to write the amount in numbers and in words, as explained in the Reading for Living section.

In his notebook, have S. make a dollar sign followed by a short blank. Under this, have him make a long blank followed by the word *Dollars*. Then ask him to fill in the amount $6.75 in numbers and in words.

Have S. make another set of blanks like this and fill in $20.39 in numbers and in words. Have him make a third set of blanks and fill in $100.00 in numbers and in words.

PRACTICE: Page 18

Have S. read the title and the directions for the first exercise. Go over the sample item with him. Then let him do the exercise by himself. Check his work. Follow the same procedure for the second exercise.

HOMEWORK: Page 19

Go over the directions for each exercise with S. Ask him to complete this page at home. Also, encourage him to read the story and the Reading for Living section over again and to practice writing words and amounts for checks as given in the Writing Lesson.

CHECKING PROGRESS

To check the student's ability to apply phonics skills, make flash cards for these words: *bay, hay, lay, say, way, clay, gray, pray, tray, stay, spray.* Begin by asking S. to say some words that end with the sound /ā/. He will probably say words from the lesson, such as *day, pay, May*. List the words he says. Ask him what letters stand for the sound /ā/ at the end of a word [*ay*]. Give him the flash cards, one at a time, and ask him to read each word. Make note of any words he has difficulty with, but don't drill on them. You are trying to see if S. can apply his knowledge of consonant sounds, consonant blends, and the long sound for *a* by blending the sounds together to form words.

Also, you may make flash cards for *Sunday, Monday, Friday, Saturday.* Tell S. that the names of the days of the week end with *-day*. Have S. read each word by sounding it out. Give help as needed in dividing the word into syllables. Point out that the *o* in *Monday* stands for the sound /u/ and that the *i* in *Friday* has the long vowel sound /ī/.

MEETING INDIVIDUAL NEEDS

If S. needs more practice in word recognition, make flash cards for the chart words in Lesson 3, similar to those you made for previous lessons. Also make flash cards for *Mason, today, payday, yesterday,* and *checks.*

Follow the suggestions for using flash cards given in the first two lessons. Ask a question that can be answered with one of the words, and have S. find it. Also have S. ask a question that can be answered with one of the words.

In the *Workbook for Skill Book 3*, the exercises for Lesson 3 may be used at this time.

In *Focus on Phonics-3*, Practices 3A-3B may be used after Lesson 3. They give practice with the word family *-ay*.

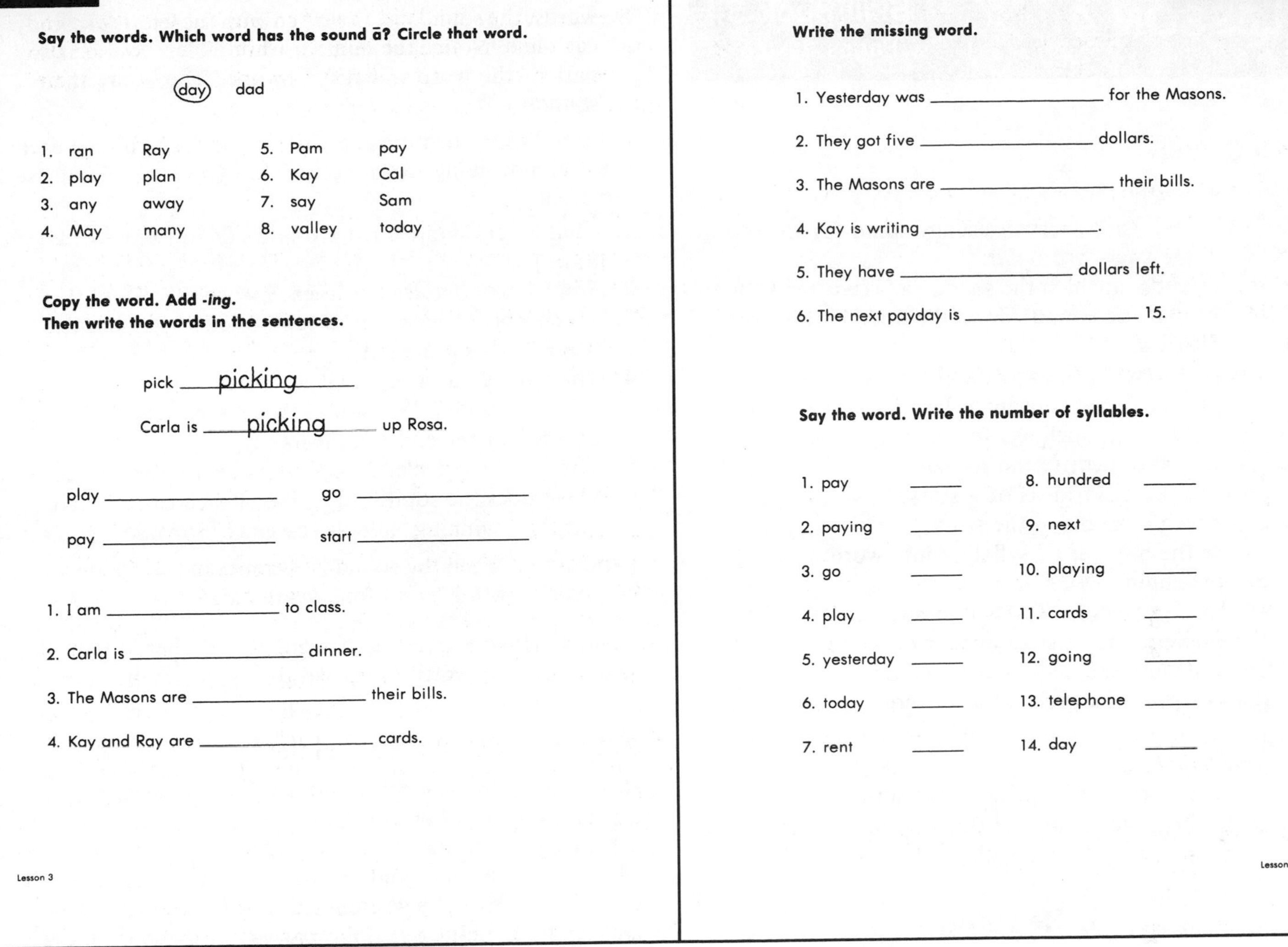

Practice

Say the words. Which word has the sound ā? Circle that word.

(day) dad

1.	ran	Ray	5.	Pam	pay
2.	play	plan	6.	Kay	Cal
3.	any	away	7.	say	Sam
4.	May	many	8.	valley	today

Copy the word. Add *-ing*.
Then write the words in the sentences.

pick picking

Carla is picking up Rosa.

play ______ go ______

pay ______ start ______

1. I am ______ to class.
2. Carla is ______ dinner.
3. The Masons are ______ their bills.
4. Kay and Ray are ______ cards.

18 Lesson 3

Homework

Write the missing word.

1. Yesterday was ______ for the Masons.
2. They got five ______ dollars.
3. The Masons are ______ their bills.
4. Kay is writing ______.
5. They have ______ dollars left.
6. The next payday is ______ 15.

Say the word. Write the number of syllables.

1. pay ___	8. hundred ___
2. paying ___	9. next ___
3. go ___	10. playing ___
4. play ___	11. cards ___
5. yesterday ___	12. going ___
6. today ___	13. telephone ___
7. rent ___	14. day ___

Lesson 3 19

Another thing you can do to give S. practice in reading word families is to make a slip strip. This simple device, pictured here, can be made from two 3-by-5-inch index cards. Fold one card in half from side to side, and tape or staple the sides together. Print *ay* in about the middle of the card, with letters about 1/8" high. In front of the *ay*, cut out a "window" about 3/8" high and 1/2" wide. The window should be high enough to hold a tall letter like *h*, low enough for a letter like *j*, and wide enough for a three-letter consonant blend like *spr*.

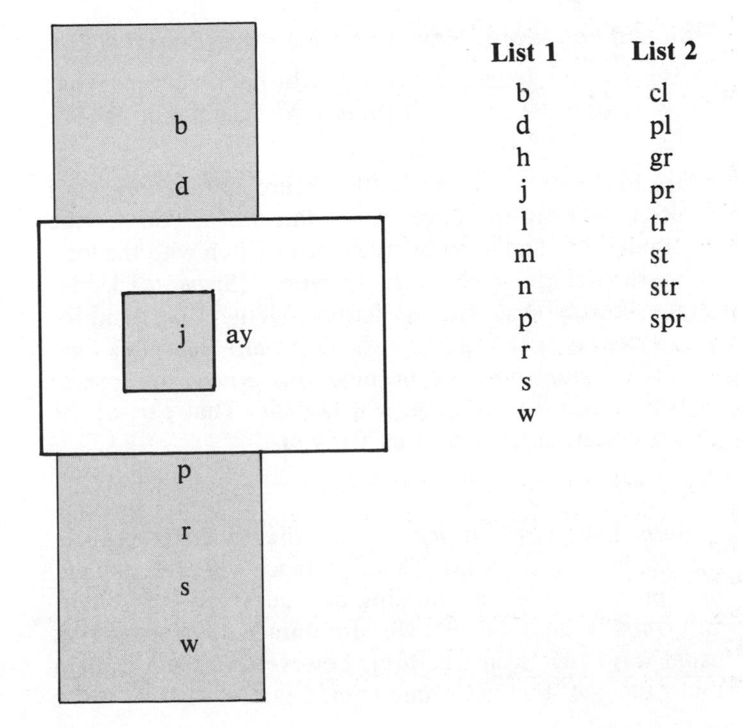

Cut another card in half lengthwise. Starting at the top of one strip, copy the consonants in List 1 in a column. Make the letters the same size as the *ay*. Place them on the strip so that they will appear in the window when the strip is inserted in the folded card. Leave about 1/4" between letters so that only one letter at a time will show. On the other strip, copy the consonant blends from List 2 in the same way.

Have S. read the words formed by moving the slip up and down.

LESSON 4 — Skill Book 3, Pages 20-25

OBJECTIVES

To help your student:

- recognize that the letters *ai* usually stand for the sound /ā/ as in the key word *paint*.
- read the words in which the sound /ā/ is written with *ai*.
- recognize that the sound /ā/ in the middle of a word is often written *ai*.
- distinguish between the short and long sounds for *a*.
- review the beginning consonant blends *bl, pl, gr, st*.
- review *er, ir, ur* as spellings for the sound /er/.
- read dialog and identify the speaker.
- summarize the main ideas of a story.
- recall or locate details in the story.
- recognize the number of syllables in a word.
- review the ending *-ed*.
- write short answers to Yes/No questions.
- write complete sentences to answer questions.
- write words and sentences from dictation.
- read and write prices related to different quantities.

INTRODUCTION

T: You have learned that the letters *ay* stand for the sound /ā/. In this lesson, you will find out another letter that is used with *a* to stand for the sound /ā/.

I. Reading

CHART: Page 20

Title and key word. Have S. read the title *Lesson 4.*

T: Look at the letters in the top right-hand corner. What two letters are together? [S: *ai.*] What sound do the letters *ai* equal? [S: /ā/.]

T: (Point to *paint.*) Look at the picture and the key word at the top of the page. After this word, you see the equal sign. Then you see the word written with the long mark over the *a*. What is the word? [S: *paint.*] Under the word, you see the two letters together that stand for the sound /ā/. What are they? [S: *ai.*] Read this line. [S: *ai* equals *ā*.] From now on, when you see *ai* together in a word, you will say /ā/. That part of the word will not be rewritten for you.

Lines 1-6

Note: The sound for *ai* before *r* is slightly different from the regular long *a* sound. This difference will probably not be a problem to S. in sounding out the words *hair, chair,* and *stairs* in lines 4-6. He will pronounce the words in his usual way. If it seems helpful, however, you can explain that *r* changes the /ā/ sound somewhat.

T: Look at the other words in the chart. In each of these words, the sound /ā/ is written with the letters *ai*. Study each line. Notice the number of syllables. Notice if any part of the word is written in a different way than it sounds.

After S. has studied the chart silently, have him read each word aloud, going down column 2. Then ask him these questions:

1. What letters stand for the sound /ā/ in these words? [S: *ai.*]
2. How many syllables are in each word? [S: One.]
3. Which word begins with a capital letter? [S: Gail.] Why? [S: It's a name.]
4. Which word has a part that is written in a different way than it sounds? [S: stairs.] Which part is different? [S: The *s* at the end sounds like *z*.]
5. What consonant blend does *stairs* begin with? [S: *st.*]
6. Where does the sound /ā/ come in each of these words —at the beginning, middle, or end? [S: Middle.]

Explain that when the sound /ā/ comes in the middle of a one-syllable word, it is often written *ai*.

Review. Have S. read each word in the chart again, including the key word. Go down the last column.

STORY: Pages 21-22 (Painting)

Have S. read the story title and new words aloud. Call attention to the number of syllables in each word. If a word has a long vowel sound, have S. tell what the sound is and what letter or letters stand for the sound. Point out that the expression *OK* can be written with just the capital letters *O* and *K*. Also, point out that *landlady* is made up of two smaller words, *land* and *lady*.

Directed silent reading. Ask S. to read the whole story to himself to find out who the people are and what they did. After he tells who the people are, ask him to summarize the story in a few sentences. His summary should include the following main points:

> [Jason and Gail planned to get married. They wanted to paint the kitchen in the apartment they had rented. The landlady said she would pay for the paint and nails if they would fix the stairs and paint the kitchen and stairs. Jason and Gail got some paint and nails, and the landlady paid for them. Jason and Gail got ready to paint.]

Have S. give the summary orally. Do not write it.

Oral reading. Explain that this is another story that is mostly people's conversation. Ask S. to tell who is speaking in each of the first four paragraphs. In the first paragraph, note that although the story says *They said*, probably only one of them spoke.

Have S. read the part of either Jason or the landlady in the first four paragraphs, while you read the other part. In the rest of the story, ask S. to read either the part of Gail or

Lesson 4

ai = ā

paint = pānt

ai = ā

nail	nail	nail
Gail	Gail	Gail
paid	paid	paid
hair	hair	hair
chair	chair	chair
stairs	stairz	stairs

20 Lesson 4

Painting

shall	ever (ev er)	OK (ō kay)
gray	never (nev er)	landlady (land lady)

Gail Fisher and Jason Hunt planned to get married. They rented an apartment. They said to the landlady, "We will paint the kitchen. Will you pay for the paint?"

The landlady asked, "Have you ever painted a kitchen?"

Jason said, "No, I have never painted a kitchen. But I have painted stairs."

"OK," said the landlady. "You get the paint and some nails. You can fix the stairs first. Then you can paint the stairs and your kitchen. I'll pay you for the paint and the nails."

"Shall we paint the kitchen red?" asked Jason.

"No, let's not," said Gail. "Let's paint it pink. What color shall we paint the stairs?"

Jason said, "Let's paint the stairs gray. Shall we get some black paint? We can paint the table and chairs black."

Lesson 4 21

Jason while you read the other part. Then reverse roles. If you have more than one student, then others can read the parts.

If S. has trouble reading just the dialog, have him underline the parts between the quotation marks.

Reading between the lines. Ask these questions. Let S. look back at the story if he needs to.

1. What did Jason and Gail offer to do at first? [Paint the kitchen.] What did the landlady want them to do besides this? [Fix and paint the stairs.]
2. What did the landlady agree to pay for? [Nails to fix the stairs, paint for the kitchen and stairs.]
3. What else did Gail and Jason decide to paint? [Table and chairs.] Was this part of their agreement with the landlady? [No.] Did she pay for this paint? [No.]
4. Which of these jobs did Gail do by herself? Which did Jason do by himself? Which did they do together?
   a. Paint the kitchen [Together.]
   b. Fix the stairs [Jason.]
   c. Paint the stairs [Jason.]
   d. Paint the table and chairs [Gail.]
5. Do you think the agreement Jason and Gail made with their landlady was a good deal both for them and for her? Why or why not?
6. What do you remember about Jason from another story in this book? (If S. doesn't remember, have him skim the Lesson 1 story. Then ask questions to elicit these facts: He works at a market. He goes to night class. He has a car. He is friends with David Miller and Carla Lopez.)

"OK," said Gail.

Jason and Gail got the paint and the nails. Gail paid for them.

The landlady paid Gail for the pink and gray paint. She paid Gail for the nails.

Gail and Jason got ready to paint. Gail covered her hair.

"Have you ever had paint in your hair?" Jason asked.

Gail said, "No, I never have. I cover my hair when I paint. Shall we paint the table and chairs first?"

Jason said, "No, let's not. Let's paint the kitchen first. Then you can paint the table and chairs. I have never painted chairs. I'll fix the stairs and paint them."

Story Checkup

Write a short yes or no answer.

Has Jason ever painted a kitchen? No, he has not.

1. Have Gail and Jason rented an apartment? ____________
2. Will they paint the kitchen red? ____________
3. Has Jason ever painted chairs? ____________
4. Did Gail cover her hair? ____________
5. Did the landlady pay for the gray paint? ____________
6. Did the landlady pay for the black paint? ____________
7. Will Jason paint the table and chairs? ____________

Reading for Living

quart (quort) gallon (gal un)

Pink Paint: $3 a quart, $10 a gallon

Gray Paint: $4 a quart, $14 a gallon

Black Paint: $5 a quart, $18 a gallon

Write the missing number with $.

1. Gail and Jason got one gallon of pink paint.
   They paid ____________ for it.
2. They got one gallon of gray paint.
   They paid ____________ for it.
3. They got two quarts of black paint.
   They paid ____________ for it.
4. The pink, gray, and black paint cost ____________.
5. Their landlady paid them for the pink and gray paint.
   She paid them ____________.

STORY CHECKUP: Page 22

Have S. read the title and directions. Go over the sample question with him. Then let him complete the exercise by himself. Tell him that he may look back at the story if he doesn't remember an answer. Check his work. If he has an error, refer him to the story and have him write the answer correctly.

READING FOR LIVING: Page 23

Have S. read the title and new words. Ask him how many syllables are in *quart* and *gallon*. Be sure S. knows that a gallon is larger than a quart. If he doesn't already know, explain that there are four quarts in a gallon.

Ask S. to read to himself what is written on each can of paint and what is written under it. Then have him tell the color of each paint and the price for each quantity (quart and gallon). Ask which paint costs the most and which costs the least. Explain that the different prices are probably for different kinds of paint and different brands. For example, Jason and Gail wanted black paint for their table and chairs. So the black paint they bought was probably enamel, which is used to paint furniture and costs more than paint for walls.

Have S. read the directions and do the exercise. Do the first item with him if he doesn't understand what to do. Check his answers, and help him correct any errors.

II. Skills Practice

T: Please close your book. We will have some practice exercises on the new things in this lesson, and we'll review some blends and endings.

PRACTICE 1: Distinguishing the Long Sound for *a*

Write the following pairs of words. Have S. read each pair and tell which word has the short sound for *a* and which has the long sound. Then, working with one pair at a time, say one of the words, and have S. point to it.

man	*main*	*pad*	*paid*
pan	*pain*	*bat*	*bait*
ran	*rain*	*am*	*aim*

PRACTICE 2: Identifying Rhyming Words

Write *nail*, and have S. read it. Then, say the following pairs of words, and have him tell which word in each pair rhymes with *nail*.

paid, sail	*tail, take*	*pail, pal*
pill, pail	*fell, fail*	*girl, Gail*

Write *hair*, and have S. read it. Then say the following pairs of words, and have him tell which word in each pair rhymes with *hair*.

are, air	*chair, chart*	*pair, part*
far, fair	*star, stair*	

PRACTICE 3: Identifying the Number of Syllables

Say each word below, and have S. tell how many syllables it has. If he has difficulty, say the word again, and have him tell how many vowel sounds—or beats—it has.

ever	[2]	*never*	[2]	*quart*	[1]
paint	[1]	*lady*	[2]	*gallon*	[2]
painting	[2]	*landlady*	[3]	*writing*	[2]

PRACTICE 4: Beginning Blends *bl, pl, gr, st*

Write *black* and *play*. Ask S. what consonant blend each begins with. As he answers, underline *bl* and *pl*.

T: I will say two words that begin with the same blend. Which blend do they begin with, *bl* or *pl*:

blank, blow?	*plus, plum?*	*plenty, plastic?*
plan, please?	*black, blond?*	*blister, blanket?*

Write *gray* and *stairs*. Ask S. which consonant blend each begins with. As he answers underline *gr* and *st*.

T: Which word begins with the consonant blend *gr:*

glass, grass?	*grave, brave?*	*train, grain?*
grace, race?	*trip, grip?*	*green, cream?*

T: Which word begins with the consonant blend *st:*

star, tar?	*stand, sand?*	*thing, sting?*
ship, step?	*stick, chick?*	*sack, stack?*

PRACTICE 5: Review *er, ir, ur* Spellings for /er/

The following words with the sound /er/ were introduced in Lessons 1-4 or were used in the Lesson 4 story. Write the words. Have S. read each one and tell what letters stand for the sound /er/. As he answers, underline the letters *er, ir,* or *ur* in the word. Be sure S. notices both the *ur* and the *er* in *hamburger*.

her	*water*	*ever*	*first*	*yesterday*
cover	*answer*	*never*		*hamburger*

PRACTICE 6: Ending *-ed*

Write these words in a column: *play, pick, ask, paint, rent, start*. Have S. read the words. Then ask him what each word would be with the ending *-ed*. As he answers, write the *-ed* words in a second column.

Point to *play, played*. Have S. read both words and tell how many syllables are in each. [One.]

T: We see two vowel letters in *played*, but we hear only one vowel sound. The *-ed* ending does not add a syllable when added to the root word *play*. But *-ed* does add a syllable when added to some root words.

Have S. read aloud each pair of words and tell the number of syllables in the root word and the *-ed* form. If he has trouble telling whether *-ed* adds a syllable, ask him how many beats he hears in the word.

Note: If S. pronounces *asked* with two syllables or as /axt/, do not comment or try to change his pronunciation. If he pronounces the words with two syllables, say /askt/ and have him tell how many syllables he hears you say.

III. Writing

CHECK HOMEWORK: Page 19

Check this page with S. Have him correct any errors. Make note of the type of errors for more practice. If S. didn't do the page at home, give him time in class.

WRITING LESSON (In Notebook)

Have S. arrange his page as in previous lessons, writing the titles *Lesson 4* and *Words* and then writing the numbers 1 to 10 in two columns.

Words

T: What letters stand for the sound /ā/ in the chart words in this lesson? [S: *ai*.] Please spell the word *paid*. [S: *p-a-i-d*.] Good. (Write *paid* on the board.) I will write the word again and leave out one letter. (Write *pad*.) What letter did I leave out? [S: *i*.] You can see that the *i* is very important. Without the *i*, *a* followed by a consonant will probably have the short sound.

T: You probably will not need to study the chart words. But let's go over three other words you will write.

Help S. study *gray, landlady,* and *apartment*. Have him tell how to spell each word, and write it on the board as he answers. For *gray*, have S. tell what letters stand for the sound /ā/. For *landlady*, have S. spell the first syllable, *land*, and then *lady*. For *apartment*, have S. spell each syllable: *a/part/ment*.

Then dictate these words for S. to write:

1. paint	6. chair
2. nail	7. stairs
3. Gail	8. gray
4. paid	9. landlady
5. hair	10. apartment

Have S. check his work by looking back at the chart and story. Have him circle the number in front of any word he missed. Then have him erase the whole word and write it again correctly.

Sentences. Have S. write the title *Sentences* and number from 1 to 4. Dictate these sentences.

1. The landlady paid for the nails.
2. Jason will paint the stairs gray.
3. Gail will paint the chairs black.
4. Gail will cover her hair.

Check what S. has written. Circle any word with an error. Have S. erase it and write it correctly. Have him correct any errrors in punctuation or capitalization.

Study. At the bottom of the page, have S. write this title and any words he missed in the first two parts.

Practice

Say the words. Which word has the sound ā? Circle that word.

1. paint	pan	5. chair	Chan
2. starts	stairs	6. neck	nail
3. Gail	girl	7. hair	has
4. pack	paid	8. gray	grass

Copy the word. Add *-ed*.
Then write the words in the sentences.

play played

They played cards.

paint ______ ask ______

rent ______ cover ______

1. Jason and Gail ______ an apartment.
2. Jason has never ______ a kitchen.
3. Gail ______ her hair.
4. "Shall we paint the kitchen red?" ______ Jason.

Homework

Answer with a sentence.

1. What did Gail and Jason rent? ______
2. What color will they paint the kitchen? ______
3. Who will paint the stairs? ______
4. Who will paint the chairs? ______

Say the word. Write the number of syllables.

1. paint	____	6. asked	____
2. painted	____	7. covered	____
3. stairs	____	8. landlady	____
4. chairs	____	9. paid	____
5. rented	____	10. never	____

PRACTICE: Page 24

Have S. read the title and the directions for the first exercise. Have him do the first exercise, and then check his work. Go over the directions for the second exercise with S. and have him read the sample. Then have him add *-ed* to each word in the list before he fills in the missing words in the sentences. Check his work.

HOMEWORK: Page 25

Have S. read the first direction. Explain that a complete sentence tells *who did it* and *what they did*. Have S. read the first question aloud, answer it orally with a sentence, and then write the sentence. Accept either *Gail and Jason* or *They* in his answer. Then have S. read the directions for the second exercise.

CHECKING PROGRESS

Use these activities to see how well S. can apply the phonics skills he is learning to new words.

• Make flash cards for *nail, Gail, pail, mail, tail, jail, fail, sail, rail*. Have S. read *nail* and *Gail*. Then give him the other cards. Tell him these words rhyme with *nail* and *Gail*, and have him read them. Note his ability to blend the beginning consonant with *ail* to form a new word. If a word gives him trouble, help him sound it out. But do not drill on these words.

• Make flash cards for these items: *Wet Paint, Main Street, Mailbox, Rain Today, Fair on Sunday, Bills to Pay, Bills Paid*. Tell S. these are some words he may see on signs or in other everyday situations. Some of these words are new, but they are like words he knows. Ask him to see how many he can read.

Let S. know that reading these words and signs is something more than the lesson. If he was able to cover the lesson reasonably well, his progress is satisfactory.

MEETING INDIVIDUAL NEEDS

You may make flash cards for the chart and story words in Lesson 4. Use them as in previous lessons.

For a game with rhyming words, make a flash card for each of these words:

Gail, nail	*me, he*	*hair, chair*	*paid, laid*
rain, train	*day, say*	*paint, faint*	*gray, play*

Mix the cards, and spread them out face down. Have S. turn up two cards and read them aloud. If they rhyme, he may keep them. If not, he should put them back face down. Take turns with S. The player with the most pairs wins.

In the *Workbook for Skill Book 3*, the exercises for Lesson 3 may be used at this time.

In *Focus on Phonics-3*, Practices 4A-4D may be used after Lesson 3. They give practice with *ai* word families.

LESSON 5 Skill Book 3 Pages 26-31

OBJECTIVES

To help your student:

- recognize that the letters *a* and *e* separated by one consonant (*a-e*) usually stand for the sound /ā/.
- read words in which the sound /ā/ is represented by *a-e*, as in the key word *cake*.
- distinguish between the long and short sounds for *a*.
- determine the number of syllables in a word.
- understand that two vowel letters in a one-syllable word usually represent a long vowel sound.
- recognize that, after a long vowel sound, the letter *k* is used for the sound /k/, rather than *ck*.
- review the beginning blends *cl, gl, pl, br, dr, fr, pr*.
- review adding *-ing* to words ending in silent *e*.
- read dialog and identify the speakers.
- recognize the main idea of a story and the supporting details.
- read and write a short thank you letter.
- write words and sentences from dictation.

INTRODUCTION

T: You have learned three ways that the sound /ā/ is written. How is /ā/ written in the word *paper?* [S: *a*.] In the word *day?* [S: *ay*.] In the word *paint?* [S: *ai*.] Today you will learn another way the sound /ā/ is written.

I. Reading

CHART: Page 26

Title and key word. Have S. read the title *Lesson 5*.

T: Look at the letters in the top right-hand corner. What are they? [S: *a* and *e*.] Notice that there is a dash between the *a* and the *e*. The dash stands for a consonant. When *a* and *e* are separated by one consonant, they stand for the sound /ā/.

T: Look at the picture and the key word. What is the word? [S: *cake*.] What consonant separates *a* and *e?* [S: *k*.]

T: (Point to *a-e* = *ā*.) We can say that *a* and *e* separated by one consonant equal the sound /ā/. Now let's look at the other words in the chart in which the sound /ā/ is written this way.

Line 1

T: Look at the first picture and word. Look at the third column for help in sounding out the word. What is it? [S: bake.] What is the vowel sound? [S: /ā/.] What consonant is between *a* and *e*? [S: *k*.]

T: In the third column, a line is drawn from *a* to *e* under the word *bake*. (Point to the line.) This is to remind you that these two letters go together for the sound /ā/.

T: Read the word again in the last column. [S: bake.]

Line 2

T: Look at the next word. If you need help, study column 3. What is the word? [S: take.] What letters stand for the sound /ā/? [S: *a* and *e*.] What consonant is between them? [S: *k*.] Read the word again in the last column. [S: take.]

Lines 3-6. Go over the rest of the words in the same way.

Review. Have S. read each word in the chart again, including the key word. Go down the last column.

Call attention to the rhyming words and the blend *pl* in *plate*. Ask S. how many syllables there are in each of the chart words [one]. Call attention to the use of *k* in *cake, bake, take*. Point out that, after a long vowel sound, the letter *k* is used for the sound /k/.

Point out that all of the chart words are root words; they do not have any endings added to them. Explain that the *a-e* spelling for the sound /ā/ comes at the end of root words. If you add an ending to the root word, the vowel sound is still /ā/. Write *cakes, plates, Jane's, baked,* and have S. read these words with endings added.

STORY: Pages 27-28 (The Wedding)

Have S. read the story title and the new words aloud. Call attention to these points:

- the beginning consonant blend *st* in *still*.
- the *a-e* spelling in *came* and *gave*.
- *where* and *there* end with the same sound: /âr/. They rhyme with *care* in the chart and with *hair* and *chair* in the previous lesson, but they are spelled differently from how they sound.
- the *dd* in *wedding* stands for just one /d/ sound.
- *yourself* is made up of two smaller words: *your* and *self*.
- the number of syllables in each word.

Directed silent reading. Have S. read the whole story silently and then summarize it in two or three sentences. Ask him to read aloud the paragraph that gives the main idea [paragraph 1]. Point out that the rest of the story fills in the details.

T: The story tells us some of the conversation at the party. Name the people who said something in the story. [S: Jane, Sam, Carla, Gail, Jason, Gail's father.]

Oral reading. Have S. read the parts of one or two of the characters while you read the others. Then reverse roles.

Reading between the lines. Discuss these questions. Let S. look back at the story to find the answers.

1. What was there to eat and drink at the wedding party? [Wedding cake, sandwiches, coffee, and other drinks.]
2. What guests at the wedding are mentioned in the story? What is their relationship to Gail or Jason? [Gail's sister Jane, Jason's little brother Sam, Gail's uncle, Carla (friend), Jason's mother, Gail's father.]
3. In what ways did family members help? [Jason's mother baked the wedding cake. Gail's uncle took pictures. Gail's sister Jane seemed to be in charge of the party.]
4. Who did Gail's father mean when he spoke of "my little girl"? [Gail.] What did Jason call Gail's father? [Dad.]
5. What wedding customs are shown in the story? What are some other wedding customs that are not in the story?

STORY CHECKUP: Page 28

Have S. read the title, new word, and directions. Go over the sample question with him. Then have him do the rest of the exercise by himself. Tell him that he may look back at the story if he doesn't remember an answer. Check his work, and have him correct any errors.

READING FOR LIVING: Page 29

Have S. read the title and new words aloud. Call attention to the *fr* blend in *frame* and the *a-e* spelling for /ā/ in *frame* and *date.* Then have S. read the introductory paragraphs first silently and then aloud.

T: This is one of the thank you letters that Gail wrote. Please read it to yourself.

When S. has finished the letter, have him read each question aloud and give the answer orally. Then have him write the answers. Check his written answers.

II. Skills Practice

T: Please close your book. We will have some practice exercises on the new things in this lesson, and we'll review some blends and endings.

PRACTICE 1: Distinguishing the Long Sound for *a*

Write the following pairs of words. Have S. read each pair and tell which word has the short sound for *a* and which has the long sound. Then, working with one pair at a time, say one of the words, and have S. point to it.

at	*ate*	*can*	*cane*	*Sam*	*same*
rat	*rate*	*Jan*	*Jane*	*mad*	*made*

PRACTICE 2: Identifying Rhyming Words

Write *cake* and have S. read it. Then, say the following pairs of words, and have him tell which word in each pair rhymes with *cake.*

came, bake	*make, made*	*snake, snack*
take, tack	*rack, rake*	*cape, lake*

Write *ate,* and have S. read it. Then say the following pairs of words, and have him tell which word in each pair rhymes with *ate.*

let, late	*gate, get*	*plate, plan*
hate, hat	*fat, fate*	*mat, mate*

PRACTICE 3: Identifying the Number of Syllables

Say each word below, and have S. tell how many syllables it has. If he has difficulty, say the word again, and have him tell how many vowel sounds—or beats—it has.

gave	[1]	*little*	[2]	*wedding*	[2]
date	[1]	*table*	[2]	*yourself*	[2]
person	[2]	*frame*	[1]	*sandwiches*	[3]
still	[1]	*party*	[2]	*building*	[2]
glasses	[2]	*plates*	[1]	*writing*	[2]

PRACTICE 4: Beginning Blends *cl, gl, pl*

Write *clock, glass, plate.* Have S. read each word and tell what blend it begins with. As he answers, underline *cl, gl, pl.*

T: I will say two words that begin with the same blend. Which blend do they begin with—*cl, gl,* or *pl:*

clip, class?	*glad, Glen?*	*glaze, glare?*
plan, play?	*plus, place?*	*clap, climb?*

PRACTICE 5: Beginning Blends *br, dr, fr, pr*

Write *brother, drink, friend, pretty.* Have S. read each word and tell what blend it begins with. As he answers underline *br, dr, fr, pr.*

T: I will say two words that begin with the same blend. Which blend do they begin with—*br, dr, fr,* or *pr:*

free, front?	*praise, prize?*	*bride, bridge?*
dry, dress?	*drive, drop?*	*fresh, Frank?*
bread, bright?	*Fran, friend?*	*practice, press?*

PRACTICE 6: Spellings with *k* and *ck*

Write these pairs of words, and have S. read them:

back	*bake*	*Jack*	*Jake*
tack	*take*	*snack*	*snake*

Remind S. of the rule learned in *Skill Book 2*: after a short vowel sound, the sound /k/ is written with *ck.* Point out that, after a long vowel sound, the sound /k/ is written with *k.* Then, say each word below, and have S. tell whether the sound /k/ is written with *k* or *ck.*

lake	*make*	*sack*	*black*	*stack*
pack	*wake*	*fake*	*shake*	*track*

a–e = ā

cake = cāk

a–e = ā

	bake	bake bāk	bake
	take	take tāk	take
	Jane	Jane Jān	Jane
	ate	ate āt	ate
	plate	plate plāt	plate
	care	care cār	care

The Wedding

yet	came	where (whāre)	church	wedding (wed ing)
still	gave	there (thāre)	party (par ty)	yourself (your self)

Jason and Gail got married in Gail's church. Jason's family and friends came to the wedding. Gail's family and friends came. After the wedding, there was a party. The party was in a building next to the church.

At the party, there was a big wedding cake. It was on a pretty glass plate. There were little sandwiches, coffee, and other drinks. There were paper plates and cups.

"Take a plate and help yourself to sandwiches," said Gail's sister Jane. "And help yourself to drinks."

"May I have some cake?" asked Jason's little brother Sam.

"No, not yet," said Jane. "Jason and Gail have to cut the cake first."

"Where are they?" asked Sam.

"They are still in the church," Jane said. "Gail's uncle is still taking pictures of them. He will take a picture of the wedding cake when they cut it."

"Who baked the wedding cake?" asked Carla.

Jane said, "Jason's mother baked it. She bakes many wedding cakes."

Just then, Jason and Gail came from the church. They cut the wedding cake. Jason gave Gail some cake, and she gave him some. They ate their cake.

Jason's little brother said, "I have not had any cake yet." Jason gave him some.

Gail said to the others, "Come and help yourself to some cake." Their family ate cake. Their friends ate cake.

Jason said to Gail, "Let's go!"

Jason's little brother said, "Where are you going?"

"Away," Jason said.

"You cannot go yet," said Gail's father. "I still have not kissed my little girl." He kissed Gail and said, "Take care of her, Jason."

Jason said, "Yes, Dad, I will take care of her. And she will take care of me."

Story Checkup

right (rīt)

Circle the letter of the right answer.

Who got married?
- (a.) Jason and Gail
- b. Carla and David

1. Where was the wedding?
   - a. in Gail's church
   - b. in Carla's apartment
2. Where was the party?
   - a. in the church
   - b. in a building next to the church
3. Where was the wedding cake?
   - a. on a paper plate
   - b. on a glass plate
4. Who was taking pictures?
   - a. Gail's father
   - b. Gail's uncle

Reading for Living

frame	much
date	dear (dēr)

Gail and Jason got many wedding gifts. Some of the gifts were glasses, plates, curtains, a chair, a table, a rug, a clock radio, and a picture frame.

Gail is writing thank you letters for the gifts. First, she writes the date. She puts the date at the top of the letter. She starts the letter with the word *Dear* and the person's name.

May 21, 1986

Dear Carla,

Thank you very much for the picture frame. Jason and I think that it is very pretty. We will put a wedding picture in the frame.

Thank you very much for coming to the wedding. You are a dear friend.

With love,
Gail

1. What is the date on the letter? ______
2. Who is the letter to? ______
3. What was the gift? ______
4. Who is Gail's dear friend? ______

PRACTICE 7: Dropping Final Silent *e* Before *-ing*

Write these words in a column: *have, come, live, give.* Have S. read the words. Then have him say each word with the ending *-ing* added. Remind S. of the rule learned in *Skill Book 2:* when a word ends in silent *e,* we usually drop the *e* before adding *-ing*. Have S. tell you how to write each word with *-ing*. As he answers, write *having, coming, living, giving* in a second column.

Follow the same procedure with *bake, take, care, name, write.* Point out that whether the root word has a short or long vowel sound, we usually drop the silent *e* at the end before adding *-ing*.

III. Writing

CHECK HOMEWORK: Page 25

Check this page with S. Have him correct any errors. Make note of the type of errors for further practice. If S. didn't do the page at home, give him time in class.

WRITING LESSON: (In Notebook)

Have S. write titles *Lesson 5* and *Words* and then write the numbers 1 to 12 in two columns.

Words. Ask S. what letters stand for the sound /ā/ in this lesson [*a* and *e* separated by a consonant]. Then have him spell *cake.*

Tell S. that you will say the chart words and four other words with the sound /ā/ spelled the same way. Also, you will say one other word with a different vowel sound. Then, dictate these words for S. to write:

1. cake	7. care
2. bake	8. came
3. take	9. gave
4. Jane	10. date
5. ate	11. frame
6. plate	12. church

Have S. check his work by looking at the chart, story, and Reading for Living. Have him circle the number in front of any word he missed, erase the whole word, and write it again correctly. Give S. time to study any words he missed he will need for the sentence dictation. Also, have him study *where* and *there.*

Sentences. Have S. write this title and number from 1 to 4. Dictate these sentences:

1. Gail baked a cake.
2. He is taking pictures of the wedding.
3. Where is the party?
4. There were paper plates and cups.

Check what S. has written. Circle any word with an error. Have S. erase it and write it correctly. Have him correct any errrors in capitalization or punctuation.

Study. At the bottom of the page, have S. write this title and any words he missed in the first two parts.

Writing a thank you letter. Help S. write a short thank you letter similar to the one in the lesson. Or, have him copy the one on page 29.

PRACTICE: Page 30

Have S. read the title and directions for the first exercise. Go over the sample with him. Let him do the others by himself. Check his work, and help him correct any errors.

Have S. read the directions for the second exercise. Go over the sample with him. Have him add *-ing* to each word before he fills in the missing words in the sentences. Check his work, and help him correct any errors.

HOMEWORK: Page 31

Go over the directions with S., and ask him to do this page at home. Also, encourage him to study any words he missed in the writing lesson and to reread the story.

CHECKING PROGRESS

Use these activities to see how well S. can apply the phonics skills he is learning to new words.

• Make a flash card for each item listed below. Tell S. that these are words and instructions he may find on forms he needs to fill out. He has had all of the words except *state,* but he may not recognize them in this form. Encourage him to sound them out.

Write the date	*Last name*	*Street, City, State*
Write your name	*First name*	

• Make a flash card for each item listed below. Tell S. that these are signs he may see. Have him read each sign. Give help where needed, such as in dividing the words into syllables. Point out that *ment* sounds the same in *apartment* (which he knows), *basement, pavement.*

One Way	*For Sale*	*Apartment for Rent*
Gate 4	*Bake Sale*	*Wet Pavement*
		Stairs to Basement

• List these words in a column on a 3-by-5-inch card: *at, hat, mat, Jan, plan, mad, tap, Sam.* At the edge of another card, write the letter *e.* First, have S. read all of the words with the short sound for *a.* Then have him place the *e* after each word to make a new word with the long sound for *a.* Have him read the long *a* words.

MEETING INDIVIDUAL NEEDS

If S. needs more practice in word recognition, make flash cards for the chart words in Lesson 5 and for *came, gave, church, where, there.* Follow the suggestions in previous lessons for using them.

Add the following words to the card game with rhyming words described in Lesson 4, and play the game again: *cake, bake, ate, plate, date, late, frame, came.*

Practice

Say the words. Circle the words with the sound ā.

(bake)	back	(gave)	bank
1. came	cake	gave	bank
2. gray	Gail	girl	care
3. check	chair	hair	Chan
4. Sam	Ray	Jane	Ann
5. ham	plate	play	class

Copy the word but not the e. Add *-ing*.
Then write the words in the sentences.

have having

They are having a party.

take ______ give ______

bake ______ write ______

1. Jason's mother is ______ a cake.
2. Gail's uncle is ______ pictures.
3. Gail is ______ a letter.
4. Jane is ______ Sam some cake.

Homework

Answer with a sentence.

1. Where was the wedding? ______
2. Who baked the wedding cake? ______
3. Who cut the wedding cake? ______
4. Who gave Sam some cake? ______

Say the word. Write the number of syllables.

1. baked ___	6. much ___
2. wedding ___	7. taking ___
3. yourself ___	8. baking ___
4. came ___	9. party ___
5. kissed ___	10. writing ___

In the *Workbook for Skill Book 3*, the exercises for Lesson 5 may be used at this time.

In *Focus on Phonics-3*, Practices 5A-5H may be used after Lesson 5. They give practice with *a-e* word families.

You may also want to make slip strips with the beginning letters shown here for these word families:

-ake family: *b, c, f, l, m, r, s, t, sh, sn*
-ate family: *d, g, h, l, m, r, pl, st*
-ame family: *c, f, g, l, s, t, sh, bl, fl, fr*

LESSON 6 — Skill Book 3, Pages 32-33

OBJECTIVES

To help your student:

- review the sound /ā/ and its most regular spellings: *ay, ai, a-e.*
- read short stories that review words introduced in Lessons 1-5, especially words with the sound /ā/.
- read silently to answer a specific question.
- recognize the main idea of a story.
- read dialog and identify the speakers.
- read orally with expression.
- interpret facts and draw inferences.
- review reading such practical material as prices, menu, check, package directions.
- develop sight recall of words first learned by sounding them out.
- distinguish between the long and short sounds for *a*.
- review the beginning blends *cl, pl, dr, fr, gr, pr, sp, st, str* and the ending blends *lk, nk, nt, st.*
- determine the number of syllables in a word.
- add the endings *-s,* or *-es, -d* or *-ed,* and *-ing* to known root words.
- recognize root words to which the endings *-s, -es, -d, -ed,* and *-ing* have been added.
- develop further skill in writing words, sentences, questions, prices, and money amounts for checks.
- apply phonics skills in practice exercises containing new words with familiar sound-letter relationships.

INTRODUCTION

T: In today's lesson, you will review the sound /ā/ and the main ways it is written. You will read four very short stories that have many words with the sound /ā/. There is only one new word in the stories, so you will be able to read them easily. We'll also review some other things you studied in the first five lessons.

I. Reading

CHART: Page 32

Have S. read the new word *more* and the titles *Lesson 6* and *More Reading with ā.*

T: (Point to *paper.*) Read this word. [S: paper.] How many syllables are in *paper?* [S: Two.] What is the vowel sound in the first syllable? [S: /ā/.] How is it written? [S: *a* by itself.] Good. (Point to *ā.*) Say the sound again. [S: /ā/.] What does the mark over the *a* mean? [S: The vowel sound is long.]

Have S. read the other key words and tell how the sound /ā/ is written in each of them.

STORIES: Pages 32-33

T: The stories in this lesson are about the people you met in the first five lessons. You will learn more about what happened to them.

Story 1: Dinner for Two. Have S. read the story title and the new word *TV.* Point out that *TV* can be written with just the capital letters *T* and *V.*

T: Remember the story about Carla? Someone was coming for dinner. In this story, you will find out about the dinner.

Silent reading. Ask S. to read the whole story silently and then summarize it in two or three sentences. After this summary, ask these questions to check details:

1. Who came to Carla's for dinner?
2. Where was Carla's baby?
3. What did David and Carla have for dinner?
4. What did they do after dinner?
5. Tell who said each of the following:
   "Your hair looks pretty."
   "Where is Rosa?"
   "Help yourself to coffee."
   "Dinner is ready."
   "I'll drink milk."

Oral reading. Have S. read the part of one speaker while you read the other. Then reverse roles.

Story 2: The Card Party. Have S. read the title.

T: Remember the story about the Masons paying their bills? They talked about what they could do for fun without spending much money. This story tells about something they did.

Silent reading. Ask S. to read the story silently and then summarize it by telling *who* the people are, *where* they are, and *what* they do. After his summary, ask these questions to check details:

1. Did Carla bring her baby?
2. Did the friends watch TV while they played cards?
3. Who baked the cake?

Oral reading. Have S. tell who the speakers are in the story. Then have him choose one of the parts to read while you read the others. Reverse roles.

Story 3: Three Days at Snake River

Note: The procedure for teaching stories 3-4 is somewhat different. It will help to have a copy of these stories that you can mark and make notes on as S. reads.

T: Remember that the Masons discussed going away at the end of May? In story 3, you'll find out if they did.

Oral reading. Have S. read the story aloud without reading it silently first. Give these directions:

T: Read story 3 aloud. Think about what you are reading. Then tell in a few sentences what the Masons did. There are no new words. If you can't remember a word, don't stop to sound it out. Just go on. I'll mark the word, and you can study it later.

more (mor)

More Reading with ā

paper	cake	paint	day
ā	a-e	ai	ay

1. Dinner for Two

TV

David came to Carla's apartment for dinner. When he came in, he kissed Carla. He said, "Your hair looks very pretty."

"Thank you, dear," said Carla. "My landlady cut my hair yesterday."

"Where is Rosa?" asked David.

"She is in bed," Carla said. "Dinner is ready. Help yourself to coffee, and I'll drink milk."

David and Carla ate their dinner. They had ham, potatoes, and salad.

After dinner, they had coffee and watched TV.

2. The Card Party

Carla and David came to the Mason's apartment. They came to play cards. They did not bring Carla's baby with them. The baby-sitter was taking care of her.

Ray Mason put four chairs at the card table. The friends played cards and listened to music on the radio. After they played cards, they ate some cake. They had coffee with their cake.

"Kay, did you bake this cake?" asked David.

"No," said Kay. "Ray baked it today."

"Your plates are very pretty," Carla said.

"Thank you very much," said Kay. "My mother gave them to me."

After they ate their cake, David and Carla thanked the Masons and left.

3. Three Days at Snake River

The Masons' payday was May 15. They put their checks in the bank and paid their bills. They went away for the last three days in May.

Kay and Ray went to Snake River. They had fun there. They fished in the river. They played in the water. They picked up pretty rocks.

When they came back, Ray said, "We spent a hundred dollars. But it was fun."

4. In the Kitchen

It was a month after the Hunts' wedding. Gail and Jason were sitting in their kitchen. They were having a snack. There were some sandwiches and a quart of milk on the table.

The landlady came up the stairs. Jason said, "Come in and have a snack with us."

"No, thanks," she said. "But may I look at your kitchen? I am happy that you painted it pink. I have a gallon of paint. Will you paint my kitchen? I will pay you for it."

"OK," said Jason. "We will paint it next month."

As S. reads orally, mark your copy as suggested below. Later, you can use this record to plan extra practice.

1. Underline any place where S. hesitates.
2. Mark through a word if S. says the wrong word. If you have time, write the word he substitutes.
3. Mark through any ending that is omitted or wrong.
4. Circle any words that are omitted or any punctuation marks not observed.
5. Note his ability to read fluently and with expression.

Summarizing. After S. gives his summary, record whether or not it was accurate and reasonably complete. You might like to write down his summary.

Making inferences. Ask how much the Masons' trip cost and how long they were away. Then ask S. if he thinks they probably camped out or stayed at a resort.

Story 4: In the Kitchen

T: Remember that Gail and Jason rented an apartment and did some painting in it? Story 4 tells about something that happened after they got married and moved in.

Follow the same procedure as for story 3. Make the same type of notations. Then ask these questions:

1. Do Gail and Jason seem to be on good terms with their landlady? What makes you think so?
2. Was the landlady pleased with the paint job Gail and Jason did in their apartment? How do you know?

READING FOR LIVING: Review

Turn back to the Reading for Living sections in the first four lessons, and review by asking questions similar to those in the exercises. (Some questions are suggested below.) Let S. answer orally.

Menu (page 6, Lesson 1)

1. How much does a hamburger cost? [$1.70.]
2. How much does a ham sandwich cost? [$2.00.] How much do a ham sandwich and a cup of coffee cost? [$2.50.]
3. How much does an egg salad sandwich cost? [$1.00.] How much do an egg salad sandwich and a glass of milk cost? [$1.70.]

Package directions (page 11, Lesson 2). Have S. tell the amount of each ingredient to use to prepare instant potatoes for *one* person.

Check (page 17, Lesson 3). Have S. look at the top check and answer these questions:

1. What is the date on the check?
2. Who wrote this check?
3. Who is the check written *to?*
4. How much is the check for?
5. What is the name of the bank? Where is the bank?
6. What is the number of the check?
7. Could either Ray or Kay Mason sign this check? How do you know?

Also, review how the money amount is written in numbers and in words.

If you think that reading this check would be too easy for S., you can make out a different check. Be sure to use only words that he can read. You may also want to bring a check from a local bank and help S. read what is printed on it.

Paint prices (page 23, Lesson 4). Have S. tell the cost of the following:

1. One quart of the pink paint [$3]
2. One gallon of the gray paint [$14]
3. One quart of the black paint [$5]
4. One gallon of the black paint [$18]
5. Two gallons of the pink paint [$20]
6. Two quarts of the gray paint [$8]
7. One gallon of the pink paint and one quart of the black paint [$15]

Remind S. that there are four quarts in a gallon. Then ask: "If you need a gallon of one of these paints, is it cheaper to buy one gallon can or four quart cans?" (You may skip this question if you think it would be too hard.)

II. Skills Practice

T: Now we'll have listening exercises to review some of the things you have covered so far in this book.

PRACTICE 1: Distinguishing the Long Sound for *a*

T: Which of these words has the long sound for *a:*

man, main?	*baby, daddy?*	*let, late?*
day, Dan?	*April, after?*	*jell, jail?*
pan, pain?	*tablet, table?*	*pain, pen?*
lake, lack?	*paper, packing?*	*fed, fade?*

PRACTICE 2: Identifying Rhyming Words

Say each of the following words, and have S. give a word that rhymes with it: *pay, Gail, hair, bake, ate, came.*

PRACTICE 3: Identifying the Number of Syllables

Say each word below, and have S. tell how many syllables it has. If he has difficulty, say the word again, and have him tell how many vowel sounds—or beats—it has.

David	[2]	*thanked*	[1]	*yesterday*	[3]
radio	[3]	*painted*	[2]	*apartment*	[3]
kissed	[1]	*dinner*	[2]	*hundred*	[2]
played	[1]	*landlady*	[3]	*sandwiches*	[3]

PRACTICE 4: Review Beginning and Ending Blends

Say each word below, and have S. tell what blend it *begins* with. As he answers, write the blend. If he makes an error, say the word again and give two other words that begin with the same blend.

class	*drink*	*gray*	*spent*	*street*
plate	*frame*	*pretty*	*stairs*	

Say each word below, and ask S. what blend it *ends* with. As he answers, write the blend. If he makes an error, repeat the word and give another with the same blend.

milk	*drink*	*cost*	*rent*

PRACTICE 5: Endings *-s, -ing, -d,* or *-ed*

Write these words in a column: *name, paint, bake, play, nail.* Have S. read each word. Then have him tell what the word would be with the ending *-s*. Write the *-s* form next to the root word. Have him do the same thing with the endings *-ing,* and *-d* or *-ed.* Have him read the *-ed* words and tell how many syllables are in each word.

PRACTICE 6: Recognizing Root Words

Write these words in a column: *baking, taking, sitting, dishes, sandwiches, writing, plates, paying.* Have S. read each word and tell what the root word is. Ask him to spell the root word as you write it by the word with the ending.

III. Writing

CHECK HOMEWORK: Page 31

Check this page with S. Have him correct any errors. Make note of the type of errors for further practice. If S. didn't do the page at home, give him time in class.

WRITING LESSON (In Notebook)

Words. Have S. write the titles *Lesson 6* and *Words* and then write the numbers 1 to 20 in two columns. Dictate the following words:

1. paper	6. plate	11. care	16. April
2. day	7. nail	12. away	17. snack
3. paint	8. hair	13. gray	18. taking
4. cake	9. chair	14. take	19. hundred
5. ate	10. pay	15. played	20. table

Check his work, and have him correct any errors.

Sentences. Have S. write this title and number from 1 to 5. Have him cover the words he wrote. Then dictate these sentences for him to write:

1. Jane baked a cake yesterday.
2. Where is the baby?
3. What is today's date?
4. When was the Masons' payday?
5. The landlady came up the stairs.

Check his work, and have him correct any errors. Then have S. write the title *Study* and any words he missed in the word and sentence dictation.

Prices. Have S. write the following prices:

$3.50	$12.35	60¢	90¢
$6.25	$25.10	87¢	32¢
$7.05	$19.99	49¢	5¢

Amounts of money for checks. Have S. write the following money amounts as they would appear on a check in numbers and in words:

$225.50 Two hundred twenty-five and $\frac{50}{100}$

$600.75 Six hundred and $\frac{75}{100}$

REVIEW PRACTICE

1. Have S. circle all of the words that have the sound /ā/ in story 2 on pages 32-33. Before he begins, point to the word *they*, and explain that it has the sound /ā/, but it is spelled with *ey* instead of *ay*.

2. Write out the exercise below or copy it from page 140 in the appendix. Go over the first item with S. as an example. Then let him complete the exercise himself. Check his work, and help him correct any errors.

Write the missing word in the sentence.

back	bake	1. Gail will ___ a cake for the party.
hat	hate	2. Kay will pay for the ___.
at	ate	3. Jason ___ a ham sandwich.
man	Main	4. My friend lives on ___ Street.
ran	rain	5. Gail ___ up the stairs.
back	bake	6. When are you coming ___?
tack	take	7. I put up the picture with a ___.
pan	pain	8. Ray has a ___ in his neck.
car	care	9. I am taking ___ of my friend's cat.

HOMEWORK (In Notebook)

Explain to S. that the homework for this lesson is to be done in his notebook. Ask him to write one question about each story in Lesson 6. Ask him to study the words that he missed in the dictation and then to write sentences using four of those words. If he didn't miss any words, he may choose any four words from the list.

CHECKING PROGRESS

Keeping a record. If you have not already started a record sheet of your student's progress in *Skill Book 3*, this is a good time to do so. There will be three more review lessons similar to this one. A record will help you keep track of the skills S. has mastered and those he needs to work on.

Comprehension. If S. was able to summarize the stories in this lesson, his progress is satisfactory. If he had difficulty, recheck comprehension by asking some questions to bring out the main ideas. Perhaps he understands the story but finds it hard to express himself.

Word recognition. If S. missed three words or less in oral reading of story 3 and five words or less in oral reading of story 4, he is doing well. If he missed more words, note the type of errors. If errors are similar, plan extra practice exercises for help in the skill needed. If errors are more general, supplementary material using the same vocabulary may be helpful.

Also, check recognition of new chart and story words by using flash cards. Sort the cards into three piles: those S. can read instantly, those he needs to sound out, and those he cannot read. Record the number of each. You can keep the cards separated and recheck periodically.

Long vowel sounds. The skills practice in this lesson will help you know whether S. usually recognizes the long sound for *a* and the ways it is written. He may not have mastered this sound yet, but he should be able to distinguish it from the short vowel sounds.

Short vowel sounds and consonant sounds. Now that S. is reading words with both short and long vowels, he may slip up on some of the short vowel sounds. If so, list these on a separate sheet, and plan some extra practice. You may want to use exercises from *Focus on Phonics-2A* for short vowel sounds and from *Focus on Phonics-1* for individual consonant sounds if you have not already used these supplements. Charts from *Skill Books 1* and *2* can be kept on hand for reference.

Consonant blends and word endings. List any beginning or ending blends that S. has difficulty with. Some of these will be reviewed in the next lessons. You can plan extra practice for the others. You may want to use exercises from *Focus on Phonics-2B* for this practice.

List any endings that S. has difficulty with. Note whether his problem is in recognizing the ending, adding it correctly to a root word, or recognizing the root word to which the ending has been added.

Syllables and rhyming words. Note how well S. responds to these items. There will be more practice in the next lessons, so do not give extra work at this time.

Writing. S. should be encouraged to refer to his notebook for the words he needs to study. Note which punctuation marks he uses correctly and which he does not. If his writing is legible, it is satisfactory.

MEETING INDIVIDUAL NEEDS

If S. did fairly well in this lesson, let him go on to Lesson 7. If he needs help in many areas, plan another review lesson. Use the supplements suggested here, or create your own, but do not repeat skill book lessons. Encourage S. and help him feel that a supplementary lesson will help his progress. But do not hold him back unnecessarily. The next lessons will give much review.

In the *Workbook for Skill Book 3*, the exercises for Lesson 6 may be done at this time.

In *Focus on Phonics-3*, Practice 6 may be used after Lesson 6. It reviews words in which the sound /ā/ is spelled with *ay, ai,* or *a-e*.

LESSON 7 — Skill Book 3, Pages 34-39

OBJECTIVES

To help your student:

- recognize the long sound for *e* as in *we* and *see*.
- recognize that *ee* stands for the sound /ē/.
- read words in which the sound /ē/ is written with *e* or *ee*.
- distinguish between the long and short sounds for *e*.
- recognize the contractions *I'll, let's, it's, wasn't, didn't* and the words from which they are made.
- review the digraphs *th* and *wh* as in *think* and *wheel*.
- recognize the consonant blend *thr* as in *three*.
- review the consonant blends *dr, gr, tr, tw, sl*.
- summarize a story in his own words.
- interpret the feelings of characters in a story.
- relate the story to personal experiences and values.
- read orally with expression.
- read number words to *one hundred*, and recognize the meaning of *-teen* and *-ty* in number words.
- write words, numbers, and sentences from dictation.

INTRODUCTION

T: You have had several lessons about the long vowel sound /ā/ and the ways it is written. Today, your lesson is about another long vowel sound.

I. Reading

CHART: Page 34

Title and key word. Have S. read the title *Lesson 7*.

T: Look at the letter in the top right-hand corner. What is the name of the letter? [S: *e*.] What is the sound? [S: /ē/.] How do you know the sound is /ē/ and not /e/? [S: There is a long mark over it.]

T: (Point to the key word *we*.) What is this word? [S: we.] (Point to *ē* under *we*.) What is the vowel sound? [S: /ē/.] Where does the vowel sound come in the word—at the beginning, middle, or end? [S: At the end.]

T: (Point to *ee* = *ē* in the top right-hand corner.) Here is another way to write the sound /ē/. Read it. [S: *ee* = *ē*.]

T: (Point to the key word *see*.) Read this word. [S: see.] What is the vowel sound? [S: /ē/.] What letters stand for the sound /ē/ in the word *see*? [S: *ee*.] Good. (Point to *ee* = *ē*.) Read this. [S: *ee* = *ē*.]

Lines 1-6. Tell S. that most of the words in the chart have two *e*'s together for the sound /ē/. All of the words are written the way they sound. Ask him to read the words to himself. After he has studied the chart silently, have him read each word aloud. Call attention to these points:

1. The number of syllables in each word.
2. How the sound /ē/ is written in *he*. Point out that the sound /ē/ is written with only one *e* in only a few one-syllable words. Write the words *we, me, he, she, be,* and have S. read them.
3. The consonant blends *tr* in *tree* and *sl* in *sleep*.
4. The *wh* for the sound /wh/ in *wheel* and the *th* for the sound /th/ in *teeth*.
5. The rhyming words *we, he, see, tree*. Ask S. which ones have the sound /ē/ spelled the same way.

Review. Have S. read each word aloud, including the key words. Go down the last column of the chart.

STORY: Pages 35-36 (Lee's Lesson)

Have S. read the story title and new words. Call attention to the sound /ē/ and how it is written in the words with that sound. Point out that *Green* is written with a capital letter here because it is used as a name in the story. When we use *green* as a color, we write it with a small *g*. Help S. read the contractions, but do not explain them at this time. Have S. tell how many syllables are in the words that are divided into syllables.

Directed silent reading. Ask S. to read the whole story to himself and be ready to tell it in his own words. Also, ask him to think about the characters in the story and how he would describe the way they act. When S. finishes reading, have him summarize the story.

Reading between the lines. Discuss these questions:

1. When does the story take place—in the afternoon or at night? How do you know? [At night. Although the story doesn't actually say it's night, Mrs. Green is in bed, and she's worried because her son isn't home.]
2. What are some facts the story tells us about Lee? [He's 16. He goes to class. He has a job. He has a car. He lives at home. He plays cards with friends.]
3. From reading this story, do you think that Mrs. Green is or is not a single parent? What makes you think so? [She seems to be a single parent. Lee's father is not mentioned, and Mrs. Green makes decisions by herself about how to discipline her son.]
4. How did Lee act toward his mother: was he polite or disrespectful? Did he seem calm or excited?
5. When Lee came in, how did his mother act toward him: was she calm or excited? Did she give him a chance to explain or did she start accusing him first?
6. Look at paragraphs 5 and 6. What do you think was Lee's main reason for saying, "OK, let's go to bed"?
   a. He was concerned about his mother's sleep.
   b. He wanted to end the conversation and avoid a lecture.

we

ē

ē

ee = ē

see = sē

ee = ē

	he	hē	he
	tree	tree	tree
	wheel	wheel	wheel
	teeth	teeth	teeth
	sleep	sleep	sleep

Lee's Lesson

Lee	need	be	late	again (u gen)	wasn't (wuz unt)
Green	beer	it's	face (fase)	angry (ang gry)	didn't (did unt)

Mrs. Green was in bed, but she wasn't sleeping. "Where is Lee?" she was thinking. "It's half past three."

Lee was 16. He had a job after class. He had his first car.

Mrs. Green heard a car. When Lee came in, she got up. "Where were you?" she yelled. "It's half past three. Were you drinking beer?"

"No, Mother," said Lee. "I wasn't drinking beer. I was just playing cards with my friends."

Mrs. Green said, "I cannot sleep when you come in late. You need to be in bed. You need your sleep."

"OK," said Lee. "Let's go to bed."

"What is that?" his mother said. "Do I see a cut on your face? Yes, I *do* see a cut."

"It's just a little cut," Lee said. "I went to sleep at the wheel. I didn't see the tree. My car hit the tree. My face hit the wheel. But I wasn't going fast. And I wasn't drinking beer!"

Mrs. Green said, "Did you hit your teeth on the wheel?"

"No, I didn't hit my teeth," Lee said. "My teeth are OK, and my face will be OK. My car still runs, but the tree looks bad."

Lee said, "Do not be angry with me, Mother. I have had a hard lesson. I will not be late again."

7. Which statement best describes the way Lee told his mother about his accident?
   a. He was eager to tell her everything that happened.
   b. He didn't offer much information until she asked a question about something, but then he told the truth.
   c. He tried to hide the facts even when she asked questions.
8. Did Lee take his accident seriously or not? What did he say that lets you know? ["I've had a hard lesson."]
9. In your opinion, was the way Mrs. Green handled Lee too harsh, too lenient, or just right? Give reasons.

Oral reading. Have S. read the part of one character while you read the part of the other. Encourage him to read with expression in the way that he thinks the person would speak. Discuss the punctuation, and help S. observe it as an aid to reading clearly and with expression. Then reverse roles.

STORY CHECKUP: Page 36

Have S. read the title and directions. Encourage him to do this exercise without looking back at the story. Check his answers. If he has any items wrong, have him find the part in the story that gives the answer.

"I was very angry," said Mrs. Green. "And I am still angry. Do not be late again, or I will take your car away."

"But, Mother, I need my car to go to work," said Lee.

"Then do not be late again," she said. "And you will have to pay for that tree."

Story Checkup

Circle the letter of the right answer.

1. Did Lee have a car?
   a. Yes, he had a car.
   b. No, he didn't have a car.
2. Was Mrs. Green sleeping?
   a. Yes, she was sleeping.
   b. No, she wasn't sleeping.
3. Did Lee hit his teeth?
   a. Yes, he hit his teeth.
   b. No, he didn't hit his teeth.
4. Was Mrs. Green angry?
   a. Yes, she was angry.
   b. No, she wasn't angry.
5. Is Lee's face cut?
   a. Yes, it's cut a little.
   b. No, it's not cut.

1 one	11 eleven (ē lev en)	10 ten
2 two	12 twelve	20 twenty
3 three	13 thirteen	30 thirty
4 four	14 fourteen	40 forty
5 five	15 fifteen	50 fifty
6 six	16 sixteen	60 sixty
7 seven	17 seventeen	70 seventy
8 eight (āt)	18 eighteen	80 eighty
9 nine (nīn)	19 nineteen	90 ninety
10 ten	20 twenty	100 one hundred

Write the number.

nine	9	thirteen	13	seventy-seven	77
nineteen	____	thirty	____	ninety-nine	____
ninety	____	fifteen	____	sixty-six	____
eight	____	fifty	____	eighty-eight	____
eighteen	____	fourteen	____	fifty-five	____
eighty	____	forty	____	forty-four	____
eleven	____	sixteen	____	thirty-three	____
seven	____	sixty	____	thirteen	____
seventeen	____	eleven	____	fifteen	____

READING FOR LIVING: Page 37

Note: The number words *one* through *seven, ten, twelve, twenty, seventy,* and *hundred* have been taught in earlier lessons in this and previous skill books. The other number words were introduced briefly in *Skill Book 1.*

Number words for 1-10. Have S. read the first column of number words from *one* to *ten.* Have him tell which words have long vowel sounds (*three, five, eight, nine*). Also, ask him how many syllables each word in this column has.

Number words for 11-20. Have S. read the first two words (*eleven, twelve*) in the second column.

T: Read the next word. [S. thirteen.] What letters stand for the sound /ē/? [S: *ee.*] Look at the words from *thirteen* to *nineteen.* What part is the same in all these words? [S: teen.] What does the ending *-teen* mean in these words? [S: Ten.] *Thirteen* means ten and what? [S: Three.] What does *fourteen* mean? [S: Ten and four.]

T: In the number word, *-teen,* meaning ten, comes at the end. In the number (point to 14), the ten comes first; the number 1 in front of the 4 stands for one ten.

Have S. read the rest of the words in the second column. If he seems to understand their meaning, it is not necessary to have him tell the value of each number.

Number words from 10-100, by 10s. In the third column, have S. read *ten* and *twenty.* Then ask him to look at the words from *twenty* to *ninety* and tell what part is the same [*ty*]. Point out that, while the ending *-teen* means *ten and,* the ending *-ty* means *tens. Thirteen* means *ten and three. Thirty* means *three tens.*

Have S. read *forty* and tell what it means. Then have him read the rest of the words in the third column.

Review. Have S. read all of the number words going down each column again. Then have him read across each line (*one, eleven, ten; two, twelve, twenty,* and so on).

Call attention to the consonant blend *tw* in *twelve* and *twenty.*

Write the number. In the exercise, have S. write the number for each number word, going down the columns. (The first blank in each column is filled in as an example.) Check his work, and help him correct any errors.

Discussion. Ask S. in what instances he needs to read numbers and number words, and discuss how this lesson may help him. Remind him that checks have the dollar amount written in both numbers and words.

II. Skills Practice

T: Please close your book. We will have some listening exercises on some things in this lesson.

PRACTICE 1: Distinguishing the Long Sound for *e*

T: Which of these words has the long sound for *e:*

sleep, slip?	*bet, beet?*	*three, third?*
grin, green?	*fed, feed?*	*whirl, wheel?*
teen, tin?	*seed, said?*	*tree, tray?*

PRACTICE 2: Identifying Rhyming Words

Write *we,* and have S. read it. Then say each pair of words below, and have him tell which word rhymes with *we.*

me, may	*sit, see*	*Lee, lie*	*throw, three*
bet, be	*tree, try*	*shy, she*	*knee, know*

Write the words *wheel, teeth, sleep, green, need.* Say each of the following words, and have S. tell which word in the written list rhymes with it: *creep, feel, seen, wreath, seed.*

PRACTICE 3: Identifying the Number of Syllables

Say each word below, and have S. tell how many syllables it has. If he has difficulty, say the word again, and have him tell how many vowel sounds—or beats—it has.

angry	[2]	*thinking*	[2]	*again*	[2]
yelled	[1]	*eleven*	[3]	*twenty*	[2]
faces	[2]	*fifteen*	[2]	*three*	[1]

PRACTICE 4: Digraphs *th* and *wh*

Write *think* and *wheel.* Have S. read each word, tell what sound it begins with, and what letters stand for the sound. As he answers, underline *th* and *wh.* For each one, remind S. that the two letters together stand for one sound. Then say each word below, and have S. tell whether it begins with the same sound as *think* or *wheel.*

where	*thin*	*what*	*thief*	*white*
thank	*when*	*why*	*thirty*	*thought*

Write *teeth.* Have S. read the word, tell what sound it ends with, and what letters stand for that sound. As he answers, underline *th* at the end of *teeth.*

T: Which word *ends* with the sound /th/ as in *teeth:*

both, boat?	*bath, bat?*	*cloth, cough?*
mat, math?	*with, off?*	*death, deaf?*

PRACTICE 5: Beginning Consonant Blend *thr*

T: Listen to this word, and tell me how many consonant sounds you hear before the vowel: *three.* [S: Two.] What is the first sound? [S: /th/.] What letters stand for the sound /th/? [S: *th.*] What is the next consonant sound in *three?* [S: /r/.] What letter stands for the /r/ sound? [S: *r.*] Good. (Write *three.*) What consonant blend does *three* begin with? [S: *thr.*] Good. (Underline *thr* in *three.*)

T: Which word begins with the blend *thr* as in *three*:

red, thread?	*thaw, threw?*	*true, through?*
rob, throb?	*thrill, thin?*	*throw, though?*
throat, wrote?	*thought, throat?*	*Fred, thread?*

PRACTICE 6: Beginning Blends *dr, gr, tr, tw, sl*

Write the words *drink, green, tree, twenty, sleep.* Have S. read each word and tell the blend it begins with. As he answers underline *dr, gr, tr, tw, sl.*

Say each word below, and have S. tell which of these blends it begins with.

train	*twin*	*sleeve*	*twist*	*slowly*
gray	*dream*	*twelve*	*trust*	*greedy*

PRACTICE 7: Contractions

In a column, write *let's, it's, wasn't, didn't, I'll.* Have S. read them.

T: Notice that there is an apostrophe in each of these words. (Point to the apostrophe in each word.) In these words, the apostrophe doesn't mean that something belongs to someone. It means that a letter has been left out. The word *let's* is made from two words. (Write *let us* next to *let's.*) Read the two words. [S: let us.] When these two words are put together to make *let's,* what letter is left out? [S: u.]

Write the words *it is* next to *it's.* Have S. read them and tell what letter is left out in *it's.* Follow the same procedure for *wasn't, didn't, I'll.*

T: When one word and part of another word are put together to make a new word, we call the new word a *contraction.* You had these contractions in today's story. Please read them again. [S. reads.]

III. Writing

CHECK HOMEWORK (In Notebook)

Check the questions and sentences S. wrote in his notebook for his assignment. Note whether he used correct punctuation and capitalization. Have him correct any errors. If he didn't do the assignment, have him write at least one question and one sentence about the Lesson 6 story before he goes on to the next part.

WRITING LESSON (In Notebook)

Have S. write the titles *Lesson 7* and *Words* and then write the numbers 1 to 12 in two columns.

Words. Dictate the words below for S. to write. For number 11, tell S. to write *Green* as he would when it is used as a name. When he has finished, check his work and have him correct any errors.

1. we	4. tree	7. sleep	10. Lee
2. see	5. wheel	8. need	11. Green
3. he	6. teeth	9. be	12. she

Sentences. Have S. write this title and then number from 1 to 5. Dictate these sentences:

1. I went to sleep at the wheel.
2. Lee didn't hit his teeth.
3. It's half past three.
4. Mrs. Green was very angry.
5. He didn't see the tree.

Check his work, and have him correct any errors. Then have S. write the title *Study* and any words he missed in the word and sentence dictation.

Number words. Help S. study the number words on page 37 of the skill book. Go across each line of the chart, pointing out the similarities and differences between the root word and the forms with *-teen* and *-ty,* as below:

one, eleven, ten — These words are not at all alike. Have S. spell *eleven* (a new word) aloud.

two, twelve, twenty — All three words begin with *tw,* but *two* is not pronounced the way it is spelled.

three, thirteen, thirty — *Three* begins with the blend *thr,* but this changes to *thir* in *thirteen* and *thirty.*

four, fourteen, forty — The root word *four* stays the same in *fourteen,* but the *u* is dropped in *forty.*

five, fifteen, fifty — The root word *five* is changed to *fif* in *fifteen* and *fifty.*

six, sixteen, sixty through *nine, nineteen, ninety* — In each case, the root word does not change when the endings *-teen* and *-ty* are added. Have S. spell *eight.*

ten, twenty, one hundred — These are not alike at all.

Practice

Say the words. Which word has the sound ē? Circle that word.

1.	Ned	need	5.	bed	beer
2.	well	wheel	6.	teeth	tent
3.	see	send	7.	sleep	seven
4.	Lee	let	8.	ten	teen

Say the word. Write the two words that it comes from.

let's ___let___ ___us___

1. it's ______ ______
2. wasn't ______ ______
3. didn't ______ ______
4. I'll ______ ______

Fill in the word: *let's, it's, wasn't, didn't, I'll.*

1. ______________ not a bad cut.
2. Lee ______________ see the tree.
3. He ______________ drinking beer
4. ______________ pay you for the paint.
5. ______________ not go to the party.

Homework

Answer with a sentence.

1. Who was angry? ______________
2. Who went to sleep at the wheel? ______________
3. What did Lee's car hit? ______________
4. Who will have to pay for the tree? ______________

Say the word. Write the number of syllables.

1. seventeen ____
2. nineteen ____
3. nine ____
4. fourteen ____
5. sleeping ____
6. fifty ____
7. drinking ____
8. yelled ____
9. better ____
10. need ____

Have S. copy the numbers in each column of the chart and then write the words for those numbers. Encourage him to write as many words as he can without looking at the book, but tell him he can look whenever he needs to.

PRACTICE: Page 38

Have S. read the title and the directions for the first exercise. Have him do all eight items, and then check his answers. If he made an error, have him read both of the words in the pair aloud and listen carefully for the vowel sound. Also, call his attention to the way the vowel sound is written. Point out that one *e* in the middle of a one-syllable word is almost always short.

Ask S. to read the directions for the second exercise and the sample item. Have him write the two words for each contraction. Check his work. Then have him read the next direction and fill in the right contraction in each sentence. Have him read the completed sentences aloud. Help him correct any errors.

HOMEWORK: Page 39

Go over the directions with S. Ask him also to study any words he missed in his writing lesson and to study the number words.

CHECKING PROGRESS

To see how well S. can apply phonics skills, make flash cards for *beef, feel, feet, peel, seed, seem, weed, weep.* Have S. read each word by blending the sounds.

Also, make a flash card for each item below. Tell S. these are words he may see on signs. Have him read each card. Then talk about where these might be seen on signs.

Help Needed *Deep End* *Speed Limit*
Do Not Feed *Keep Away*

MEETING INDIVIDUAL NEEDS

Make flash cards for the chart words and these new story words: *Lee, Green, need, be, beer.* Have S. read each word. Spread the cards face up. Ask questions that can be answered with one of the words.

Make slip strips for the word families and beginning letters listed below. Give the meaning for *heel, reel, steel* so S. doesn't confuse them with *heal, real, steal.*

-eed family: *d, f, n, s, w, bl, br, sp*
-eel family: *f, h, p, r, wh, st*
-eep family: *b, d, j, k, p, w, cr, st*

In the *Workbook for Skill Book 3,* the exercises for Lesson 7 may be used at this time.

In *Focus on Phonics-3,* Practices 7A-7E may be used after Lesson 7. They give practice with *ee* word families.

LESSON 8

Skill Book 3
Pages 40-45

OBJECTIVES

To help your student:

- recognize that the letters *ea* usually stand for the sound /ē/ as in *eat*.
- read words in which the sound /ē/ is written with *ea*.
- distinguish between the long and short sounds for *e*.
- summarize the main ideas of the story by answering the questions *who, what, when, where,* and *why*.
- recall details to support the main idea of the story.
- recognize the vowel sound in each syllable of a word.
- recognize that, after a long vowel sound, the final consonant is not doubled before *-er* is added.
- recognize that verb forms ending in *en* are related to known verbs, as *eat, eaten; take, taken*.
- read a grocery ad, locating items and their prices.
- write words, sentences, prices, and a grocery list from dictation.

INTRODUCTION

T: In the last lesson, you learned two ways that the sound /ē/ is written. How is it written in the word *we?* [S: With one *e*.] How is it written in the word *see?* [S: With two *e*'s.] In this lesson, you will learn another way that the sound /ē/ is written.

I. Reading

CHART: Page 40

Title and key word. Have S. read the title *Lesson 8*.

T: Look at the letters in the top right-hand corner. What two letters are together? [S: *ea*.] What sound do the letters *ea* equal? [S: /ē/.] Look at the picture and the key word at the top of the page. (Point to *eat*.) After this word, you see the equal sign. Then you see the word written with a long mark over the *e*. What is the word? [S: eat.]

T: Under the word, you see the two letters together that stand for the sound /ē/. What are they? [S: *ea*.] Read this line. [S: *ea* equals *ē*.] From now on, when you see *ea* together in a word, you will say /ē/. That part of the word will not be rewritten for you.

Lines 1-6

T: Look at the other words in the chart. In each of them, the sound /ē/ is written with *ea*. Study each line. Notice the number of sounds in each word and the number of syllables. Notice if any part of the word is written in a different way than it sounds.

After S. has studied the chart silently, have him read each word aloud, going down column 2. Then ask these questions:

1. What letters stand for the sound /ē/ in these words? [S: *ea*.]
2. Where does the sound /ē/ come in most of these words—at the beginning, middle, or end? [S: In the middle.]
3. In which word does the sound /ē/ come at the end? [S: tea.]
4. Which words have some part written in a different way than it sounds? [S: beans, please.] What sound does *s* stand for in these words? [S: /z/.]
5. Which word starts with a consonant blend? [S: please.] What is the blend? [S: *pl*.]
6. Which word has more than one syllable? [S: teacher.] How many syllables does it have? [S: Two.]

Review. Have S. read each word in the chart aloud, including the key word. Go down the last column.

STORY: Pages 41-42 (The Class Party)

Have S. read the story title and new words aloud. Call attention to the number of syllables in each word. If a word has a long *e* sound, have S. tell how it is written. Point out that *something* is one word made up of two smaller words, *some* and *thing*. Ask S. what letters stand for the sound /ch/ in *cheese* and *cheap*.

Directed silent reading

T: The title of the story gives some idea of what it is about. Read the whole story to yourself, and find out who is having a party and why.

Have S. read the whole story silently and then answer the question. Emphasize the main point: Carla's class is having a dinner party so they can get together for a big meal and have fun.

T: Every story has one main idea. If you understand the main idea, then you understand the important part of the story. The rest of the story tells more about the main idea. Usually, a story will answer the questions *who, what, where, when, why,* and *how*.

Continue as indicated below. Write the question words *Who? What? Where? When? Why? How?* in a column. After each one, write the answer that S. suggests.

T: *Who* is the story about? [S: Carla's class.]

T: *What* is the story about? [S: A dinner party.]

T: Does the story tell *where* the party is held? [S: No.] From what is told, where do you think it is held? [S: In the classroom or another room in the building.] Do you think they are sitting at a table? [S: Yes.] Why? [S: They're passing the food.] Since we're not sure about the building, I'll write *At a table* after *Where*.

T: Does anything in the story suggest *when* the party is held? [S: Yes, since it's a dinner party, it's probably in the evening.] (Write *Evening* or *Dinner time.*)

T: *Why* is the class having this party? Do they seem to be celebrating any special occasion? [S: No.] So what can we say their reason is? [S: To have fun.]

T: *How* do the people in the class provide food for the dinner? [S: Each person brings something to eat. Each person helped to pay for the meat.]

Have S. read the question words and answers.

Oral reading. Have S. scan the story to find the names of the people who say something. List the names on the board: *Ray, Kay, Ms. Smith, Jason, Gail, Carla.* Have S. read what each person says.

Reading between the lines. Discuss these questions.

1. Classify the foods mentioned in the story: What was the main dish? [Meat.] Does the story tell what kind of meat it was? [No.] What kind of salad was there? [Green salad.] What vegetables were there? [Beans, baked potatoes.] What did they have for dessert? [Apples and cheese.] What beverages, or things to drink, were there? [Coffee and tea.]
2. What clue in the story tells you whether or not this is the only party this class has ever had? [Carla says, "This is the best party that we have ever had." This tells us that the class has had other parties.]
3. Do you think the way the class provided the food is a good way for a group to have a party? Why or why not?
4. If you were going to a party like this, what food would you like to bring?

STORY CHECKUP: Page 42

T: You have talked about the main ideas in the story. In the Story Checkup, you will have some questions about some of the details. Read the directions for the first exercise. Then answer as many of the questions as you can without looking back at the story.

After S. finishes, have him check his answers by looking back at the story. Also, have him find any answers he could not remember.

Have S. read the directions for the second exercise and fill in the blanks. Have him read the completed sentences aloud.

READING FOR LIVING: Page 43

Have S. read the title and the new word *ad.*

T: This is a supermarket ad like the one you would see in a newspaper. The name of the store is in the upper left-hand corner. What is it? [S: Green Hills Market.] You have had all of the words that are in the ad.

Have S. read the instruction aloud. Then have him look over the ad and read the names of the items and their prices to himself. After he has studied the ad, have him read it aloud. Help him sound out any word that he doesn't remember, or refer back to the lesson in which the word was introduced, if it is in this book.

Let S. do the exercise by himself. When he has finished have him read each question and answer aloud. Have him find the correct answer in the ad for any item he missed.

II. Skills Practice

Have S. close his book before doing these exercises.

PRACTICE 1: Distinguishing the Long Sound for *e*

T: Which of these words has the long sound for *e:*

met, meat?	*net, neat?*	*catch, each?*
cheap, chip?	*bit, beat?*	*tea, ten?*
eat, at?	*beans, bins?*	*sit, seat?*

PRACTICE 2: Identifying Vowel Sounds in Syllables

T: Listen to each word I say. Tell how many syllables are in the word. Also, tell what the vowel sound is in each syllable. In these words, the vowel sound will be short or long, or it will be the sound /er/.

cheese	[1—/ē/]	*teacher*	[2—/ē/, /er/]
baked	[1—/ā/]	*eighteen*	[2—/ā/, /ē/]
ever	[2—/e/, /er/]	*hamburger*	[3—/a/, /er/, /er/]
meal	[1—/ē/]	*something*	[2—/u/, /i/]

PRACTICE 3: Noun Ending *-er*

Write *teacher*, and have S. read it. Ask what the word would be without the *-er* ending. Write *teach* to the left of *teacher*, to start column 1.

Under *teach*, write these words in column 1: *run, read, bake, write.* Have S. read each word and tell what it would be with the ending *-er* added. As he answers, write *runner, reader, baker, writer* in column 2 under *teacher*.

Point out that when a root word ends in *e*, as the words *bake* and *write* do, we add just *-r*, not *-er*.

T: Is the final consonant doubled in any of these words before *-er* is added? [Yes, in *runner*.] Is the vowel sound in *run* short or long? [S: Short.]

T: Look at *read* and *reader*. Is the final consonant in *read* doubled before *-er* is added? [S: No.] Is the vowel sound in *read* short or long? [S: Long.]

T: When the vowel sound is short, you double the final consonant before adding *-er*. When the vowel sound is long, the final consonant is not doubled before *-er*.

T: I will say a root word and its form with *-er*. Listen for the vowel sound in the root word, and tell whether the final consonant is doubled before *-er* is added.

sit, sitter	[S: Yes.]	*speak, speaker*	[S: No.]
lead, leader	[S: No.]	*shop, shopper*	[S: Yes.]
bat, batter	[S: Yes.]	*beat, beater*	[S: No.]
zip, zipper	[S: Yes.]	*wait, waiter*	[S: No.]

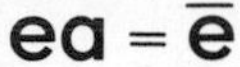

eat = ēt

ea = ē

	meat	meat	meat
	meal	meal	meal
	beans	beanz	beans
	tea	tea	tea
	teacher	teach er	teacher
	please	pleaz	please

The Class Party

each	eaten (eat en)	cheese (cheez)	best
cheap		people (pē pul)	something (some thing)

Carla's class is having a dinner party. There will be a big meal.

Each person brings something to eat. Carla brings beans. David brings a green salad. Jason and Gail bring baked potatoes. The Masons bring apples and cheese. Other people bring something to eat.

Ms. Smith, the teacher, brings the meat. The meat wasn't cheap. Each person helped to pay for the meat.

There are eighteen people at the party. They are having fun and eating a big meal.

"Please pass the meat," says Ray. "I have not eaten any meat for three days."

Kay says, "That is right. Meat is not cheap. For many meals, we have eggs, beans, or cheese. They are pretty cheap."

The teacher says, "Please pass the beans. Carla's beans are the best beans that I have ever eaten."

Jason says, "This is the best salad that I have ever eaten."

The people at the party eat their dinner. Then Ray passes apples and cheese. The teacher brings coffee and tea to the table. She asks each person, "Will you have coffee or tea?"

"I'll have tea, please," says Gail. "And Jason will have coffee."

"This is the best party that we have ever had," says Carla. "Let's have another one."

Story Checkup

Write a short answer.

1. Who is having a party? ____________
2. What does Carla bring? ____________
3. What do Jason and Gail bring? ____________
4. Who brings the meat? ____________
5. Who pays for the meat? ____________

Read this list of words.
Then write one of the words in each sentence.

eat, meal, tea, please, cheap

1. The people are eating a big ____________.
2. Each person brings something to ____________.
3. ____________ pass the meat.
4. Will you have coffee or ____________.
5. The meat wasn't ____________.

Reading for Living

ad

Please read this ad. Then write the answers.

1. Hamburger is in the ad. What other meat is there? ____________
2. What three things to drink are in this ad? ____________
3. What does a quart of milk cost? ____________
4. What does a half gallon of milk cost? ____________
5. What does the bread cost? ____________
6. What does a box of 100 tea bags cost? ____________
7. What do three cans of green beans cost? ____________
8. What does a jar of instant coffee cost? ____________

PRACTICE 4: Recognizing Verb Forms Ending in *en*

Write the following words in two columns:

eat	*eaten*
take	*taken*
give	*given*
got	*gotten*

T: In the first column are some action words that you have learned. Another name for an action word is *verb*. Read the verbs in the first column. [S. reads.]

T: In the second column is another form of these verbs. For these verbs, this is the form we use after *has* or *have*. Listen to these sentences: *Have you eaten dinner yet? Yes, I have eaten dinner.*

T: How many syllables are there in *eat*? [S: One.] How many in *eaten?* [S: Two.] Look at all of the verbs in the second column. Notice that they all end with *en*. The *en* adds a syllable.

Have S. read each pair of words: *eat, eaten,* and so on. Point out that the *t* at the end of *got* is doubled in *gotten* because there is a short vowel sound before the *t*.

Note: From now on, you should use the term *verb* when talking about words that are verbs. This will help S. learn to recognize verbs. This manual will indicate places where this is appropriate. But, do *not* try to define verbs or expect S. to identify them.

III. Writing

CHECK HOMEWORK: Page 39

Check this page with S. Have him correct any errors. If S. didn't do the work at home, give him time in class.

WRITING LESSON (In Notebook)

Have S. write the titles *Lesson 8* and *Words* and then write the numbers 1 through 12 in two columns.

Words. Help S. study the words *please, cheese,* and *people* before you dictate the words. After he has finished the dictation, have him check what he has written by looking at the chart and story words.

1. eat	4. beans	7. please	10. each
2. meat	5. tea	8. cheese	11. eaten
3. meal	6. teacher	9. people	12. cheap

Sentences. Have S. write the title *Sentences* and number from 1 to 5. Dictate these sentences:

1. Please pass the meat.
2. The people will eat a big meal.
3. Ray passes apples and cheese.
4. The teacher brings coffee and tea.
5. Beans are cheaper than meat.

Check what S. has written, and have him correct any errors, including those in punctuation and capitalization.

Have S. write the title *Study* and any words that he missed in the word and sentence dictation.

Be sure to praise S. for what he has written correctly. Encourage him to note his own progress. If he misses many words, dictate fewer words at a time, and give him more help studying the words beforehand.

Making a grocery list. Tell S. that many people like to make a list of things they need to buy at the grocery store before they go shopping. Dictate the shopping list below for him to write. (Tell him where to put the commas.) Check the list he has written, and help him correct any spelling errors. (Since a shopping list would be for his own use, it doesn't matter if he starts words with a capital or small letter.)

Eggs	Bread
Butter	Jelly
Cheese	Coffee
Milk, half gallon	Tea
Ham	Apples
Hamburger	Potatoes
Sandwich meat	Green beans, 2 cans

Note: You may, instead, read the list aloud to S., let him choose any 6 or 8 items he would want to buy, and have him write them. Read the list as many times as necessary.

PRACTICE: Page 44

Have S. read the directions for the first exercise to himself and then do it. Check his answers. If he has any wrong, have him read the pair of words aloud. Note how he pronounces the words. Give another similar pair of words and have him listen. Keep a record of the sounds he confuses for later practice.

Go over the directions and sample item for the second exercise with S. Have him add the *-er* ending to the words and then fill in the correct words in the sentences. Have him read the completed sentences aloud and correct any errors.

HOMEWORK: Page 45

Go over the directions with S. Encourage him to read the story and grocery ad again at home and to practice writing any words he missed.

CHECKING PROGRESS

To see how well S. can apply phonics skills, write the list below (or, put each item on a flash card). Tell S. that these are labels he might see on foods in a grocery store. Have him read each item.

Ham	*Beans*	*Baked Beans*	*Milk*
Beef	*Peas*	*Sweet Potatoes*	*Cream*
Veal	*Beets*	*Instant Tea*	*Peaches*
		Peanut Butter	

Practice

Say the words. Which word has the sound ē? Circle the word.

1. it eat
2. tea ten
3. dark dear
4. red read
5. meat men
6. plate please
7. bill meal
8. bean best

Copy the word. Add -r or -er.
Then write one of the words in each sentence.

farm ___farmer___ write ___writer___

Mr. Arthur is a ___farmer___. Ann is a ___writer___.

teach __________ bake __________

paint __________ read __________

1. Ms. Smith is Carla's __________.
2. The __________ is painting the apartment.
3. The __________ is baking bread.
4. She can read the story quickly.

   She is a fast __________.

Homework

Answer with a sentence.

1. What do the Masons bring? __________
2. Who brings a salad? __________
3. What does Ms. Smith bring to the table? __________

Say the word. Write the number of syllables.

1. tea ____
2. people ____
3. eat ____
4. something ____
5. eaten ____
6. baked ____
7. baking ____
8. baker ____
9. read ____
10. reader ____
11. teacher ____
12. potatoes ____

MEETING INDIVIDUAL NEEDS

Make flash cards for the chart words in Lesson 8 and for the new story words with the sound /ē/. Ask questions that can be answered with the words.

Add flash cards for the following words to those you made for the game on rhyming words in Lesson 4:

eat, meat	*bean, mean*	*each, teach*
meal, seal	*cheap, heap*	*please, tease*

If S. needs practice with the ending *-er*, make up a worksheet. Write the root words *bake, make, play, bank, rent, write, work, read, give, paint* in a column on a sheet of paper. Across the top, write the instruction *Add -r or -er*. Have S. read each root word aloud, say the word with the ending added, tell whether to add *-r* or *-er*, and then write the word.

A similar exercise can be made for the endings *-s* and *-es* with these words: *class, check, day, box, chair, plate, match, church, meal, sandwich*.

To give additional practice in writing the number words, make up the following worksheet. Have S. work *across* each line, reading the words that are given and filling in the missing ones. From time to time, give a similar worksheet, gradually reducing the number of words that are given as cues until S. can write all of the number words by himself.

Write the missing number words.

1 one	11 eleven	10 ten
2 two	12 twelve	20 ______
3 three	13 thirteen	30 ______
4 four	14 ______	40 forty
5 five	15 fifteen	50 ______
6 six	16 ______	60 sixty
7 ______	17 seventeen	70 ______
8 eight	18 ______	80 ______
9 nine	19 ______	90 ______
10 ______	20 twenty	100 ______

In the *Workbook for Skill Book 3*, the exercises for Lesson 8 may be used at this time.

In *Focus on Phonics-3*, Practices 8A-8E may be used after Lesson 8. They give practice with *ea* word families.

LESSON 9 — Skill Book 3, Pages 46-51

OBJECTIVES

To help your student:

- recognize that two *e*'s separated by one consonant (*e-e*) usually stand for the sound /ē/, as in *Pete*.
- recognize that the letters *ey* usually stand for the sound /ē/ as in *key*.
- read words in which the sound /ē/ is represented by *e-e* or *ey*.
- distinguish between the long and short sounds for *e* and distinguish both from the sound for *i*.
- recognize the main idea of a paragraph and recall supporting details.
- recall the sequence of events in a story.
- read and understand a bill for repair services.
- identify the number of syllables in a word and the vowel sound in each syllable.
- recognize the root word in a word ending with *-ing* or *-ed*.
- write words, sentences, and money amounts from dictation.

INTRODUCTION

T: You have learned three ways that the sound /ē/is written. (Write *he, tree, eat.*) How is the sound /ē/ written in each of these words? [S: *e, ee, ea.*] In today's lesson, you will learn two other ways.

I. Reading

CHART: Page 46

Title and key words. Have S. read the title *Lesson 9.*

T: Look at the first two letters in the top right-hand corner. What are they? [S: *e-e.*] What does the dash between the *e*'s mean? [S: The two *e*'s are separated by a consonant.] Two *e*'s separated by a consonant equal what sound? [S: /ē/.]

T: (Point to *Pete.*) Read the first key word. [S: Pete.] What letter separates the two *e*'s in *Pete*? [S: *t*.] What kind of letter is *t*? [S: A consonant.] (Point to *e-e* = *ē*.) Two *e*'s separated by a consonant equal what sound? [S: /ē/.]

T: Read the second key word. [S: key.] (Point to *ey* = *ē*.) What letters together equal the sound /ē/? [S: *ey*.]

Lines 1-3. Ask S. to study the first three lines and notice how the sound /ē/ is written in these words. After S. has studied the lines, have him read each word aloud, tell how the sound /ē/ is written, and how many syllables the word has.

Lines 4-5. Ask S. to study the last two lines and notice how the sound /ē/ is written in these words. After he has studied the lines, have him read the words aloud. Ask him how the sound /ē/ is written and the number of syllables in each word.

Review. Have S. read the words aloud, including the key words. Go down the last column. Call attention to the consonant blend *st* in *Steve.*

STORY: Pages 47-48 (Steve's Job)

Have S. read the story title and new words. Have him tell what long vowel sound is in each word and how the sound is written. Call attention to the consonant blend *cl* in *clean* and the number of syllables in *repair* and *Saturday*.

Main idea of paragraphs. Ask S. to read paragraphs 1-4 silently and notice the main thing each paragraph tells about Steve's job. When he has finished, have him tell the main points about Steve's job. These should include:

Par. 1. Where Steve works — Pete's Valley Repair Shop
Par. 2. What his job is — To keep the place clean
Par. 3. When he works — Nine to six in the evenings and on Saturdays
Par. 4. How much he makes — $60 a week
(Par. 4 also tells how much Steve has saved and why, but that is not about his job.)

Summarizing. Have S. read the rest of the story to himself. Then have him summarize it by telling the main events in the order in which they happened.

Reading between the lines. Discuss these questions:

1. Pete left Steve in charge of the shop. What does this indicate that Pete thought of Steve? [He trusted him.] Do you think the way Steve handled this responsibility showed that he was worthy of Pete's trust? Give reasons for your answer.
2. Why do you think Pete let Steve keep the money for fixing Mrs. Green's radio?

STORY CHECKUP: Page 48

Have S. read the direction for the first exercise to himself and then write the answers. Check his work. Have him scan the story to find the correct answer for any item he has wrong. Ask him to read aloud the part that answers the question.

Go over the directions for the second exercise with S. Tell him to read all of the statements before he starts numbering them. If he doesn't remember the order in which events happened, let him look back at the story.

READING FOR LIVING: Page 49

Have S. read the title, new words, and instructions. Explain that this is one of the bills that Pete made out for his repair service. Have S. read aloud everything that is on the bill. Then have him do the exercise.

Lesson 9

Pete = Pēt
e-e = ē

e-e = ē
ey = ē

key = kē
ey = ē

Steve	Steve	Steve
these	theze	these
evening	eve ning	evening
valley	val ey	valley
money	mun ey	money

Steve's Job

clean, teach, keep, week, here, make, save, place (plase), repair (rē pair), Saturday (Sat ur day)

Steve is seventeen. He has a job at Pete's Valley Repair Shop. Pete repairs radios, TVs, and other things.

Steve's job is to keep the place clean. He keeps the shop clean. He keeps the stairs clean. Pete is teaching him to repair radios. Next, Pete will teach him to repair TVs.

Steve works from six to nine in the evening. And he works on Saturday.

Steve does not make much money at his job. He makes $60 a week. Steve saves some of his money. He has worked at the repair shop for six weeks. In six weeks, he has saved $120 dollars. He is saving his money to get a color TV.

One evening, Pete gives Steve some keys. "These are the keys to the shop," Pete says. "I will not be here on Saturday. You can take care of the place."

"OK," says Steve. "I will be here at eight on Saturday. I will take care of the place very well."

Pete says, "A lot of people will come in to pick up their things. These radios are ready. These TVs are ready. I was going to repair Mrs. Green's radio yesterday, but I didn't. You can fix it."

On Saturday, Mrs. Green comes in. Steve gives her the radio that he fixed. Other people come in. Steve gives them their things and takes their money.

That evening, Pete comes back. Steve says, "Here are your keys. Here is the money that I got today. I fixed Mrs. Green's radio, and she picked it up."

Pete says, "You can keep the money she gave you. You worked hard today."

Story Checkup

Write a short *yes* or *no* answer.

1. Is Steve fifteen? ______________________
2. Has Steve saved $120? ______________________
3. Did Pete work in the shop on Saturday? ______________________
4. Did Steve repair Mrs. Green's radio? ______________________
5. Is Pete teaching Steve to repair radios? ______________________

Read these five sentences. What happened first? You will see a number 1 next to that sentence. What happened next? Put a number 2 next to that sentence. Put the right numbers next to the other sentences.

______ Steve fixes Mrs. Green's radio.
___1___ Pete gives Steve some keys.
______ Steve gives Mrs. Green the radio.
______ Steve gives Pete the keys.
______ That evening, Pete comes back.

Reading for Living

second (sec und), third, tax, part, labor (lā ber)

PETE'S VALLEY REPAIR SHOP
332 Second Street
Garden City

Name Jane Fisher
Address 332 Third Street
Date April 16, 1986
For TV repair

Parts	$12.14
Labor	30.00
	42.14
Tax	2.32
	$44.46

Please read this bill. Then write short answers.

1. What is this bill for? ______________________
2. What do the parts cost? $ __________
3. What does the labor cost? $ __________
4. What is the tax? $ __________
5. Which costs more, the parts or the labor? __________
6. Which costs more, the parts or the tax? __________
7. What does Jane Fisher have to pay? $ __________
8. What is the date on the bill? ______________________
9. Is the repair shop on Second Street? ______________________
10. Does Jane Fisher live on Third Street? ______________________

Check what S. has written. Help him find the correct answer for any item he has wrong. Then have him write the correct answer.

II. Skills Practice

Have S. close his book before doing these exercises.

PRACTICE 1: Distinguishing the Long Sound for *e*

T: I will say three words. Which one has the long sound for *e*:

bit, bet, beet?	*key, kiss, Ken?*
Eve, Ed, if?	*pen, peel, pin?*
kept, keep, kick?	*tin, ten, teen?*
week, wet, with?	*this, then, these?*

PRACTICE 2: Identifying Vowel Sounds in Syllables

T: Listen to each word I say. Tell how many syllables are in the word. Also, tell what the vowel sound is in each syllable. In these words, the vowel sound will be short or long, or it will be the sound /er/.

Saturday	[3—/a/, /er/, /ā/]	*valley*	[2—/a/, /ē/]
evening	[2—/ē/, /i/]	*repair*	[2—/ē/, /ā/]
labor	[2—/ā/, /er/]	*cleaned*	[1—/e/]
sixteen	[2—/i/, /ē/]	*fixing*	[2—/i/, /i/]
Fisher	[2—/i/, /er/]	*money*	[2—/u/, /ē/]

PRACTICE 3: Subtracting the Endings *-ing* and *-ed*

Write these words in a column: *teaching, keeping, saving, making, needed, cleaned, fixed, saved.* Have S. read each word and tell what the root word is. (If necessary, remind him that the root word is the word without the ending.) As he answers, write the root words in a second column.

III. Writing

CHECK HOMEWORK: Page 45

Check this page with S. Have him correct any errors.

WRITING LESSON: (In Notebook)

Have S. write the titles *Lesson 9* and *Words* and then write the numbers 1 through 12 in two columns.

Words. Have S. study the word *money*. Have him tell how the sound /ē/ is written in *here, keep, week,* and the way it is written in *clean* and *teach*. Then dictate the words below. Check what S. has written. Have him correct any errors.

1. Pete	4. these	7. money	10. week
2. key	5. evening	8. here	11. clean
3. Steve	6. valley	9. keep	12. teach

Sentences. Have S. write the title *Sentences* and number from 1 to 6. Dictate these sentences:

1. Steve keeps the shop clean.
2. He works three evenings each week.
3. Pete will teach him to repair TVs.
4. These are the keys to the shop.
5. I will not be here on Saturday.
6. Mrs. Green gave Steve the money.

Check what S. has written. Have him correct any errors in spelling, punctuation, or capitalization. Then have S. write the title *Study* and any words that he missed in the word and sentence dictation.

Money amounts in a column

T: Sometimes you may need to write amounts of money in a column in order to add them. It is important to line up the numbers in the right way.

Demonstrate by writing the column of numbers shown below. Point out that the periods (decimal points) should line up and that the number of 10's, 1's and cents should line up. Explain that it is not necessary to write the dollar sign each time. It should appear in the first amount and in the total.

```
$31.25
  2.00
   .75
------
```

T: I will say three amounts for you to write in a column. Please listen carefully, and write each amount as I say it: $13.10, $5.75, $.50. Draw a line under the last amount, but you do not need to add the numbers.

Check what S. has written. Have him rewrite any amount that is not correct. If the numbers are not lined up properly, have him recopy the whole column.

Then dictate these numbers for him to write in a different column: $17.35, $.99, $8.09. Check his work, and have him correct any errors.

PRACTICE: Page 50

Have S. read the directions for the first exercise to himself and then do it. Check his answers. If he has any wrong, have him read the word aloud. Notice how he pronounces the vowel sound. If the vowel sound is not clear or accurate the way he says it, say another word with that sound, and ask him to listen and tell you the sound that he hears. Keep a record of the sounds that he confuses for further practice.

Have S. read the directions for the second exercise and then do it. After he finishes, have him read aloud each word with an ending and its root. Have him correct any errors.

HOMEWORK: Page 51

Go over the directions with S. Encourage him to reread the story and repair bill at home and to practice writing any words that he missed.

Practice

Say the words. Circle the words with the sound ē.

1.	clean	class	please	last
2.	money	meat	key	month
3.	well	week	went	with
4.	these	here	her	this
5.	pet	Pete	teach	pick

Drop *-ing* or *-ed*. Write the word that is left.

1. keeping ________
2. painted ________
3. eating ________
4. played ________
5. drinking ________
6. reading ________
7. repaired ________
8. needed ________
9. paying ________
10. yelled ________
11. cleaned ________
12. teaching ________

Homework

Answer with a sentence.

1. Where does Steve work? ________
2. What is Steve saving his money for? ________
3. Who repaired Mrs. Green's radio? ________
4. Who gave the keys to Steve? ________

Say the word. Write the number of syllables.

1. cleaned ____
2. repaired ____
3. money ____
4. saved ____
5. seventeen ____
6. Saturday ____
7. week ____
8. yesterday ____
9. fixed ____
10. labor ____

CHECKING PROGRESS

From today's lesson, you can check the student's progress in the following comprehension skills:

1. Summarizing a story
2. Identifying the main idea of a paragraph
3. Recalling details
4. Remembering the sequence of events (This skill is not completely new, but this is the first time S. has had to remember the sequence independently.)

Note which type of skills he needs most help in, and plan extra practice for that skill. Comprehension skills will be reviewed in the next lessons.

MEETING INDIVIDUAL NEEDS

Make flash cards for the Lesson 9 chart and story words. Have S. read each word and tell what long vowel sound it has and how the sound is written.

Mix these cards with those from earlier lessons, omitting those from Lesson 1. Spread the cards out face down. Have S. turn up two cards. If they have the same long vowel sound written the same way, he keeps them and takes another turn. If the cards don't match, he puts them back face down, and then the next player has a turn. If you set a time limit, the winner is the player with the most cards matched when the time is up. Or, you can play until all cards that can be matched are matched.

If S. needs help with sequence of events, write out the sentences below. Have him scan the story in Lesson 7 and number the sentences in order. (Put in the number 1 to get him started.) Point out that he should give the order in which the events actually happened, not the order in which they're told in the story.

__2__ Lee's car hit a tree.
__4__ Lee came in at half past three.
__6__ After listening to her son, Mrs. Green said, "Do not be late again, or I will take away your car. And you will have to pay for that tree."
__3__ Lee's face hit the wheel.
__5__ Mrs. Green got up and asked Lee what happened.
__1__ Lee Green went to sleep at the wheel of his car.

For more practice in comprehension, you may want to give supplementary reading. You can get a list of local literacy councils that publish material correlated to the Laubach Way to Reading series from LLA, Laubach Literacy International, Box 131, Syracuse, NY 13210.

You may want to give another worksheet on number words similar to the one described in Lesson 8.

In the *Workbook for Skill Book 3*, the exercises for Lesson 9 may be used at this time.

In *Focus on Phonics-3*, Practices 9A-9B may be used now. They cover word families with *ey, e-e, ee-e,* and *ea-e*.

LESSON 10 — Skill Book 3, Pages 52-53

OBJECTIVES

To help your student:

- review the sound /ē/and its most regular spellings: *e-e, ea, ee, ey.*
- review the sound /ā/ and its most regular spellings: *a-e, ai, ay.*
- read short stories that review words introduced in Lessons 7-9, especially words with long *e*.
- summarize the main ideas of a story.
- interpret facts and draw inferences.
- interpret the feelings of characters in the stories.
- develop sight recall of words first learned by sounding them out.
- develop further skill in reading a grocery ad.
- distinguish between the long and short sounds for *e*.
- distinguish the long *a* sound from short *a* and long *e*.
- identify rhyming words.
- determine the number of syllables in a word.
- review the beginning consonant blends *cl, pl, sl, dr, gr, tr, thr, sp, st, str,* and *tw.*
- review the endings *-er* and *-ing* and how to add them to root words.
- review the ending *-ed* and the three ways it is pronounced, as in *yelled, passed, needed.*
- recognize the root word in a word with an ending.
- review contractions.
- develop further skill in writing words, sentences, money amounts, and number words.
- apply phonics skills in practice exercises containing new words with familiar sound-letter relationships.

INTRODUCTION

T: In today's lesson you will review the sounds /ā/and /ē/ and the main ways they are written. You will read two short stories that have many words with these sounds. We'll also go over some of the other things that you have studied in the last three lessons. You'll find the stories easy to read as there are only a few new words in them.

I. Reading

CHART: Page 52

Have S. read each key word and tell what the long vowel sound is and how it is written.

STORIES: Pages 52-53

T: In these stories, you will learn more about the people you met in Lessons 7 through 9.

Story 1: A Teenager Pays. Have S. read the story title and the new word *teenager*.

T: Remember the story about Lee Green? What did Lee's car hit when he fell asleep at the wheel? [S: A tree.] In this story, you'll find out what Lee did about it.

Silent reading. Ask S. to read the whole story silently and then summarize it in a few sentences. After his summary, ask these questions to check comprehension:

1. What day of the week was it?
2. Where did Lee go?
3. Why was the woman angry?
4. What statements did the woman make about teenagers in general? Do some teenagers do these things? Did Lee do these things? Is it fair to judge all members of a group by the actions of some?
5. How much did the woman say it would cost to get another tree?
6. What made the woman change her feelings about Lee?

Oral reading. Have S. find the different punctuation marks that are in the story. Review what each mark means. Discuss the importance of observing punctuation marks in order to read with meaning and expression. Have S. read the whole story aloud. Note whether he interprets the feelings of the characters by the way he reads.

Story 2: Pete's Story

Note: It will help to have a copy of this story that you can mark as S. reads aloud. The procedure for teaching it is the same as that used for stories 3-4 in Lesson 6.

T: Remember the story about Steve, who works in the TV repair shop? This story is about the man he works for.

Have S. read the title and new words first to himself and then aloud. Note how many words he is able to sound out. Underline any with which he needs help.

Oral reading. Have S. read the story aloud without reading it silently first. Tell him to be ready to tell Pete's story in a few sentences. As S. reads aloud, mark your copy of the story as suggested below. Later, you can use this record to plan extra practice.

1. Underline any place where S. hesitates.
2. Mark through a word if S. says the wrong word. If you have time, write the word he substitutes.
3. Mark through any ending that is omitted or wrong.
4. Circle any words that are omitted or any punctuation marks not observed.
5. Note his ability to read fluently and with expression.

Summarizing. After S. gives his summary, record whether or not it was accurate and reasonably complete. You might like to write down his summary. Also, note whether he told the events in the order they happened.

Scanning for main ideas. Ask S. how many paragraphs are in the story [7]. Have him number the paragraphs so that he can answer your next questions more easily. Then have him scan the story to find each part asked for.

Lesson 10

More Reading with ā and ē

paper	cake	paint		day
ā	a‿e	ai		ay
we	Pete	eat	see	key
ē	e‿e	ea	ee	ey

1. A Teenager Pays

teenager (teen āj er)

It was Saturday. Lee Green went to see the tree that he hit. When he got there, a woman was standing next to the tree. She looked angry. "Are you the teenager that hit my tree?" she asked.

"Yes, I am." said Lee. "I went to sleep at the wheel."

"You teenagers!" she yelled, and her face got red. "You do not care what you do! You drink beer! You go fast in your cars! You do not need cars!"

"I am a teenager," said Lee. "But I wasn't drinking beer. I wasn't going fast. And I do care. I came to pay for your tree."

"We cannot save this tree," said the woman. "It will not live. It will cost a hundred dollars to get another one."

"That is a lot of money," said Lee. "I can pay you twenty dollars today. I have a job. I can pay you twenty dollars a week."

The woman said, "I am happy that you came back. You are OK."

2. Pete's Story

team	hockey (hock ey)	Canada (Can u du)
year	player (play er)	

I am Pete. I run the repair shop on Second Street. Steve works for me in the evenings. He keeps the place clean. I am teaching him to repair things.

Let me tell you my story. I was a teenager in the 1940s. I lived with my mother in Canada. My father was dead. When I was nineteen, I got a job with a hockey team in Canada. I was going to be a big hockey player and make a lot of money.

My mother left Canada and came back to Garden City. Then she got sick. She needed me to take care of her. I came to Garden City. I got a job at a TV factory. I started repairing TVs. I repaired them in the evening at the kitchen table.

Many years passed. My mother did not get well. I never went back to my hockey team. After fourteen years, I started my repair shop.

When I think back, I am not very happy. I was going to be a big hockey player. Many people were going to see me play. I was going to make a lot of money. These things never happened.

But I am happy with the hockey team that I have today. There are fifteen teenagers on my team. I am teaching these boys to play hockey. They think that I am the best hockey player there is.

"Not the best," I tell them. "But I still have my teeth, and a lot of hockey players do not. And I have you. We will be the best hockey team in the valley. And next year we will play in Canada."

1. Which paragraph tells what Pete planned to be when he was nineteen. [2]
2. Which two paragraphs tell why Pete had to give up his dream of being a big hockey player? [3-4]
3. Which paragraph tells why Pete is not happy when he thinks back? [5]
4. Which paragraph tells what makes Pete happy now? [6]
5. Which paragraph tells what Pete's hopes are for the hockey team he coaches? [6]
6. Which paragraph tells how Pete earns a living now and who works for him? [1]

Making inferences. Discuss these questions with S. Ask him to find reasons for his answers in the story.

1. Which way of describing Pete is more accurate:
   a. Is Pete a selfish or an unselfish person?
   b. Do you think he is ambitious or unambitious?
   c. Do you think Pete is bitter about losing his dream or fairly satisfied with the life he has today?
2. Which idea about life does this story try to show:
   a. There is no point in making big plans for your life because they are sure to fail.
   b. Although a person's life may not turn out the way he wanted, he can still find satisfaction.
   c. A person should look out for himself first and not worry about others.

READING FOR LIVING (Supplementary Materials)

Collect some supermarket ads from newspapers. Circle (in red if possible) all the items that S. should be able to read or sound out. These include words with regular spellings for short vowel sounds; long *a* and long *e*; *er, ir,* or *ur* for the sound /er/; and *ar* for the sound /ar/. You may include a few sight words, also, especially if they go together with items you want to use, such as *ice* in *ice cream* or *ground* in *ground beef.*

Have S. read the items you have circled and their prices. You may want to explain a few of the common abbreviations—such as *qt.* for *quart, lb.* for *pound,* and *oz.* for *ounces*—so that the prices are more meaningful.

If it is not possible to bring ads, review the ad on page 43. Ask questions that S. can answer orally, and make your questions different from those in the exercise.

You may also want to bring in a bank deposit slip, and have S. fill it out for practice in writing money amounts in a column. You can show him how to fill in the other parts. You can make up a blank check for him to fill out for practice in writing money amounts in both numbers and words. Also, you can have him read a sample check that you have written.

II. Skills Practice

T: Now we'll have some listening exercises to review some things you have covered in the last few lessons.

PRACTICE 1: Distinguishing the Long Sound for *e*

T: Which of these words has the long sound for *e*:

check, cheek?	*peek, pick?*	*step, steep?*
meat, met?	*dip, deep?*	*green, grin?*
bed, beat?	*feel, fill?*	*it, eat?*

Write the following pairs of words. Have S. read each pair and tell which word has the short sound for *e* and which has the long sound.

red	*read*	*Ned*	*need*	*pet*	*Pete*
bed	*bead*	*fed*	*feed*		
men	*mean*	*ten*	*teen*		

PRACTICE 2: Distinguishing the Long Sound for *a*

T: Which of these three words has the long sound for *a*:

at, ate, eat?	*plan, play, please?*
hate, hat, heat?	*frame, from, Fran?*
land, let, late?	*pepper, paper, popper?*

Write the following pairs of words. Have S. read each pair and tell which has the short sound for *a* and which has the long sound.

at	*ate*	*man*	*main*
hat	*hate*	*ran*	*rain*
mad	*made*	*am*	*aim*

PRACTICE 3: Identifying Rhyming Words

Say each of the following words, and have S. give a word that rhymes with it: *see, sleep, meat, teach.*

Note: Accept answers that end with the same vowel and consonant sounds even if they are not spelled the same way. For example, *cheap* rhymes with *sleep.*

PRACTICE 4: Identifying the Number of Syllables

Say each word below, and have S. tell how many syllables it has. If he has difficulty, say the word again, and have him tell how many vowel sounds—or beats—it has.

hockey	[2]	*drinking*	[2]	*Saturday*	[3]
cleaned	[1]	*teacher*	[2]	*yesterday*	[3]
needed	[2]	*teenager*	[3]	*something*	[2]
labor	[2]	*started*	[2]	*nineteen*	[2]

PRACTICE 5: Review of Beginning Consonant Blends

T: (Write *cl, pl, sl.*) Listen as I say two words. Which of these blends do they begin with:

place, please?	*clean, class?*	*sleep, slip?*

T: (Write *dr, gr, tr, thr.*) Listen as I say two words. Which of these blends do they begin with:

tree, tray?	*green, gray?*	*three, throw?*
drink, drop?	*thread, through?*	*train, trust?*

T: (Write *sp, st, str.*) Listen as I say two words. Which of these blends do they begin with:

still, story?	*street, strip?*	*spell, speak?*
spent, spoke?	*Steve, stairs?*	*stream, stray?*

T: (Write *tw.*) Listen as I say two words. Which word begins with the blend *tw:*

win, twin?	*tin, twin?*	*twenty, thirty?*
twig, wig?	*twice, dice?*	*twist, trust?*

PRACTICE 6: Endings *-ing* and *-er*

Write these words in a column: *bake, keep, teach, paint, read, play, run, sit.* Have S. read each word and tell what it would be with the ending *-er* added. Ask in which of these words the final consonant should be doubled before *-er.* Write the *-er* words in a second column, and have S. read them.

Do the same thing with the ending *-ing.* Ask in which of these words a change must be made in the root word before *-ing* is added. Write the *-ing* words in a third column, and have S. read them.

PRACTICE 7: Ending *-ed*

Write the words *yelled, passed, needed* in a row. Have S. read each word and tell the following: the root word, the ending, how the ending is pronounced, the number of syllables in each word. Under each word, write the way the ending is pronounced: *d, t, ed.*

Say each word below, and have S. tell the sound for the *-ed* ending:

painted	*repaired*	*saved*	*named*
baked	*reached*	*started*	*kissed*
played	*crashed*	*wished*	*wanted*

PRACTICE 8: Recognizing the Root Word

Write these words in a column: *thinking, passes, having, fixed, repairing, teacher, saving, asked.* Have S. read each word and tell what the root word is. Ask him to spell the root word as you write it by the word with the ending.

PRACTICE 9: Contractions

Write these contractions in a column: *I'll, let's, it's, wasn't, didn't.* Have S. read each contraction and tell the two words it is made from. Write the two words.

Read each sentence below to S. Have him tell what contraction is used in the sentence and what two words the contraction is made from.

1. Let's have another party next month.
2. The meat wasn't cheap.
3. I'll be there at eight on Saturday.
4. Pete didn't repair the radio.
5. It's half past three.

III. Writing

CHECK HOMEWORK: Page 51

Check this page with S. Notice whether he has used correct punctuation and capitalization. Have him correct any errors. Note the type of errors for further practice. Be sure to give praise for sentences well written. If he didn't do the work, give him time in class.

WRITING LESSON (In Notebook)

Words. Have S. write the titles *Lesson 10* and *Words* and number from 1 to 20 in two columns. Dictate the following words for him to write. (If you prefer, you may substitute words from his "Study" list in the last few lessons.)

1. sleep	6. people	11. money	16. keep
2. need	7. teacher	12. seventeen	17. here
3. teeth	8. beans	13. evening	18. make
4. see	9. these	14. valley	19. week
5. please	10. keys	15. clean	20. place

Check his work, and have him correct any errors.

Sentences. Have S. write the title *Sentences* and number from 1 to 5. Have him cover the words he wrote. Then dictate these sentences for S. to write:

1. This bill is for the repair on my car.
2. I saved some money this week.
3. Mrs. Green keeps a list of the things she needs.
4. Steve wasn't late for work.
5. Will Lee pay twenty dollars for the tree?

Check his work, and have him correct any errors. Then have him write the title *Study* and any words he missed in the word and sentence dictation.

Money amounts. Dictate each group of money amounts below. Ask S. to write the amounts in a column.

$60.90	$20.75	$125.00
$ 6.56	$ 8.26	$ 6.28
$19.09	$ .95	$ 40.02

Check the numbers he has written, and note if they are lined up properly in each column.

Number words. Make a worksheet on number words similar to the one described in the Meeting Individual Needs section of Lesson 8. Leave blank as many of the words as you think S. can spell correctly at this point.

REVIEW PRACTICE

Write out the exercises shown at the right. Go over the directions with S. Let him do the page by himself. Check his answers for the first exercise, and have him correct any errors. For the second exercise, have him read each sentence with the word he filled in.

HOMEWORK (In Notebook)

Explain to S. that the homework is to be done in his notebook. Ask him to write a short summary (three or four sentences) about the first story. Ask him to write two questions about the second story. Encourage him to study any words he missed in the dictation.

CHECKING PROGRESS

Comprehension. If S. was able to summarize the stories and answer most of the questions, his progress is satisfactory. If he had difficulty, note the reasons. He may not have recognized enough words to understand the meaning. Or, he may have difficulty in keeping the order of events in mind or in expressing himself orally. Plan extra practice in needed skills.

Word recognition. If S. missed five words or less in the oral reading of story 2, he is doing well. If he missed more words, note the types of errors. If they are similar, plan extra practice in the skill needed. If errors are more general, supplementary material using the same vocabulary may be helpful.

See Lesson 6 for suggestions on checking word recognition with flash cards.

Recording progress. Follow the suggestions in Lesson 6 for recording progress in comprehension and phonics skills. Also, record the number of words and sentences S. wrote correctly in the dictation. Note which punctuation marks S. uses correctly in his writing.

MEETING INDIVIDUAL NEEDS

If S. did fairly well in this lesson, let him go on to Lesson 11. If he needs help in many areas, plan another review lesson. Use the supplements suggested here, or create your own, but do not repeat skill book lessons. Encourage S. and help him feel that a supplementary lesson will help his progress. But do not hold him back unnecessarily. The next lessons will give much review.

In the *Workbook for Skill Book 3*, the exercises for Lesson 10 may be done at this time.

In *Focus on Phonics-3*, Practice 10 may be used after Lesson 10. It reviews words in which the sound /ē/ is spelled with *-e, ee, ea, e-e, ee-e,* and *ea-e.*

Read each sentence. Circle the words with the sound ē.

1. Mrs. Green lives on Second Street.
2. Lee will eat a cheese sandwich.
3. Will you have coffee or tea with your meal?
4. Turkey is cheaper than beef.
5. Steve worked three evenings this week.

Write the missing word in each sentence.

weeds	seeds	1. The farmer will plant some ____.
peas	fleas	2. Mrs. Green brings a can of ____.
jeep	deep	3. That river is very ____.
cream	steam	4. Ed puts ____ in his coffee.
bees	beach	5. Let's look for shells on the ____.
chair	cheer	6. I'll ____ for Pete's hockey team.

LESSON 11 Skill Book 3 Pages 54-59

OBJECTIVES

To help your student:
- recognize the long sound for *i* as in key word *I*.
- recognize that *i* at the end of a syllable usually stands for /ī/, as in *bicycle*.
- recognize that the letters *i* and *e* separated by one consonant (*i-e*) usually stand for the sound /ī/, as in the key word *time*.
- read words in which the sound /ī/ is written *i* or *i-e*.
- read a factual article to obtain information.
- recognize the difference between fact and fiction.
- distinguish between the long and short sounds for *i*.
- determine the number of syllables in a word.
- review adding the endings *-er* and *-ing* to words.
- recognize the root word in words with the endings *-er* and *-ing*.
- recognize that verb forms ending in *en* are related to known verbs, as *write, written*.
- review the beginning consonant blends *dr, tr, pl, gl, st, str* and the ending blend *st* as in *test*.
- read and fill in a simple application form.
- write words and sentences from dictation.
- write dates and addresses.

INTRODUCTION

T: In today's lesson, you will study another long vowel sound. Turn to Lesson 11, and find out what it is.

I. Reading

CHART: Page 54

Title and key words. Have S. read *Lesson 11* and tell what long vowel sound the lesson is about.

T: Read the first key word. [S: I.] How is the sound /ī/ written? [S: The letter *i* by itself.]

T: (Point to *i-e* = ī.) What is another way the sound /ī/ is written? [S: *i* and *e*.] What does the dash mean? [S: *i* and *e* are separated by a consonant.] The letters *i* and *e* separated by a consonant equal what sound? [S: /ī/.]

T: (Point to *time.*) Read this key word. [S: time.] What consonant separates *i* and *e* in *time?* [S: *m*.] Good. (Point to *i-e* = ī.) The letters *i* and *e* separated by a consonant equal what sound? [S: /ī/.]

Lines 1-2. Have S. study the first two lines and notice how the sound /ī/ is written in these words. After he has studied the lines, have him read each word aloud and tell how the sound /ī/ is written.

Line 3

T: Look at the next line. This is the same word as the one you just read with an ending added. What is the word? [S: driver.] What is the ending? [S: *-er*.] Remember, when the root word ends in *e*, as *drive* does, we just add -r.

Lines 4-5. Have S. study the words silently and then read them aloud. Ask him to tell how the sound /ī/ is written and the number of syllables in each word.

Review. Have S. read the words aloud, including the key words. Go down the last column of the chart. Call attention to the blend *dr* in *drive* and *driver*.

STORY: Pages 55-56 (Getting a Driver's License)

Have S. read the story title and new words. Call attention to the meaning of the word *eye*, and to the beginning blend *st* in *state* and the ending blend *st* in *test*.

T: Up to now, the stories that you have read have been what we call *fiction*. This means that the story was imagined and made up by the author.

T: The reading material in today's lesson is not fiction; it is *fact*. The author has written a factual article to give information about getting a driver's license.

Directed silent reading

T: Read the first paragraph to yourself, and find out what three questions this article will answer. Also, find out if the answers are the same in all states.

Have S. read silently and then tell what the questions are. Be sure he understands that the article will describe what is generally true in many of the states. But, because each state can make different rules, the information may not be true of every state.

Ask S. to finish reading the article silently and find the answers to the three questions. When he has finished, have him summarize the information about getting a driver's license. His summary might be as follows:

[You get your license from the state you live in. You must take tests. The eye test tells if you need glasses to drive. Another test is a written test. If you pass the written test, you can get a permit to drive with a licensed driver in the car. The last test is a driving test. If you pass the driving test, you can get a driver's license. If you do not pass the test, you can take it again.]

If S. did not include the important points in his summary, have him scan certain paragraphs to find the information.

Discuss with S. the information in the article about who needs a driver's license and license plates. Point out that the information about license plates was probably included in this article about getting a driver's license to distinguish between the two types of licenses.

I
i

Ī
i–e = ī

time
i–e = ī

ride	rīde rīd	ride
drive	drīve drīv	drive
driver	drīv er	driver
license	lī sens	license
bicycle	bī sic ul	bicycle

Getting a Driver's License

eye (ī)	same	test	written (rit en)
if	state	tester (test er)	permit (per mit)

Who needs a driver's license? What do I have to do to get one? Do I need license plates? The answers are not the same in each of the 50 states. But the answers are the same in many states.

You need a license to drive a car. You need a license to drive a truck. You do not need a license to ride a bicycle.

You must have license plates for your car. You must have license plates for a truck. In some places, you have to have license plates for a bicycle. In other places, you do not have to have license plates for a bicycle.

You get license plates from the state that you live in. You get your driver's license from your state.

To get a driver's license, you must take tests. One test is an eye test. To take this test, you have to read letters on a chart. The eye test tells if you need glasses to drive.

Another test is a written test. If you do not pass the written test the first time, you must not drive. But you can take this test again.

If you pass the written test, you get a permit to drive. A permit is not a license. But with a permit, you can start driving. Another person must ride with you. That person must have a driver's license.

The last test is a driving test. You are ready to take it when you can drive well. A tester will ride with you. The tester tells you where to drive and when to turn. The tester watches your driving and parking.

If you pass the driving test, you will get a driver's license. Many people do not pass this test the first time. If you do not pass the first time, you can take the driving test again. You can take it again and again.

Story Checkup

Circle yes or no.

1. Do you need a license to ride a bicycle? Yes No
2. Do you have to take tests to get a driver's license? Yes No
3. If you do not pass the written test, can you take it again? Yes No
4. Do you have to take an eye test to get a driver's license? Yes No
5. Do you have to take a test to get license plates? Yes No
6. Is a permit a license? Yes No
7. Can you take the driving test two times? Yes No
8. Do you have a driver's license? Yes No

Reading for Living

birth	Dallas (Dal us)	zip code (cōd)
sex	Texas (Tex us)	application (ap li cā shun)

State of Texas
Application for Driver's License

Baker — Last name
Ann — First name
Date of birth: May 9, 1962 (Month/Day/Year) Sex: ☐ M ☒ F Eye color: Green
Address: 3214 Church Street (Number and Street)
Dallas — City Texas — State 75203 — Zip code

This is part of an application for a driver's license. Read the application, and write short answers.

1. What is this person's first name? ______
2. What is this person's last name? ______
3. Which box did this person mark for Sex? ______
4. Is this person a man or a woman? ______
5. What is her date of birth? ______
6. What is her street address in Dallas? ______
7. Is Texas a city or a state? ______
8. What is Ann's zip code? ______
9. What is your sex? Put an X in one box. ☐ M ☐ F
10. What is the year of your birth? ______

Relating the story to everyday life. It will be helpful for you to have an up-to-date edition of your state driver's manual. Also, you should know where in your area to get information about driver's licenses.

1. If the procedures for getting a driver's license in your state are different from those described in the article, discuss this with S.
2. If S. is particularly interested, you might want to find out what the rules are for licensing motorcycles and various types of motor bikes in your state. Point out that these are not mentioned in the article in the skill book.
3. Discuss with S. where in your community a person can get information about driver's licenses. You may want to help him find the number in the phone book.

STORY CHECKUP: Page 56

Have S. read the directions and circle the right answers according to the information given in the article in the skill book. Check his work. Have him find that part that answers the question for any item he has wrong. Emphasize the importance of reading the question carefully and thinking through what it means before circling the answer.

READING FOR LIVING: Page 57

Have S. read the title of the page. Explain that this is a sample of part of an application for a driver's license. Even if he already has a license, this sample will help him read and fill out other kinds of applications.

Have S. read the new words and tell how many syllables are in each word. Then have him read the titles at the top of the application and each item that is printed on it: *Last name, First name, Date of birth*, and so on. Be sure he knows that *M* and *F* stand for *Male* and *Female*. Then have S. read each printed item again along with the information that is filled in for it.

Ask S. to read the directions below the application and write the answers. Tell him that if he doesn't want to answer question 10, he may leave it blank. On an actual form, however, he should give the date; since a driver's license is often used for identification, information on it should be correct. When he has finished, check his answers. If any are wrong, refer him to the application.

II. Skills Practice

Have S. close his book before doing these exercises.

PRACTICE 1: Distinguishing the Long Sound for *i*

T: Which of these words has the long sound for *i*:

bite, bit? | *fine, fish?* | *mean, mine?*
lick, like? | *mill, mile?* | *pine, pain?*
dim, dime? | *pick, pike?* | *time, tame?*

PRACTICE 2: Identifying the Number of Syllables

Say each word below, and have S. tell how many syllables it has. If he has difficulty, say the word again, and have him tell how many vowel sounds—or beats—it has.

permit	[2]	*tester*	[2]	*bicycle*	[3]
drive	[1]	*state*	[1]	*application*	[4]
driver	[2]	*getting*	[2]	*license*	[2]
Texas	[2]	*birth*	[1]	*written*	[2]

PRACTICE 3: Beginning Consonant Blends

Write *drive, truck, plates, glasses, state, street.* Have S. read each word and tell what blend it begins with. As he answers, underline *dr, tr, pl, gl, st, str.*

Say each pair of words below, and have S. tell which of these blends the words begin with.

drip, drop | *plan, please* | *glad, glide*
steep, steam | *tree, train* | *strike, strange*

PRACTICE 4: Ending Blend *st*

Write *test.* Have S. read and tell what blend it ends with. As he answers, underline *st.*

T: Which word ends with the blend *st* as in *test*:

lit, list? | *pass, past?* | *best, bench?*
nest, net? | *must, much?* | *reached, rest?*
less, last? | *rush, rust?* | *mask, mast?*

PRACTICE 5: Endings *-er* and *-ing*

Write *drive, test, ride, write, bake, help* in a column and have S. read them. Ask him what each word would be with the ending *-er* added. As he says the word, write it by the root word. Have him note which words require only *-r* and which require *-er.*

Follow the same procedure for the ending *-ing*, but before you write the word, ask S. to spell it.

PRACTICE 6: Recognizing the Root Word

Write *taking, making, living, driving, riding* in a column. Have S. read each word, and tell what the root word is and how to spell it. Write the root word by the word with the ending.

In another column, write *teacher, driver, maker, rider, tester, singer, worker.* Have S. read each word and tell what the root word is and how to spell it. Write the root word by the word with the ending.

PRACTICE 7: Recognizing Verb Forms Ending in *en*

Write the words *write, ride, drive* in one column and *written, ridden, driven* in a second column.

T: In column 1 are some verbs, or action words, you have learned. Read the verbs in column 1. [S. reads.]

T: In column 2 is another form of these verbs. For these verbs, this is the form we use after *has* or *have.* Listen to these sentences. *I write to my mother every week. I have written to her three times this month.*

T: How many syllables are there in *write*? [S: One.] How many in *written*? [S: Two.] Look at all of the verbs in column 2. Notice that they all end with *en*. The *en* adds a syllable.

T: This group of verbs has a long *i* sound in the root word. The vowel sound changes to short *i* in the form with *en*: *write, written*.

Have S. read each pair of words: *write, written,* and so on. Point out the double *t* after the short vowel sound in *written* and the double *d* after the short vowel sound in *ridden*. The *v* in *drive* is not doubled, however; the letter *v* is almost never doubled in English.

III. Writing

CHECK HOMEWORK (In Notebook)

Check the summary of story 1 and the two questions about story 2 in Lesson 10 that S. was asked to write. If he did not write them, ask him to give them orally. Allow time for him to scan the story before he gives the oral summary or asks the questions.

WRITING LESSON (In Notebook)

Have S. write the titles *Lesson 11* and *Words* and then number from 1 to 12 in two columns.

Words. Help S. study the words *license, eye,* and *bicycle*. Then dictate the words below for him to write. Give a sentence for *I* and *eye*.

1. I	4. rider	7. bicycle	10. date
2. ride	5. driver	8. license	11. birth
3. driver	6. test	9. state	12. eye

Check his work, and have him correct any errors.

Sentences. Have S. write the title *Sentences* and number from 1 to 5. Dictate these sentences:

1. Do you have a driver's license?
2. Did you pass the driving test the first time?
3. What is the date of your birth?
4. I passed the eye test.
5. Must I get a license for my bicycle?

Check his work, and have him correct any errors. Have him write the title *Study* and any words that he missed in the word and sentence dictation.

Writing dates. On another page of his notebook, have S. practice writing dates. Write *March, April, May* on the board, and have S. read them. Write the dates below, and have S. read them. Call attention to the placement of the commas.

April 1, 1980   March 15, 1982   May 3, 1959

Read these sentences, and ask S. to write only the date.

1. Her birth date is April 19, 1969.
2. John graduated from high school on May 30, 1980.
3. Jane and Bill were married on March 21, 1981.

Also, have S. write today's date. If the name of the month is difficult to sound out, write it on the board for him to copy. Or, write the abbreviation.

Writing addresses. Help S. write several addresses, such as his own address, the address where he works, the address of a friend or relative, or some other address that he would like to write.

PRACTICE: Page 58

Have S. read the directions for the first exercise to himself and do it. Check his work, and have him correct any errors.

Go over the directions for the second exercise with S., and then have him do it independently. Check his work, and have him correct any errors.

HOMEWORK: Page 59

Go over the directions with S., and ask him to do the page at home. Also, encourage him to study any words that he missed and to read over the lesson again at home.

CHECKING PROGRESS

Use these activities to see how well S. can apply the phonics skills he is learning.

- List the following words in a column on a 3-by-5-inch card: *rid, rip, win, fin, pin, dim, bit, kit*. At the edge of another card, write the letter *e*.

First, have S. read all of the words with the short sound for *i*. Then have him place the card with *e* on it after each word to make a new word with the long sound for *i*. Have him read the long *i* words.

- Put the items listed below on flash cards. Tell S. that these are items he may see on forms and applications. Explain that different kinds of forms ask for different information. Many kinds of forms ask for similar information, but the instructions may be worded differently. Have S. read each card. Help him sound out the new words. Assure him that with practice he will be able to read the forms that he may need to fill out.

Last name	*Place of birth*	*Sex*
First name	*Date of birth*	*Male*
Middle name	*Birth date*	*Female*
Please print	*Eye color*	*Hair color*
Today's date	*Color of eyes*	*Color of hair*

MEETING INDIVIDUAL NEEDS

Make flash cards for the chart and story words in this lesson. Follow the suggestions given in previous lessons for using them.

If S. needs practice with the endings *-s* and *-es*, make up a worksheet. Write the root words *state, eye, glass, driver, sex, bicycle, watch, test, place, license* in a column on a sheet of paper. Across the top, write the instruction *Add -s*

Practice

Say the words. Circle the words with the sound ī.

1. ride	drive	ring	sick
2. I	if	eye	first
3. driving	living	driver	river
4. fit	time	license	with
5. building	bicycle	written	write

Copy the word. Add *-r* or *-er*.
Then write one of the words in each sentence.

ride ________________ drive ________________

test ________________ play ________________

1. A bicycle ________________ does not need a license.
2. The ________________ will ride with you when you take the driving test.
3. The ________________ of a car must have a license.
4. Pete is a hockey ________________.

Homework

Write short answers.

1. What is your first name? ________________
2. What is your last name? ________________
3. What is your street address? ________________
4. What is the name of your state? ________________
5. What is your zip code? ________________
6. Do you have a driver's license? ________________

Say the word. Write the number of syllables.

1. driver ____	6. license ____
2. bicycle ____	7. state ____
3. written ____	8. letters ____
4. tester ____	9. glasses ____
5. ride ____	10. application ____

or *-es*. Have S. read each root word aloud, say the word with the ending added, tell whether to add *-s* or *-es*, and then write the word.

A similar worksheet can be made for the endings *-r* and *-er* with these words: *drive, read, ride, make, truck, start, time, play, help.*

If S. needs practice in recognizing root words, give him this list of words: *driver, tester, driving, runner, zipper, getting, reading, making*. Have him tell what the root word is and how to spell it. Have him tell when the final silent *e* is part of the root word and when the final consonant of the root word was doubled before the ending was added.

If S. still needs practice writing number words, make another worksheet similar to the one described in Lesson 8. Ask S. how the long *i* sound is spelled in *five* and *nine.*

In the *Workbook for Skill Book 3*, the exercises for Lesson 11 may be used at this time.

In *Focus on Phonics-3*, Practices 11A-11C may be used after Lesson 11. They give practice with some *i-e* word families.

LESSON 12

Skill Book 3
Pages 60-65

OBJECTIVES

To help your students:

- recognize that the letters *i* and *e* separated by one consonant (*i-e*) usually stand for the sound /ī/, as in the key word *time*.
- read more words in which the sound /ī/ is written *i-e*.
- distinguish between the long and short sound for *i*.
- contrast the sounds for *ire* and *ir*.
- determine the number of syllables in a word.
- review the beginning blends *sm, sn, br, pr, fr,* and the ending blend *nd* as in *husband*.
- review adding the ending *-er* to adjectives.
- review adding the endings *-ed* and *-ing* to words that end in silent *e*.
- recognize when to spell the sound /k/ at the end of a word with *k* or *ck*.
- recognize rhyming words.
- recognize the main idea of a story and its paragraphs.
- read factual material to obtain information about the purpose of an application and how to fill it out.
- read and fill out another type of application.
- write words and sentences from dictation.
- write dates using a number for the month.
- write addresses.

INTRODUCTION

Write the words *bicycle* and *ride*. Have S. read each word and tell how the sound /ī/ is written.

T: In today's lesson, you will have more words with the sound /ī/ written the way it is in *ride*.

I. Reading

CHART: Page 60

Title and key words. Have S. read *Lesson 12,* the vowel sound and spelling, and the key word *time*.

Lines 1-6. Tell S. that most of the chart words are written the way they sound. Ask him to read them to himself and notice what consonant comes between the *i* and *e*.

After S. has studied the chart silently, have him read each word aloud. Call attention to these points:

1. The rhyming words and how he knows they rhyme. [*Mike* and *like, mile* and *smile*. The final vowel and consonant sounds are the same.] Ask S. to think of a rhyming word for *wife* and one for *nice*.
2. The use of *k* for the sound /k/ in *Mike* and *like*. Explain that, after a long vowel sound, /k/ is written with *k*. It is written with *ck* after a short vowel sound.
3. The sound /s/ for *c* in the word *nice*.
4. The blend *sm* in *smile*.

Review. Have S. read the words aloud again, including the key word. Go down the last column of the chart.

STORY: Pages 61-62 (Running)

Have S. read the story title and the new words. Call attention to these points:

1. Any long vowel sounds and how they are written. Point out that the root word for *tired* is *tire*.
2. *White* is written with a capital letter here because it is used as a name in the story. When we use *white* as a color, we write it with a small *w*.
3. *Sometimes* is one word made up of two smaller words, *some* and *times*.
4. The number of syllables in each word. Point out that although *every* is respelled here with three syllables, it may be pronounced with either two syllables (*ev ry*) or three (*ev er y*). Tell S. that when he is asked to tell the number of syllables, he should answer according to the way *he* pronounces *every*.

Directed silent reading. Ask S. to read the whole story to himself to find out who it is about and what they do. Also, ask him to tell whether it is fact or fiction.

After S. finishes reading, ask these questions:

1. Who are the characters in the story?
2. Who is the story mostly about?
3. What are three important things that the story tells about Fran's running?
4. Is this story fact or fiction?

Then without further discussion or oral reading, have S. do the Story Checkup on page 62.

STORY CHECKUP: Page 62

Have S. read the directions and do the page by himself. Check his work. Note whether he followed directions, completed the exercise, and answered the questions correctly. Have him find the part of the story that gives the answer for any items he had wrong or omitted. If he didn't understand what to do, go over the directions with him, and have him do the exercise again.

Oral reading. Have S. find the paragraph that tells the most about each of these topics and read it aloud:

1. Where Fran runs [par. 5].
2. How long Fran has been running [par. 4].
3. What Mike does while his wife runs [par. 6].
4. Why the Whites have time to do what they like [par. 1].
5. What Fran is getting ready for [par. 2].
6. Why Fran runs five miles each day [par. 3].
7. What Fran thinks of her running ability now [par. 10].

READING FOR LIVING: Page 63

Have S. read the title and new words. Explain that this is a sample of another kind of application. Ask him to read the introductory part to himself and find out what the application is for. After he finishes, have him tell what the application is for and who is eligible.

Ask S. to read the third paragraph again aloud. Make sure he understands what to do, and then have him fill in the application. (If necessary, give help in figuring out Mike's age, using his birth date and today's date.) When S. has finished, check his work and help him make any needed corrections. Note any parts that gave him difficulty, and plan extra practice later.

Note: If S. is an older person or has a close relative who is, you may want to find out if any agencies in your community issue special permits for older people.

II. Skills Practice

Have S. close his book before doing these exercises.

PRACTICE 1: Distinguishing the Long Sound for *i*

T: Listen as I say three words.
Which one has the long sound for *i*:

bit, bait, bite? *like, lick, lake?*
pine, pin, pain? *mail, mile, mill?*
win, wine, wait? *smell, still, smile?*

Note: If S. has trouble distinguishing the correct word, it may help if you use each of the words in a sentence. Also, it may be easier for him to give the number of the word (1, 2, or 3) than to repeat it.

PRACTICE 2: The Sounds for *ire* and *ir*

Write the following words in three columns, as shown:

tire	*sir*	*bird*
fire	*stir*	*third*
hire		*girl*
wire		*skirt*
		first
		birth

Explain that, when *ire* comes at the end of a word, the sound is /īr/. Have S. read the words in column 1. Give help if needed.

Explain that when *ir* or *ir* plus a consonant come at the end of a word, the sound is /er/. Have S. read the words in columns 2 and 3. Give help if needed.

PRACTICE 3: Identifying Rhyming Words

Write *like, mile, wife, nice, time, white* on the board, and have S. read them. Then say each word below, and have S. tell which word on the board it rhymes with.

while *bike* *price* *crime* *life* *Mike*
knife *bite* *smile* *quite* *rice* *lime*

PRACTICE 4: Beginning Blends *sm, sn, br, fr, pr*

Write *smile* and *snack*. Have S read each word and tell what blend it begins with. Underline *sm* and *sn*.

T: I will say two words that begin with the same blend. Which blend do they begin with, *sm* or *sn*:

snake, snack? *smash, smell?* *snap, sneeze?*
smile, smart? *snail, snug?* *smog, smoke?*

Write *breakfast, Fran, price*. Have S. read each word and tell what blend it begins with. Underline *br, Fr, pr*.

T: I will say two words that begin with one of these blends. Tell me if they begin with *br, fr,* or *pr:*

prize, pride? *brick, brake?* *from, frame?*
free, freeze? *print, press?* *bride, bright?*

PRACTICE 5: Ending Blend *nd*

Write *husband*, and have S. read it. Ask him what blend it ends with. As he answers, underline *nd*.

T: Which of these words ends with the blend *nd*:

stand, fast? *band, bent?* *wind, when?*
pink, spend? *hint, land?* *Fran, friend?*
sand, sank? *wind, rent?* *blend, been?*

PRACTICE 6: The Sound for *ce* at the End of a Word

Write *face, race, place* in one column and *nice, price* in another, lining up the *ce* in the words. Have S. read the words in each column.

T: When *ce* comes at the end of a word, *c* has the sound /s/ and the *e* is silent.

Write these words, and have S. read them: *ace, lace, space, ice, mice, rice, spice*. Give help if needed.

PRACTICE 7: Adjective Ending *-er*

Write *cheap, fast, hot, late* in a column. Have S. read each word and tell what it would be with the ending *-er*. As he answers, write *cheaper, faster, hotter, later* in a second column. With *hotter*, review doubling the final consonant when the root word ends in a short vowel and one consonant. With *later*, review adding just *-r* when the root word ends in *e*.

Then add these words to column 1: *clean, dark, big, nice, large*. Have S. read each word, tell what it would be with *-er* added, and tell how to spell the word with the ending *-er*. As he answers, write *cleaner, darker, bigger, nicer, larger*, in column 2.

Point out that the *-er* ending has different meanings. In words like *writer* and *burner*, it means a person or thing that does something. A writer is a person that writes. A burner is a thing that burns. In words like *cheaper* and *faster*, the *-er* ending means *more*. Have S. use one or two of the *-er* words in column 2 in a sentence to make sure he understands the meaning.

Finally, have S. read one or two of the root words and their *-er* forms and tell how many syllables are in each. Point out that the *-er* ending adds a syllable.

i–e = ī

time

i–e = ī

	Mike	Mike Mīk	Mike
	like	like līk	like
MILE 4 4	mile	mile mīl	mile
	smile	smile smīl	smile
	wife	wife wīf	wife
	nice	nise nīs	nice

Running

White	tired (tīrd)	race (rase)	husband (huz bund)
while	retired (rē tīrd)	been (bin)	breakfast (brek fast)
	every (ev er y)		sometimes (some times)

Fran White is retired. Fran has been retired for three years. Her husband Mike has been retired for five years. These days, the Whites have a lot of time. The Whites have time to do things that they like.

Fran likes to run. Every day, she gets up at five and runs. She is getting ready for a big race. It is a mile race for retired women.

Fran must run five miles every day. Then she will not get tired in the mile race.

Fran has been running every day for three years. Her doctor said that it was OK. At first, Fran did not run very far or very fast. Every week, she ran a little more.

Sometimes, Fran runs in the park. Sometimes, she runs in the street. Today, Fran is running in the park. It is a nice day. People in the park smile at Fran. Fran smiles back at them.

While his wife runs, Mike makes breakfast. He likes to make breakfast while his wife is not in the kitchen.

When Fran comes back, breakfast is ready. Her husband smiles and says, "Is it a nice day?"

"Yes," says his wife. "It is a very nice day."

While they are eating, Mike looks at his wife. "Are you tired, dear?" he asks. "Sometimes, you get very tired."

"Well, I didn't get tired today," Fran says to her husband. "And I am getting fast. I think I am ready for the mile race."

Story Checkup

Circle the letter of the right answer.

1. What does Fran do every day when she gets up?
   a. run
   b. makes breakfast
   c. goes for a drive
2. What is Fran getting ready for?
   a. the five-mile race
   b. the one-mile race
   c. the driving test
3. What time does Fran get up?
   a. at six
   b. at five
   c. at seven
4. What does Mike do while his wife runs?
   a. runs with her
   b. goes to work
   c. makes breakfast

Reading for Living

price (prise)	bus
sign (sīn)	age (aje)

In some places, retired people can get things for cheaper prices. At the age of 62 or 65, you can get these cheaper prices. You can ride the bus cheaper. You can get glasses cheaper. You can get many other things cheaper.

To get these cheaper prices, you need a permit. To get a permit, you have to fill in an application.

Here is an application for a bus permit. Fill it in for Mike White. He lives at 1400 Third Street in Dallas, Texas. His zip code is 75210. His date of birth is April 12, 1915. Do not sign your name. Sign his name. Give his age.

City Bus
Application for Retired Person's Permit

____
Last Name First Name

Address: ________________________________
Number and Street

____
City State Zip Code

Date of Birth: __________________ Age: _____ Sex: ☐M ☐F
Month Day Year

____
Sign Here

PRACTICE 8: Verb Endings *-ed* and *-ing*

Write *like, smile, retire, ask, live, sign, start* in column 1. Have S. read each word, tell what it would be with the ending *-ed,* and tell whether to add *-d* or *-ed* when writing the word. As he answers, write the *-ed* words in column 2. Ask S. how many syllables are in the root word and in the word with the ending *-ed*. Point out that sometimes *-ed* adds a syllable, but not always.

Have S. read each root word again, tell what it would be with the ending *-ing*, and tell how to spell the word with *-ing*. As he answers, write the *-ing* words in column 3.

Finally, have S. read all three forms of each word.

PRACTICE 9: Spellings of the Sound /k/

Write the words *back, bank, bake* at the head of three columns. Have S. read each word and tell how the sound /k/ is spelled. Then review these rules for spelling the sound /k/ at the end of a word:

1. When the sound /k/ comes after a short vowel sound, it is usually written with *ck*. (Point to *back*.)
2. When the sound /k/ comes after a consonant, it is usually written with *k*. (Point to *bank*.)
3. When the sound /k/ comes after a long vowel sound, it is usually written with *k*. (Point to *bake*.)

Read each word from the lists below, but mix up the order. Have S. tell whether the sound /k/ comes after a short vowel, a consonant, or a long vowel and whether /k/ should be written *k* or *ck*. As he answers, write the word in the appropriate column.

bake	**bank**	**back**
check	*think*	*take*
pick	*ask*	*like*
lock	*milk*	*week*
trunk	*dark*	*speak*

Then have S. read all of the words in each column. In column 1, have him tell what the short vowel sound is in each word. In column 2, have him tell what consonant comes before the sound /k/. In column 3, have him tell what the long vowel sound is. Point out that some long vowel words end with just *k*, as in *week* and *speak*, and others end with a silent *e* after the *k*, as in *take* and *like*.

III. Writing

CHECK HOMEWORK: Page 59

Check this page with S. Have him correct any errors.

WRITING LESSON (In Notebook)

Have S. write the titles *Lesson 12* and *Words* and then number from 1 to 12 in two columns.

Words. Have S. study the word *sign*. Call attention again to the *ce* at the end of *nice, price, race*. Dictate the words below for S. to write. For number 7, tell S. to write *white* as he would when it is used as a color.

1. Mike	4. smile	7. white	10. race
2. like	5. wife	8. while	11. price
3. mile	6. nice	9. tired	12. sign

Check what S. has written. Have him correct any errors.

Sentences. Have S. write the title *Sentences* and number from 1 to 7. Dictate these sentences:

1. Fran White likes to run.
2. She will run the mile race.
3. Mike smiles at his wife.
4. Is it a nice day?
5. I did not get tired while I was running.
6. Mike can ride the bus for a cheaper price.
7. Please sign your name here.

Check his work, and have him correct any errors. Have him write the title *Study* and any words that he missed in the word and sentence dictation.

Writing dates, using numbers for the month

T: On some forms, there isn't much space to write the date. But there is a short way to write it. You can use a number in place of the name of the month. The months are numbered in order from 1 to 12.

Have S. say the names of the months in order and give the number for each. (If he is not sure of the months, write them in order, using abbreviations, and put the number by each month. Go over these with him.)

Write *April 28, 1980*, and have S. read this date. Then write the following:

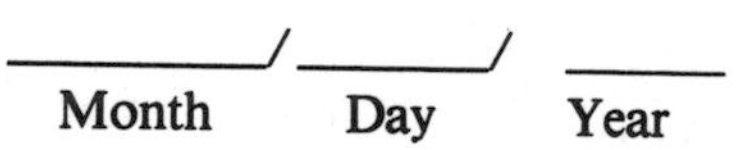

1. Point out that the date is always written in this order: month, day, year.
2. Ask S. what number to write for the month [4].
3. Ask S. what number to write for the day [28].
4. For the year, explain that you can write the whole number 1980, or you can shorten it and just write 80. If you leave off the 19, it will be understood that the date is 1980. But when you write a date in another century, such as 1880, you must write the whole number.

Fill in the blanks with 4/28/80. Then write the following dates in this form, and have S. read them:

2/14/81 12/25/82 8/30/59 7/4/76

Dictate today's date and the dates below for S. to write in the short form:

January 1, 1982	November 4, 1980	June 3, 1969
October 12, 1492	September 2, 1884	May 31, 1957

Check what S. has written, and give help where needed.

Writing addresses. Ask S. to draw two lines (blanks) on his paper. He can trace lines that are there, but have him skip a

Practice

Say the words. Circle the words with the sound ī.

1. Miller	mile	wife	with
2. Mike	milk	Smith	smile
3. while	will	tired	third
4. neck	nice	like	lift
5. price	white	pick	which

Copy the word. Add *-d* or *-ed*.
Then write one of the words in each sentence.

retire ______________ sign ______________

smile ______________ like ______________

1. Fran has been ______________ for three years.
2. Mike ______________ at his wife.
3. Mike ______________ the application.
4. Fran ______________ to run in the park.

Drop the *-e* and add *-ing*. Write the word.

1. smile ______________
2. retire ______________
3. like ______________
4. drive ______________
5. ride ______________

Homework

Write short answers.

1. What is Fran's last name? ______________
2. What is her husband's first name? ______________
3. Did the doctor say that it was OK for Fran to run? ______________
4. Did Fran run very far at first? ______________
5. What does Mike make while Fran runs? ______________
6. Does Fran sometimes get tired from running? ______________
7. Does Mike run with Fran? ______________
8. Does Fran think that she is ready for the mile race? ______________

Say the word. Write the number of syllables.

1. sometimes ____
2. every ____
3. breakfast ____
4. age ____
5. today ____
6. nice ____
7. cheaper ____
8. permit ____
9. husband ____
10. race ____

space between lines. Tell him that, for the address that you dictate, he should write the number and street on the first line and the city, state, and zip code on the second line. Dictate this address:

720 First Street
Bay City, Texas 77414

PRACTICE: Page 64

Have S. read the directions for the first exercise to himself and do it. If he has any wrong, have him read the word aloud. If he doesn't pronounce the vowel sound clearly, have him listen as you read it. Note which sounds he is confusing.

Have S. read the directions for the other exercises and do them. Check his work, and have him correct any errors.

HOMEWORK: Page 65

Go over the directions with S. Suggest that he also practice writing dates, using a number for the month.

CHECKING PROGRESS

To see how well S. can apply the phonics skills he is learning, make slip strips for the word families and beginning letters listed below.

-ice family: *d, m, n, r, pr, sl, sp, tw*
-ile family: *f, m, p, t, sm, wh*

Note the number of words S. is able to read correctly in each family. Do not give help or further practice at this time.

MEETING INDIVIDUAL NEEDS

Make flash cards for the chart words and for the words *White, Fran, makes, likes, to, run, while, breakfast, runs, five, miles, every, it, is, a, day.*

Have S. read each card. Then mix up the cards, and spread them out face up. Tell S. you will ask a question. He is to find the words to make a sentence that answers the question. After he arranges the cards, have him read the sentence. Then have him mix up the cards again before you ask the next question. Ask these questions:

1. Who likes to run?
2. How far does Fran run every day?
3. Who makes breakfast while Fran runs?
4. What kind of day is it?

In the *Workbook for Skill Book 3*, the exercises for Lesson 12 may be used at this time.

In *Focus on Phonics-3*, Practices 12A-12C may be used after Lesson 12. They give practice with some more *i-e* word families.

LESSON 13 Skill Book 3 Pages 66-71

OBJECTIVES

To help your student:

- recognize that the letter *y* following a consonant at the end of a one-syllable word usually stands for the sound /ī/ as in *my*.
- recognize that the letters *ie* in a one-syllable word usually stand for the sound /ī/ as in *tie*.
- read words in which the sound /ī/ is written *y* or *ie*.
- recognize the consonant blends *cr* and *fl*, and review the blends *dr, fr, tr, thr, str,* and *cl, gl, pl*.
- add *-es* and *-ed* to words ending in a consonant and *y*, changing *y* to *i* before adding *-es* and *-ed*.
- recall the sequence of events in a story.
- interpret the feelings of characters in the story.
- read a simple news story (obituary).
- recognize the abbreviations *a.m.* and *p.m.* and their meanings.
- read times of day written in numerals and understand how the colon is used in them, as in 2:30 and 4:00.
- understand how to use the comma when writing out a date in full, as in *May 30, 1980*.
- write words, sentences, dates, and times of day from dictation.

INTRODUCTION

T: You have learned two ways in which the sound /ī/is written. How is the sound /ī/ written in the word *bicycle?* [S: *i* by itself.] In the word *time?* [S: *i* and *e* separated by a consonant.] Good. Today you will learn two more ways that the sound /ī/ is written.

I. Reading

CHART: Page 66

Title and key words. Have S. read *Lesson 13*.

T: In *Skill Book 2,* you learned one vowel sound for *y*, the sound at the end of *city* and *happy*. In this lesson, you will have some more words in which *y* has another vowel sound. (*Point to ȳ = ī.*) The letter *y* with a line above it equals whhat sound? [S: ī.] You won't usually see *y* written with a line above it. But in this lesson, it is written that way to help you pronounce it.

T: Read the first key word. [S: *my*.] What sound does *y* stand for in *my?* [S: /ī/.] when you see *y* with a line over it, what sound will you say? [S: /ī/.]

T: (Point to *ie* = ī.) What two letters together equal /ī/? [S: *ie*.] This time, they are not separated by a consonant. Read the second key word. [S: tie.] What letters stand for the sound /ī/? [S: *ie*.]

Lines 1-3. Have S. read *cry* aloud, tell what sound *y* stands for, and then read *cry* again. Point to *cried*. Tell S. this is another form of the word. Have him read *cried*, tell what sound *ie* stands for, then read *cried* again.

Follow the same procedure for lines 2-3. Then give this rule: when *y* at the end of a word follows a consonant, *y* is changed to *i* before the ending *-ed*.

Lines 4-5. Have S. read the words. Call attention to the letter or letters that stand for the sound /ī/. Explain that we don't add *-ed* to *fly*; instead, we say *flew* and *have flown*. Ask S. to tell how *died* should be spelled.

Review. Have S. read the words aloud again, including the key words. Go down the last column of the chart. Call attention to the rhyming words *my, tie, cry, dry, try, fly, die*. Point out that they rhyme because they end with the same vowel sound even if the spelling is different. Ask S. to think of other words that rhyme with these. Then ask him to read the words in the chart that rhyme with *cried*. Also, call attention to the consonant blends in *cry, dry, try, fly*.

STORY: Pages 67-68 (A Brother Dies)

Have S. read the story title and new words. For each word that has a long vowel sound, ask him to tell what the vowel sound is and how it is written.

Directed silent reading. Ask S. to read the whole story silently and be ready to summarize it in a few sentences. After his summary, ask these questions to check comprehension of details:

1. Whose brother died? [Fran's.]
2. What was his first name? [Tom.]
3. How old was he? [55.]
4. Who telephoned Fran? [Tom's wife.]
5. Who called the airline? [Mike.]
6. Who did the packing? [Fran and Mike.]
7. What time did the Whites have to be at the airport? [Nine o'clock.]
8. What time did their flight leave? [Half past nine.]

List these names from the story: *Fran, Mike, the Whites, Tom, Ellen*. Have S. tell something that will identify each name.

Reading between the lines. Discuss these questions.

1. What emotion would you say this story is mainly about? [Grief, sorrow, sadness are suitable answers.]
2. Who else, besides her brother that died, was Fran concerned about? [Her sister-in-law Ellen.]
3. What things did Mike say to comfort Fran? Do you think these were appropriate and comforting things to say?

my = mī

ȳ = ī

ȳ = ī

ie = ī

tie = tī

ie = ī

	cry cried	crȳ cried	cry cried
	dry dried	drȳ dried	dry dried
	try tried	trȳ tried	try tried
	fly	flȳ	fly
	die	die	die

A Brother Dies

by	feel	line
why	air	o'clock (u clock)

One day, Mike got up to make breakfast. It was time for Fran to run, but she was not running. She was sitting next to the telephone. She was crying. Fran tried to dry her eyes when Mike came in.

"Why have you been crying?" Mike asked.

"My brother Tom has died," said Fran. "His wife just telephoned me. She said that he died in his sleep." Fran started to cry again.

Mike tried to make Fran feel better. "There, there, dear," he said. "Cry. You will feel better if you cry."

"He was just 55," Fran cried. "Why did he have to die? Why?"

"Try to think of the happy times that you had with him," said Mike. "Then you will feel better."

Fran cried and cried. Then she dried her eyes. "Ellen will need us," she said. "We must fly there today if we can. I'll start packing while you telephone the air line."

Mike telephoned the air line. "The air line says that we can fly at half past nine," he said to Fran. "We must be there by nine o'clock. Can we be there by nine?"

"We can be ready if we hurry." Fran said. "Tell the air line that we will be there by nine o'clock."

Fran started packing. "Where is your black tie?" she asked Mike. "You will need that tie."

"Here is my black tie," Mike said. "Let me help you. We will save time if I help you."

The Whites packed their bags. From time to time, Fran stopped to dry her eyes. But she and Mike were ready to fly by nine o'clock.

Story Checkup

Answer with the name of a person in the story.

1. Who died in his sleep? ______
2. Who telephoned Fran? ______
3. Who was Ellen? ______
4. Who was Tom's sister? ______
5. Who was Fran's husband? ______
6. Who was Mike's wife? ______

Read these six sentences.
What happened first? You will see a number 1 next to that sentence.
What happened next? Put a number 2 next to that sentence.
Put the right numbers next to the other sentences.

______ Fran answered the telephone.

______ Ellen telephoned to Fran.

______ Mike got up to make breakfast.

__1__ Tom died in his sleep.

______ The Whites were ready to fly by nine.

______ Mike telephoned the air line.

Reading for Living

a.m.	Monday (Mun day)	service (ser vis)
p.m.	Friday (Frī day)	

When Fran's brother died, this story was in the *King City Times*. Read the story, and write short answers.

King City Times, Friday, April 11, 1986

Tom J. Roberts

Tom J. Roberts, 55, of 162 Green Street, died at 4:00 a.m. today. He died in his sleep at his apartment.

Mr. Roberts worked at the Hill Bicycle Shop for 25 years.

He left his wife, Mrs. Ellen Smith Roberts; two sons, Sam of Bell Gardens and John of Apple Valley; and one sister, Fran Roberts White of Dallas, Texas.

Services will be Monday at 2:30 p.m. at the Little Church in the Valley.

1. Who died? ______
2. Where did he live? ______
3. Mr. Roberts died on Friday. What was the date? ______
4. What time on Friday did he die? ______
5. Where did he work? ______
6. Who is his wife? ______
7. Who are his sons? ______
8. Who is the dead man's sister? ______
9. Where does she live? ______
10. What time are the church services on Monday? ______
11. What will the date be on Monday? ______
12. Where will the services be? ______

4. What things did Mike do to be helpful? [He called the airline and helped with the packing.]
5. What feelings did Mike show in the things he said and did? [Sympathy, concern, tenderness.]
6. Why was it important to take Mike's black tie? [People wear black to funerals.]
7. What question that people often ask when a loved one dies is in this story? [Why did he have to die?]

Oral reading. Have S. read the part of one character while you read the other. Reverse roles. Encourage S. to interpret the feelings of the character by reading with expression.

STORY CHECKUP: Page 68

Go over the directions with S. In the second exercise, be sure he understands that he is to give the order in which things *happened*, not the order in which they appear in the story. Tell him he can look back at the story if he needs to. Check his work, and help him correct any errors.

READING FOR LIVING: Page 69

Have S. read the title of the page and the new words. Call attention to the *fr* blend and the sound /ī/ in *Friday*.

Times of day

T: The letters *a.m.* and *p.m.* are used with times of day. *A.m.* means before noon; it is used for times between midnight and noon. *P.m.* means after noon; it is used for times between noon and midnight.

T: (Write *6:30 a.m.*) When we use *a.m.* or *p.m.*, we write the time in numbers. First we write the hour, then we put a colon (point to the colon in 6:30), then we write the number of minutes. This is read as *six-thirty a.m.* It means 6:30 in the morning.

T: (Write *7:00 p.m.*) When the time is exactly on the hour, we write two zeros for the minutes. This is read as *seven p.m.* It means seven o'clock in the evening.

Write *4:00 a.m.* and *2:30 p.m.* Have S. read each one aloud and tell what it means. Point out that when we use *a.m.* or *p.m.*, we do not use the word *o'clock* or a time expression like *in the morning.*

Note: In case S. asks, *a.m.* stands for the Latin words *ante meridiem* (before noon), and *p.m.* stands for *post meridiem* (after noon).

News story (obituary). Have S. read the introductory sentences and the line at the top of the news story, first silently and then aloud. Ask him what the name of the newspaper is and on what date this story appeared.

T: Newspapers print notices when people are born, get married, and die. A death notice is called an *obituary.* The first paragraph usually answers these questions about the person's death:

Write the questions *Who? What happened? When? Where?* on the board, and have S. read them. Ask him to read the first paragraph silently to find the answers. When he has finished reading, have him give the answers. Write them on the board. Point out that the person's age and address are given in the first paragraph to help identify him. Ask S. what date *today* stands for in the paragraph [the date of the newspaper, April 11, 1986]. Explain that some obituaries also answer the question *why*, that is, they tell the cause of death. Ask if the question *why* is answered in the first paragraph [no].

Then ask S. to read the rest of the obituary to himself and be ready to tell what each paragraph is about. His answers should be similar to these:

Par. 2: where Mr. Roberts worked.
Par. 3: who his surviving relatives are.
Par. 4: when and where the services (funeral) will be.

Exercise. Let S. do the exercise by himself. Check his work. Help him find the answers if he has any wrong.

II. Skills Practice

Have S. close his book before doing these exercises.

PRACTICE 1: Distinguishing the Long Sound for *i*

T: Which of these words has the long sound for *i*:

lie, lit?	*boy, by?*	*windy, why?*
toy, tie?	*tied, Ted?*	*try, tree?*
lid, lied?	*stay, sty?*	*spy, city?*

PRACTICE 2: Consonant Blends with *r*

Write *cry* on the board. Have S. read it and tell what consonant blend it begins with. As he answers, underline *cr*. Point out that this is a new blend.

T: (Write *dry, Friday, try, three, street.*) You have had some other blends with the consonant *r*. Read each of these words, and tell what blend it begins with. (Underline *dr, Fr, tr, thr, str* as S. answers.)

Say each pair of words below, and have S. tell what blend the words begin with.

drive, dress	*tree, trail*	*throw, thrill*
trust, trap	*three, throat*	*dream, drink*
fry, frill	*creep, crime*	*cream, crust*
crack, crop	*stream, stripe*	*string, strap*

PRACTICE 3: Consonant Blends with *l*

Write *fly* on the board. Have S. read it and tell what consonant blend it begins with. As he answers, underline *fl*. Point out that this is a new blend.

T: (Write *black, clean, glass, plate.*) You have had some other blends with the consonant *l*. Read each of these words and tell what blend it begins with. (Underline *bl, cl, gl, pl* as S. answers.)

Say each pair of words below and have S. tell what consonant blend the words begin with.

blaze, blind	*claim, class*	*blame, bleak*
flare, flame	*flag, flee*	*club, clay*
play, plan	*glass, glad*	*place, please*

PRACTICE 4: Adding *-ing* to Words Ending in *y*

Write *cry, try, carry, hurry*. Have S. read each word and tell how many syllables it has. Point out that *y* at the end of a one-syllable word usually stands for the sound /ī/. At the end of a word with more than one syllable, *y* usually stands for the vowel sound /y/, as in *city*.

Ask S. to tell what each word would be with the ending *-ing* added. As he answers, write the *-ing* words. Then have him read aloud each root word and its *-ing* form.

Note: In words of two or more syllables, the sound for final *y* depends on where the stress is. If the final syllable is stressed, the sound is /ī/, as in *supply*. If the final syllable is unstressed, the sound is /y/, as in *city*. These rules will be explained in a later skill book after the study of stressed syllables.

PRACTICE 5: Changing *y* to *i* before *-es* and *-ed*

T: (Point to the words you wrote in Practice 4.) Do we make any change in the root word when we add *-ing* to these words? [S: No.]

T: But we do make a change before adding *-es* or *-ed*. (Point to *cry*.) Look at the root word, and then notice what change is made when *-es* is added. (Write *cries*.) What is changed in the root word? [S: *y* is changed to *i*.]

T: The same change is made before adding *-ed*. How do we write *cried*? [S: *c–r–i–e–d*.] Good. (Write *cried* by *cries*.)

Follow the same procedure for *try, carry, hurry*. Point out that when a consonant comes before final *y*, we change *y* to *i* before *-es* or *-ed*.

Have S. read all three forms of each word. Ask him how many syllables are in each. Point out that the *-es* and *-ed* endings do not add a syllable in these words.

PRACTICE 6: When Not to Change *y* to *i*

Write *play, plays, played*, and have S. read them. Point out that after a vowel, *y* is not changed to *i*. Write *stay*, and have S. read it. Have him tell what it would be with *-s* and *-ed* and how to write those words. As he answers, write *stays* and *stayed*.

III. Writing

CHECK HOMEWORK: Page 65

Check this page with S. Have him correct any errors. (Accept either 2 or 3 as the number of syllables in *every*, depending on how S. pronounces it.) Plan extra practice if S. needs more help in certain areas.

WRITING LESSON (In Notebook)

Have S. write the titles *Lesson 13* and *Words* and then number from 1 to 12 in two columns.

Words. Dictate the words below for S. to write. Check his work, and have him correct any errors.

1. die	4. by	7. dry	10. dried
2. tie	5. fly	8. try	11. tried
3. my	6. cry	9. cried	12. died

Sentences. Help S. study the spelling of *Monday, Friday*, and *o'clock*. (If S. asks, you can explain that an apostrophe is used in *o'clock* because it is a contraction for *of the clock*.) Then have S. write the title *Sentences* and number from 1 to 5. Dictate these sentences:

1. Why was Fran crying?
2. Tom died on Friday.
3. Did the Whites fly at nine o'clock?
4. I will try to see you on Monday.
5. Where is my black tie?

Check what S. has written, and have him correct any errors. Have him write the title *Study* and any words that he missed in the word and sentence dictation.

Writing dates. Write *March 17, 1980*. Have S. read this date. Explain that when a date is used in stories, news articles, and letters, the month is usually written out. Point out that a comma is used after the number for the day to separate it from the year. Dictate these dates for S. to write:

April 9, 1982	May 30, 1985	March 2, 1990

Check what S. has written, and help him correct any errors. Then, for practice, ask him to write each date using a number for the month as he might write it on an application.

Writing times of day. Write *8:00 a.m.* and *2:30 p.m.* Have S. read each time and tell whether it is in the morning, afternoon, evening, or night. Review the use of the colon between the hour and minutes. Then dictate these times for S. to write:

3:15 p.m.	9:45 a.m.	12:30 p.m.
7:00 a.m.	11:15 p.m.	10:00 a.m.

PRACTICE: Page 70

Have S. read the new word *change*. Let him do the first exercise by himself. Check his work, and have him correct any errors.

Go over the directions for the second exercise with S. Have him read the sample and tell what change was made in the root word. Have him do number 1. Check what he has written to make sure he understands. Then let him do the others independently. Check his work, and have him correct any errors.

Practice

change (chānj)

Say the words. Circle the words with the sound ī.

1. cry	city	by	baby
2. my	dry	play	windy
3. any	try	eye	tie
4. puppy	die	why	way
5. cried	angry	line	nine

Read the word. Change the *y* to *i*, and add *-es*. Write the *-es* word in List 1.

Read the word again. Change the *y* to *i*, and add *-ed*. Write the *-ed* word in List 2.

	List 1	List 2
cry	cries	cried
1. dry	______	______
2. try	______	______
3. carry	______	______
4. hurry	______	______
5. marry	______	______

70 Lesson 13

Homework

Fill in the missing word or number.

1. ______ got up to make breakfast.
2. Tom was just ______ when he died.
3. Tom died in his ______.
4. Mike will need his black ______.
5. The Whites were ready by ______ o'clock.

Drop *-ing*, *-d*, or *-ed*. Write the word that is left.

trying try

1. crying	______	5. died	______
2. flying	______	6. tied	______
3. drying	______	7. started	______
4. packing	______	8. telephoned	______

Lesson 13 71

HOMEWORK: Page 71

Go over the directions and the sample item in the second exercise with S. Suggest that he also practice writing times of day with *a.m.* and *p.m.*

CHECKING PROGRESS

To see how well S. can apply phonics skills, write each of the small "ads" below on a separate card. Tell S. that these are like ads he might read in a newspaper. Have him read each one and tell what kind of product or business the ad is for. Note his ability to recognize old words with endings added and to sound out new words.

Fly on Sun Air Line
We Try Harder

Ride the Safe Way Bus Line
Let Us Do the Driving

Zip Bug Killer
Kills Ants and Flies

Die-Hard Battery
Starts Your Car Every Time

Fisher's Quick-Drying Paint
Dries in Half the Time

Mason and Son, Dry Cleaners
At Your Service for 25 Years

MEETING INDIVIDUAL NEEDS

Make flash cards for the chart words and for *by, why, feel, air, line, o'clock, Monday, Friday, services*. Have S. put the words with more than one syllable in one pile, the words that rhyme with *my* in a second pile, and the words that rhyme with *cried* in a third pile. You may also use the cards in ways suggested in previous lessons.

Make slip strips for the word families and beginning letters listed below:

-y: *b, m, sh, wh, cr, dr, fr, tr, fl, sl, sp, sk*
-ie: *d, l, p, t*
-ies: *d, l, p, t, cr, dr, fr, tr, sp, fl*
-ied: *d, l, t, cr, dr, fr, tr, sp*

You may also want to put the words *die, lie, pie, tie, cry, dry, fry, try, spy, fly* on one set of cards and the words *dies, lies, pies, ties, cries, dries, fries, tries, spies, flies* on another. Have S. match each word with the ending to its root word.

In the *Workbook for Skill Book 3*, the exercises for Lesson 13 may be used at this time.

In *Focus on Phonics-3,* Practices 13A-13C may be used after Lesson 13. Practices 13A-13B cover word families with *y* and *ie*. Practice 13C covers adding endings to words that end with *y* and *ie*.

LESSON 14 — Skill Book 3, Pages 72-77

OBJECTIVES

To help your student:

- recognize that the letters *igh* usually stand for the sound /ī/, as in *night*.
- read words in which the sound /ī/ is written *igh*.
- recognize that when the letter *i* is followed by the ending blend *nd* or *ld*, it usually stands for the sound /ī/, as in *find* and *child*.
- review the other regular spellings for the sound /ī/: *i-e, ie, y*.
- distinguish between the short and long sounds for *i*.
- read a compound word by recognizing the two small words from which it is made.
- recognize the contraction *I'm* and the words from which it is made, and review the contractions *I'll, let's, it's, wasn't, didn't*.
- review adding *-es* and *-ed* to words ending in *y*.
- recognize the root word when *y* has been changed to *i* before *-es* and *-ed*.
- interpret the feelings of the character in the story.
- read a simple timetable.
- write words, sentences, and times of day from dictation.

INTRODUCTION

Write *I, time, tie, my*. Have S. read each word, tell what the vowel sound is, and tell how it is written. Tell him that he will learn another way that the sound /ī/ is written in this lesson.

I. Reading

CHART: Page 72

Title and key word. Have S. read *Lesson 14*.

T: Look at the letters in the top right-hand corner. What are they? [S: *igh*.] What sound do they equal? [S: /ī/.]

T: Read the key word. [S: night.] What is the vowel sound? [S: /ī/] What letters stand for the sound /ī/? [S: *igh*.] The key word is respelled to help you pronounce it. But after this, *igh* will not be respelled in a word. You will know that it stands for what sound? [S: /ī/.]

T: Read the part under *night*. [S: *igh* = *ī*.]

Lines 1-6. Tell S. that all of the words in the chart have the letters *igh* for the sound /ī/. Ask him to study the chart silently. When he has finished, have him read each word aloud. Call attention to these points:

1. The words that rhyme (all but *high*).
2. The consonant blend *fl* in *flight*.
3. The consonant blend *br* in *bright*.

Review. Have S. read the words aloud again, including the key word. Go down the last column of the chart.

STORY: Page 73 (A Night Flight from China)

Have S. read the story title and new words. For each word that has a long vowel sound, ask him to tell what the sound is and how it is written. For *find, behind,* and *child,* point out that when the letter *i* is followed by the ending blend *nd* or *ld*, it usually stands for the sound /ī/. Ask S. to tell what two words the contraction *I'm* is made from. (Give a sentence if he doesn't know.)

Directed silent reading. Ask S. to read the first two paragraphs to find out who the story is about, where the person is going, and why. When he has finished reading have him answer these questions. Be sure he understands that *the States* means the United States of America. Then have him tell how Lee is feeling and what probably makes him feel that way.

Have S. read the rest of the story to himself to find out what Lee thinks about during the flight. After he has finished reading, have him summarize the things Lee thinks about.

Reading between the lines. Discuss these questions.

1. What reasons does Lee give for wanting to study in the States? Is he probably coming to study at a high school or at a university?
2. How old is Lee's child now? [One year old.]
3. What does the story reveal about the kind of person Lee is?

You may also want to explain that many students from other countries who come here to study must leave their families behind. Their governments pay the expenses for the students, but not for their families.

If possible, bring a world map or globe, and help S. find China and the U.S. Compare the huge distance between them with the distance across the U.S. Help S. to understand that the great distance is probably why Lee can't afford to go for a visit during the four years he will study in the United States.

STORY CHECKUP: Page 74

Have S. do the Story Checkup before he reads the story orally. Go over the new words and directions with him, and then let him work independently. Check his work. Have him find the part of the story that gives the correct answer for any items he has wrong.

Oral reading. Have S. read the whole story aloud. Note his ability to read with expression and his observation of punctuation marks.

READING FOR LIVING: Page 75

Have S. read the title of the page and the new words. Be sure that he knows the meaning of *arrive* (come) and *depart* (go, leave). Have him tell how many syllables are in each word. Call attention to the two words that make up the word *timetable,* the long *i* sound in *arrive*, and the root word of *cities.*

Ask S. to read the introductory paragraphs first silently and then aloud. Point out that timetables in most airports, train stations, and bus depots are set up in a way very similar to the timetable in this exercise. Review the meaning of *a.m.* and *p.m.*

Before S. studies the whole timetable, have him point out these main sections in it:

1. name of airline
2. side that tells when planes arrive
3. side that tells when planes depart
4. column that shows flight numbers of arriving planes
5. column that shows flight numbers of departing planes
6. column that shows where planes are coming from
7. column that shows where planes are going to
8. gate numbers of arriving planes and departing planes
9. times that planes arrive and times that planes depart

After S. studies the timetable, have him read the first question and answer it. Check his answer to be sure he understands what to do. Then have him complete the exercise. Check his work, and help him find the correct answer in the timetable for any items he has wrong.

II. Skills Practice

Have S. close his book before doing these exercises.

PRACTICE 1: Distinguishing the Long Sound for *i*

T: I will say three words. Listen carefully. Which one has the long sound for *i*:

light, lit, late?	*knit, net, night?*
fit, fight, fate?	*sight, sit, said?*
sky, skin, scare?	*sin, same, sign?*

PRACTICE 2: Spellings of the Long *i* Sound

Write *five, sky, tie, sight*. Have S. read each word, tell how the sound /ī/ is written, and give another word in which the sound /ī/ is written the same way.

PRACTICE 3: Long *i* before Ending Blends *nd* and *ld*

T: (Write *find*, and have S. read it.) What consonant blend does *find* end with? [S: *nd*.] When the letter *i* is followed by the blend *nd*, it usually stands for the sound /ī/.

Write the words *kind, mind, blind, behind* in a column under *find,* lining up the *ind* in all the words. Have S. read each word.

T: (Write *child*, and have S. read it.) What consonant blend does *child* end with? [S: *ld*.] When the letter *i* is followed by the blend *ld*, it usually stands for the sound /ī/.

Write *wild* and *mild* under *child*. Have S. read them.

PRACTICE 4: Compound Words

T: (Write *timetable*, and have S. read it.) *Timetable* is a word made up of two small words. We call this kind of word a *compound word*. What two words is the compound word *timetable* made from? [S: *time* and *table*.] Good. (Write *time* and *table* by *timetable*.)

Write *himself, yourself, something, sometimes, payday, landlady* in a column under *timetable*. Ask S. to read each compound word and tell what two words it is made from. As he answers, write the two words.

PRACTICE 5: Contractions

Write *I'll, I'm, let's, it's, didn't, wasn't* in a column. Remind S. that these are contractions. A contraction is a word made from one word and part of another word. Have S. read each contraction and tell what two words are put together. Have S. read each contraction again and tell what letter is left out.

Remind S. that the apostrophe is used in a contraction to show that a letter is left out when the two words are put together. Have S. read each contraction again and tell what letter is left out.

PRACTICE 6: Changing *y* to *i* before *-es*

Write the word *fly*, and have S. read it. Ask him to tell what change must be made before adding the ending *-es*. Write *flies* by the root word. Follow the same procedure for the words *try, cry, city, family, baby.*

Point out that it doesn't matter whether *y* stands for the vowel sound /y/ as in *city* or /ī/ as in *fly*. When *y* comes after a consonant at the end of a word, *y* is changed to *i* before *-es*.

PRACTICE 7: Recognizing Root of *-ies, -ied* Words

Write *carried, married, hurries, ladies, parties, stories* in a column. Have S. read the word with the ending, tell what the root word is, and tell how to spell the root word. As he answers, write the root word.

III. Writing

CHECK HOMEWORK: Page 71

Check this page with S. Have him correct any errors. Note whether he needs extra practice with these kinds of exercises.

igh = ī

night = nīt

igh = ī

	high	high	high
	light	light	light
	flight	flight	flight
	right	right	right
	bright	bright	bright
	sight	sight	sight

A Night Flight from China

find (fīnd)	child (chīld)	I'm (Īm)	sky
behind (bē hīnd)	China (Chī nu)		sad

My name is Lee Chan. I am on a night flight. I'm high in the sky. The night is dark. But the bright lights of my city are still in sight. The bright lights of China are still in sight.

I am going far away, and I feel sad. I'm on a night flight from China to the States. I'm going to the States to study.

From high in the sky, I look for the bright lights again. But they are not in sight. My city is far behind me.

I think of my family that I left behind. I left my wife and my child behind. I will not see them for four years. My child will be five by then. A child needs a father, but I will not be there. Am I doing the right thing?

What will I find in the States? Will I find a place to live? Will I find friends? Am I doing the right thing?

I must not think like that. It makes me sad. I *am* doing the right thing. I'll be OK in the States. I will study very hard. When I go back to China, I'll have a better job. I can take care of my family better. I can help China. I can make things better for my child and other children.

I will not be sad any more. From high in the sky, I see a bright light again. This time, it is the sun. Day has come.

Story Checkup

question (ques chun), himself (him self)

Answer each question with a sentence.

1. Where is Lee Chan from?

____

2. Where is he going?

____

3. Why is he going there?

____

Lee asks himself some questions.
Write four questions that Lee asks himself.

1. _______________
2. _______________
3. _______________
4. _______________

Reading for Living

gate	arrive (u rive)	cities (sit yz)
	depart (dē part)	timetable (time table)

Lee Chan has arrived in the States. He has to take another flight to Dallas, Texas. He will take a flight on Sun Air Line.

Here is the Sun Air Line timetable. The timetable has flights to and from many cities on it. On the left are flights that arrive from other cities. On the right are flights that go to other cities.

Study the timetable, and write the answers. When you tell the time, put *a.m.* or *p.m.* in the answer.

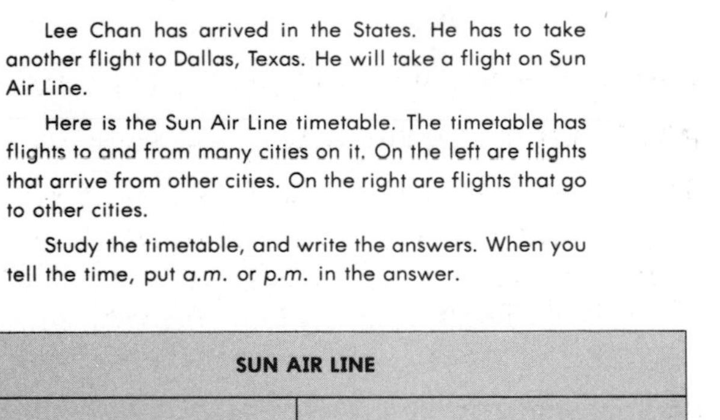

SUN AIR LINE

ARRIVE				*DEPART*			
Flight	**From**		**Gate**	**Flight**	**To**		**Gate**
740	Garden City	8:55 a.m.	2	740	Apple Valley	9:25 a.m.	2
406	Apple Valley	10:00 a.m.	5	406	Dallas	10:30 a.m.	5
505	Little Rock	12:40 p.m.	7	505	Sun Valley	1:20 p.m.	7
419	Dallas	2:00 p.m.	7	670	Dallas	2:40 p.m.	7
680	Sun Valley	2:45 p.m.	4	530	Little Rock	3:15 p.m.	4

1. What time does Flight 740 arrive from Garden City? _______________
2. What time does Flight 740 depart for Apple Valley? _______________
   If you take this flight, which gate will you go to? _______________
3. Two flights go to Dallas. Write the flight numbers. _______________
4. Which flight to Dallas departs at 10:30 a.m.? _______________
4. Which flight to Dallas departs at 2:40 p.m.? _______________
6. Lee will take Flight 670. Which gate will he go to? _______________

WRITING LESSON (In Notebook)

Have S. write the titles *Lesson 14* and *Words* and then number from 1 to 12 in two columns.

Words. Have S. study the words *child, find, behind, China,* and *sky.* Then dictate the words below for S. to write. (Give a sentence for *right.*) Check his work, and have him correct any errors.

1. night	4. right	7. high	10. find
2. sight	5. flight	8. sky	11. behind
3. light	6. bright	9. China	12. child

Sentences. Have S. study the spelling of *arrive.* Then have him write the title *Sentences* and number from 1 to 6. Dictate these sentences:

1. There are flights to many cities.
2. I am on a night flight from China.
3. My child will be five in April.
4. What time does your flight arrive.
5. I see a bright light in the sky.
6. Will I find a place to live?

Check what S. has written, and have him correct any errors. Have him write the title *Study* and any words that he missed in the word and sentence dictation.

Times of day. Write *2:00 p.m.* and *8:55 a.m.* Have S. read each time and tell whether it is in the morning, afternoon, evening, or night. Ask him for another way to say 8:55 [five minutes to nine]. Dictate these times for S. to write:

6:10 a.m.	9:00 a.m.	5:45 a.m.
7:30 a.m.	1:40 p.m.	11:15 p.m.

Check what S. has written. Give any help needed. Have him read each time aloud and tell what it means. Then ask him to write the times to show the following:

1. what time he got up this morning.
2. what time he ate breakfast.
3. what time his class starts.
4. what time his class usually ends.
5. what time he expects to go to bed.

PRACTICE: Page 76

Have S. read the title of the page and the new word *underline.* Ask him to tell the two words that make up this compound word. Explain that in the respelling the first word in the compound has not been divided into syllables so it will be easier to recognize the old word *under.* Have S. tell how many syllables are in *under* and how many are in the whole word *underline.*

Have S. read the directions and sample for the first exercise. Then have him do the exercise independently. Check his work. Have him read aloud any words that he should have marked or that he marked incorrectly. Have him correct any errors.

Go over the directions and sample for the second exercise with S., and have him do it. Check his work.

HOMEWORK: Page 77

Go over the directions with S. Make sure he understands what to do. If he seems uncertain, have him do one item under each direction at this time.

CHECKING PROGRESS

To see how well S. can apply phonics skills, make flash cards for these words: *night, flight, might, tight, fright, slight.*

Show S. the card for *night.* Have him read the word, tell what the vowel sound is, what letters stand for the sound /ī/, and what the ending sound is. Underline *ight.* Then show the other flash cards, one at a time. Make a note of any with which S. has difficulty. Help him sound out the word, but don't drill on it now.

MEETING INDIVIDUAL NEEDS

For more practice with contractions, write the sentences below on a worksheet. Leave enough space under each sentence for S. to write the sentence again, spelling out the words in full instead of using the contraction.

1. I'll try to be on time.
2. I'm going shopping.
3. It's a nice day today.
4. I didn't go to work yesterday.
5. I wasn't feeling well.

You can also work in the opposite direction, giving sentences like those below and having S. rewrite them using contractions.

1. It is getting late.
2. I am studying hard.
3. I will see you later.
4. The answer was not right.
5. We did not have fun at the party.

For more practice with compound words, write these words on separate cards or strips of paper: *sometimes, someone, something, payday, paycheck, landlady, underline, timetable, myself, yourself, himself, herself, today, tonight.* Bring scissors to class. Let S. cut apart the two small words in each compound word. Mix up the pieces, and have him put the compound words back together again.

In the *Workbook for Skill Book 3,* the exercises for Lesson 14 may be used at this time.

In *Focus on Phonics-3*, Practices 14A-14B may be used after Lesson 14. They cover word families *-igh, -ight, -ind,* and *-ild.*

Practice **underline (under line)**

Read the sentence. Underline each word with the sound ī.

I am on a night flight.

1. I left my wife and child behind.
2. My child will be five by then.
3. Am I doing the right thing?
4. I must not think like that.
5. The bright lights of China are still in sight.

Sometimes, two little words make one big word. Read the big word. Then write the two little words.

payday ____pay____ ____day____

1. himself ________ ________
2. yourself ________ ________
3. something ________ ________
4. sometimes ________ ________
5. timetable ________ ________
6. underline ________ ________

Homework

Write three other words with *igh* that have the sound ī.

high ________ ________ ________

Write three other words with y that have the sound ī.

by ________ ________ ________

Write three other words with *i—e* that have the sound ī.

time ________ ________ ________

Change the y to *i*, and add *-es*.
Write one of the words in each sentence.

party ________ baby ________

city ________ story ________

factory ________ family ________

1. I like to read funny ________.
2. My class had two ________ this year.
3. The ________ are crying.
4. There are flights to many ________.
5. Many ________ live on this street.
6. The people in the ________ work hard.

LESSON 15

Skill Book 3
Pages 78-83

OBJECTIVES

To help your student:

- review the sound / ī/ and its most regular spellings: *i-e, ie, igh, y.*
- review the sounds / ā/ and / ē/ and their most regular spellings.
- read short stories that review words introduced in Lessons 11-14, especially words with long *i*.
- recognize the sequence of events in a story.
- interpret the feelings of characters in a story.
- develop sight recall of words first learned by sounding them out.
- develop further skill in reading applications.
- distinguish between the long and short sounds for *a, e,* and *i.*
- review the beginning consonant blends *sk, sm, st, cl, fl, pl, br, cr, dr, fr, tr, pr.*
- review long *i* before the ending blends *ld* and *nd.*
- determine the number of syllables in a word.
- review changing *y* to *i* before *-es* and -ed.
- recognize *dying* and *tying* as forms of *die* and *tie.*
- review adding *-er* to adjectives, recognizing when to double the final consonant and when to add just *-r.*
- review words ending in *ce* and recognize that the *-s* ending adds a syllable, as in *price, prices.*
- recognize the root word in words with the endings *-es, -ed,* and *-er.*
- review verb forms ending in *-en,* as in *write, written.*
- develop further skill in writing words, sentences, questions, dates, and times.
- apply phonics skills to practice exercises containing new words with familiar sound-letter relationships.
- review compound words and contractions.

INTRODUCTION

T: In today's lesson, you will review the sounds / ā/ , / ē/ , / ī/ , and the main ways they are written. You will read four short stories that have many words with these sounds. We'll also go over some of the other things that you have studied in the last four lessons.

I. Reading

CHART: Page 78

Have S. read *Lesson 15* and the lesson title *More Reading with ā, ē, ī.*

Have S. read each key word in the chart and tell what the long vowel sound is and how it is written.

STORIES: Pages 79-83

T: In these stories, you will learn more about some of the people you met in Lessons 11 through 14.

Story 1: A Teenager Learns to Drive. Have S. read the story title and the new word *learn.*

T: Remember the story that told about how to get a driver's license? In this story, you'll find out what happened to one person who wanted a driver's license.

Silent reading. Ask S. to read the whole story and summarize it by telling the main events in order. His summary should include the main points in this order:

[Jill went to the state office building. She filled in an application for a driver's license. She passed the written test. She took an eye test. The tester told her she needed to wear her glasses when driving. Jill got a learner's permit. Her mother taught her to drive. Jill did not pass the driving test the first time she took it. She took it again and passed.]

If S. has difficulty, go over the story and have him tell the main points of each paragraph.

Ask these questions to check comprehension:

1. How old was Jill when she got her learner's permit?
2. Why did Jill fail the first driving test she took?
3. How did she probably feel when she got her driver's license? How does the story show how she felt?

Oral reading. Have S. read the last paragraph aloud. Note whether he observes punctuation marks and reads with expression.

Story 2: A Letter from Ellen Roberts

Note: It will help to have a copy of this story that you can mark as S. reads aloud. The procedure for teaching it is the same as for the last stories in Lessons 6 and 10.

T: You have read about Fran White's reaction to the news of her brother's death. In this story, you will see another person's reaction to this event.

Have S. read the title and the new words to himself and then aloud. Note how many words he is able to sound out. Underline any with which he needed help.

Point out that this story is written in the form of a letter. Ask S. to tell who the letter is from, the person it is written to, and the date it was written.

Oral reading. Have S. read story 2 aloud without reading it silently first. As he reads aloud, mark your copy of the story as suggested below. Later, you can use this record to plan extra practice.

1. Underline any place where S. hesitates.
2. Mark through a word if S. says the wrong word. If you have time, write the word that he substitutes.
3. Mark through any ending that is omitted or wrong.
4. Circle any words that are omitted or any punctuation marks not observed.
5. Note his ability to read fluently and with expression.

Lesson 15

More Reading with ā, ē, ī

paper	cake	paint		day
ā	a–e	ai		ay
we	Pete	eat	see	key
ē	e–e	ea	ee	ey
I	time	tie	night	my
ī	i–e	ie	igh	y

1. A Teenager Learns to Drive

learn (lern)

On the day that Jill was 16, she went to the state office building. She filled in an application for a driver's permit. She had to take a written test. The person that gave her the eye test said, "You must have your glasses on when you drive."

Jill got a driver's permit. Her mother started teaching her to drive. Jill learned to make left and right turns. She learned to watch for stop signs and red lights. She learned to watch for other traffic signs while she was driving. She learned to back up and to park.

"I'm ready to try the driving test," said Jill. But she did not pass the test the first time. The tester said that Jill did not stop at a stop sign. She had to take the driving test again. The second time, she passed. "I did it!" said Jill. "I have my driver's license!"

2. A Letter from Ellen Roberts

fine	wives (wīvz)	ago (u gō)
life	myself (my self)	stories (stor yz)

April 21

Dear Jane,

I have something sad to tell you. My husband Tom died in his sleep ten days ago. That was Friday, April 11.

I was Tom's wife for twenty-nine years. He was a fine husband. We had a happy life.

When Tom died, I telephoned his sister Fran right away. She and her husband Mike arrived from Texas that night. My two sons, Sam and John, came with their wives. The family helped me plan the services.

I liked the services. Tom looked very nice. Many friends were at the church. Tom's family and my family were there. I cried, and they cried with me. It was a sad time, but the services helped me.

After the services, my sons and their wives were standing with me. Friends stopped to say nice things. They said that Tom was a fine man. We cried some more.

My family and I left the church and went back to the apartment. Friends came with many things to eat. We ate and we listened to family stories. My sons heard some of the stories for the first time. We cried and we laughed at these stories.

The services were on Monday, April 14. That was a week ago. My sons and their wives left that night. Fran and Mike left two days ago. I am by myself for the first time.

Things happened very fast. One day, Tom was feeling fine. The next day, he was dead. I can still see his bright smile. I can still see the love in his eyes. Why did he have to die?

I will never stop thinking of Tom. But I must start thinking of myself. I have never lived by myself in my life. I have never had a job in my life. At 49, I must start my life again. I will dry my eyes and do my best.

This letter to you has helped me. I feel a little better. Jane, you are a dear friend.

Love,
Ellen

3. Studying in the States

buy (by) I.D. English (Ing glish)

Lee Chan has been in the States for two months. He is studying in Dallas, Texas.

The first week that he was there, Lee had a lot to do. He had to find a place to live. He had to buy many things. He had to sign up for classes. He had to get an I.D. card. He had to get a picture for his I.D. card.

Lee had to fill in many applications. Each application asked for his name, address, age, date of birth, place of birth, and sex. Lee got tired of filling in applications. He got tired of standing in line. But, at last, he was ready to start classes.

Lee has been going to class for five weeks. He has been studying very hard. His English is getting much better.

Lee's classes are three miles from where he lives. He had to buy a bicycle. Sometimes, he rides his bicycle to class. Sometimes, he takes the bus.

Lee misses his wife and child in China. But he is making many friends in the States. Two of his friends are Fran and Mike White. The Whites helped Lee find a place to live. They helped him find a bicycle to buy. They are helping him learn English. Lee visits the Whites every Saturday.

Lee likes his life in the States. He likes his classes. He is learning English very well. Lee thinks that prices in the States are high. But he thinks that the people are nice.

4. The Mile Race

as (az) finish (fin ish) that's

It was the day of the mile race. Fran White ate breakfast, but she didn't eat lunch. "If I eat lunch, I cannot run fast in the race," she said.

Fran's husband Mike went to the race with her. It was a nice day. The sky was bright, and the air was dry. Retired women from five cities were there for the race.

The race started at two o'clock. There were fifteen women in the race. They were at the starting line. When they heard the gun, they started running.

At first, Fran was far behind. She tried harder, and she ran faster. One by one, Fran passed thirteen women. One woman was still running next to Fran. "If I run faster, I can pass her," Fran was thinking. "But I'm running as fast as I can."

The finish line was in sight. Fran ran fast, but the other woman ran as fast as Fran. The two women passed the finish line. It was a tie!

"Nice work!" Mike said to his wife. "You were flying when you passed the finish line. A tie is just fine!"

Fran dried her face and smiled. "That's right!" she said. "It's better to be first, but a tie is not bad."

Discussion. Discuss these questions:

1. What kinds of information does Ellen give in her letter?
2. What are some things Ellen says that show her feelings toward her husband?
3. Did Tom die unexpectedly or after a long illness? What part of Ellen's letter tells you this?
4. What did Ellen's family and friends do to help her?
5. How does a funeral help bring a family closer together? What signs of this do you find in this story?
6. Besides her grief, what other feelings does Ellen hint at near the end of her letter? [Worry or fear about her future, determination to manage by herself.]
7. How do you think writing this letter helped Ellen?

Story 3: Studying in the States. Have S. read the title and new words. Point out that *I.D.* is an abbreviation for *identification* and that *English* is written with a capital letter because it is the name of a language.

Review who Lee Chan is, what country he came from, and why he came.

Silent reading. Ask S. to read the story silently and find out how Lee is getting along in the States. Time how long it takes S. to read the story. There are about 250 words. He should be able to finish in two minutes or less. Record the time, but don't comment on it.

Discussion. Discuss these questions:

1. How long has Lee been in the States?
2. How long has he been going to class?
3. Does he seem to be adjusting to life in the States? What shows that he is or isn't?
4. How far does Lee live from where his classes are? How does he get there?
5. What are some of the things Lee doesn't like about living in the States? What are some of the things that he does like?
6. How have Fran and Mike White helped him?

Note how many of these questions S. is able to answer satisfactorily. If he was not able to answer any, have him scan the story to find the answers.

Oral reading. It is not necessary for S. to read the whole story aloud. If he had difficulty finding the answer to a question, you might tell him the number of the paragraph and have him read that paragraph aloud.

Story 4: The Mile Race

Note: It will help to have a copy of this story that you can mark as S. reads aloud. The procedure for teaching it will be the same as for story 2 in this lesson.

T: Do you remember reading about Fran White, who was getting ready to run in a mile race? In this story, you'll find out how the race turns out.

Have S. read the title and new words to himself and then aloud. Note how many words he is able to sound out. Underline any with which he needed help. Ask what two words the contraction *that's* is made from.

Oral reading. Have S. read the story orally without reading it silently first. As he reads, make notes as suggested for story 2.

Summarizing. Ask S. to summarize the story in a few sentences. Record whether or not his summary is accurate and reasonably complete. You might like to write down his summary.

Discussion. Discuss these questions:

1. What was the weather like on the day of the race?
2. Why didn't Fran eat breakfast that day?
3. Who was competing in the race? [Fifteen retired women from five cities.]
4. About how old do you think these women are? [In their 60s.]
5. How did the race turn out?
6. Was Fran's husband proud of her? How do you know?
7. Do you think Fran was disappointed or pleased? What makes you think so?

Ask S. which of these four stories he liked best and why. Praise him for his progress in reading.

READING FOR LIVING (Supplementary Materials)

Make up an application form like the one in Lesson 11 and have S. fill it out for himself. If he needs any words that he hasn't learned yet, help him to spell them.

If you think S. needs more of a challenge, you may want to bring in some simple applications, news items, or ads. Try to collect samples made up mostly of words that S. knows or can sound out, with only a few sight words. Mark the parts that you expect S. to be able to read independently.

You may also want to make up a simple bus schedule, similar to the timetable in Lesson 14, using the names of some communities in your area.

II. Skills Practice

T: Now we'll have some listening exercises to review some things you have learned in the last few lessons.

PRACTICE 1: Distinguishing Long *a, e, i* Sounds

Write the words *paper, me, I.* Have S. read each word and tell what the long vowel sound is. Then say each pair of words below. Have S. tell which of the words has a long vowel sound and what the sound is.

dim, dime	*lift, life*	*gate, get*
meat, met	*bake, back*	*sleep, slip*
will, while	*chip, cheap*	*pad, paid*

Write the following pairs of words. Have S. read each pair and tell which word has the short sound for *i* and which has the long sound.

lit	*light*	*fin*	*fine*	*mill*	*mile*
sit	*sight*	*Tim*	*time*	*lick*	*like*
fit	*fight*	*rid*	*ride*	*did*	*died*

PRACTICE 2: Identifying the Number of Syllables

Say each word below, and have S. tell how many syllables it has. If he has difficulty, say the word again, and have him tell how many vowel sounds—or beats—it has.

tied	[1]	*bicycle*	[3]	*sometimes*	[2]
cried	[1]	*behind*	[2]	*application*	[4]
ago	[2]	*license*	[2]	*underline*	[3]
sleep	[1]	*timetable*	[3]	*question*	[2]
sky	[1]	*arrived*	[2]	*seventeen*	[3]
cities	[2]	*Friday*	[2]	*breakfast*	[2]

PRACTICE 3: Review Beginning Consonant Blends

T: (Write *sk, sm, st.*) Listen as I say two words. Which of these blends do both words begin with:

smile, smart? *sky, skirt?* *state, stairs?*

T: (Write *cl, fl, pl.*) Listen as I say two words. Which of these blends do they begin with:

please, place? *fly, flight* *clean, climb*

T: (Write *br, cr, dr, fr, pr, tr.*) Listen as I say two words. Which of these blends do they begin with:

free, Friday?	*try, tree?*	*price, practice?*
dries, driver?	*cry, cream?*	*bright, breakfast?*

PRACTICE 4: Long *i* before Ending Blends *nd* and *ld*

Write *child, mild, wild* in a column. Have S. read *child* and tell what blend it ends with, and tell what the vowel sound is. Point out that, when the letter *i* is followed by the blend *ld*, it usually stands for the sound / ī/ . Have S. read the other words in the column.

Write *find, kind, mind, bind, blind, grind, behind* in another column. Have S. read *find*, tell what blend it ends with, and tell what the vowel sound is. Point out that, when the letter *i* is followed by the blend *nd*, it usually stands for the sound / ī/ .

PRACTICE 5: Changing *y* to *i* before *es* and *ed*

Write *cry, dry, try, carry, marry, hurry* in a column. Point out that these are verbs, or action words. Ask S. to read each verb and tell what it would be with the ending *-es*. Have him tell what change should be made in the root word before the ending is added. Write the *-es* word by the root word. Follow the same procedure with the ending *-ed*. Then ask S. to read all three forms of each verb.

Write *baby, lady, city, story, battery, sky.* Tell S. that these are nouns. Explain that a noun is a word for a person, place, or thing. Ask S. to read each noun and tell what it would be with the *-es* ending. Have him spell the word with the ending. Write it by the root word. Then ask him to read both forms of the noun again.

PRACTICE 6: Changing *ie* to *y* before *-ing*

Write *die, tie, lie* in column 1, and have S. read them. Ask him to tell what each word would be with the ending *-s* and then the ending *-d*. As he answers, write the *-s* form in column 2 and the *-d* form in column 3.

In column 4, write *dying, tying, lying*. Explain that, for these three root words—*die, tie, lie*— the *ie* is changed to *y* before the ending *-ing*. Have S. read all four forms of each word.

PRACTICE 7: Adjective Ending *-er*

Write *high, bright, clean, cheap* in a column, and have S. read them. Have him tell what each word would be with the ending *-er* and how to spell it. As he answers, write the *-er* word next to the root word.

Follow the same procedure with *nice, late, large*. Remind S. that when the root word ends in *e*, we add just *-r*.

Follow the same procedure with *big, hot, sad*. Explain that after a short vowel sound, we double the final consonant before *-er*.

PRACTICE 8: The Sound for *ce* at the End of a Word

Write *race, face, place, price, service* in a column, and have S. read them. Remind him that when *ce* comes at the end of a word, *c* has the sound /s/ and *e* is silent.

Have S. tell what each word would be with the ending *-s*. As he answers, write each word with *-s* next to its root. Ask S. how many syllables are in the root word and in the form with *-s*. Point out that the form with *-s* has an extra syllable.

PRACTICE 9: Recognizing the Root Word

Write these words in a column: *driving, smiling, retired, arrived, hurried, cried, cities, tries, faster, sadder, nicer, dying*. Have S. read each word and tell what the root word is. Ask him to spell the root word as you write it by the word with the ending.

PRACTICE 10: Recognizing Verb Forms Ending in *en*

Write the following words in two columns:

eat	*eaten*
take	*taken*
give	*given*
got	*gotten*
write	*written*
ride	*ridden*
drive	*driven*

T: In the first column are some verbs you have learned. In the second column is another form of each verb.

Ask S. to read both forms of each verb aloud. Call attention to these points:

1. The *en* adds a syllable.
2. The first four verbs have the same vowel sound in both forms. In the last three verbs, long *i* in the root changes to short *i* in the *en* form.
3. The consonant is doubled after the short vowel sound in *gotten, written, ridden*. The *v* in *given* and *driven* is not doubled, however; *v* is almost never doubled.

Remind S. that, for these verbs, the *en* form is the form we use after *has* or *have*. Say each sentence below. Have S. listen for the verb and point to it in column 1. Then have him change the sentence, saying *I have never* and the *en* form of the verb in column 2.

I eat snake meat. [I have never eaten snake meat.]
I ride in a Jeep.
I take an eye test.
I drive a racing car.
I write to the president.

III. Writing

CHECK HOMEWORK: Page 77

Check this page with S. Have him correct any errors. The Skills Practice exercises in today's lesson should have reinforced these skills. Plan more practice if needed.

WRITING LESSON (In Notebook)

Words. Have S. write *Lesson 15* in the upper left-hand corner of his page. Have him write today's date in the upper right-hand corner. Then have him write the title *Words* and number from 1 to 20 in two columns. Dictate the following words for S. to write. (You may substitute words from his "Study" list in the last few lessons.)

1. birth	6. time	11. nice	16. fly
2. drive	7. bus	12. tired	17. why
3. ride	8. like	13. wife	18. child
4. state	9. air	14. husband	19. high
5. test	10. by	15. cried	20. night

Check his work, and have him correct any errors.

Sentences. Have S. write the title *Sentences* and number from 1 to 5. Have him cover the words he wrote. Then dictate these sentences for S. to write:

1. Why is the child crying?
2. I had to take an eye test.
3. Is Lee doing the right thing?
4. Ellen will write a letter to her friend.
5. Mr. and Mrs. White will be there by nine.

Check your student's work. Have him correct any errors. Then have him write the title *Study* and any words he missed in the word and sentence dictation.

Dates. Have S. write the following dates, spelling out the name of the month:

April 16, 1976 March 21, 1983 May 31, 1985

Have S. write these dates, using a number for the month:

December 1, 1954 February 12, 1965 July 4, 1976

Check what S. has written. Have him correct any errors.

Times of day. Dictate the following times for S. to write. When he has finished, check his work and have him correct any errors.

3:15 p.m.	10:00 a.m.	9:55 p.m.	12:10 a.m.
6:30 a.m.	1:45 p.m.	7:20 a.m.	4:25 p.m.

REVIEW PRACTICE

Write out the exercises shown below. Go over the directions with S., including the sample item for the third exercise. Let S. do the page by himself. Check his work, and have him correct any errors. (When you check the first exercise, have S. read each sentence aloud with the word he filled in.)

Write the missing word in each sentence.

kit	kite	1. Sam likes to fly a ______.
fit	fight	2. The two men started to ______
but	buy	3. Gail did not ______ the white dress.
sad	same	4. Ellen Roberts was feeling very ______.
pin	pie	5. Mike baked an apple ______.

Read the word. Write the two words that it comes from.

it's	______	______	that's	______	______
I'll	______	______	didn't	______	______
I'm	______	______	wasn't	______	______

Each word in List 1 will make a big word with a word in List 2. Write the big word.

List 1	List 2	
pay	line	1. payday
under	day	2. ______
some	table	3. ______
my	thing	4. ______
time	self	5. ______

HOMEWORK (In Notebook)

Explain to S. that the homework is to be done in his notebook. Have him copy these words: *I, eye, by, buy, right, write, ate, eight.* Ask him to read each word aloud and tell what it means. For homework, he is to write a sentence using each word. Also, encourage him to study any words he missed in the dictation and to read the stories in the lesson again.

CHECKING PROGRESS

Comprehension. Note your student's progress in the following areas, as shown in the reading of the stories in this lesson:

1. Understanding the main ideas
2. Recall of details
3. Ability to scan a story to find information
4. Understanding of sequence of events
5. Understanding implied meanings
6. Interpreting the feelings of the characters

Also, see the paragraph on comprehension in the Checking Progress section of Lesson 10. Plan reinforcement activities for the skills with which S. needs help.

Word recognition. In the oral reading of stories 2 and 4, if S. missed five words or less per story, he is doing well. If he missed more words, note the types of errors. If they are similar, plan extra practice in the skill needed. If errors are more general, supplementary material using the same vocabulary may be helpful.

Recording progress. Follow the suggestions in Lesson 6 for recording progress in comprehension and phonics skills. Also, record the number of words, sentences, dates, and times that S. wrote correctly in the dictation. Note which punctuation marks S. uses correctly.

MEETING INDIVIDUAL NEEDS

If S. did fairly well in this lesson, let him go on to Lesson 16. If he is having much difficulty with word recognition or needs help in many other areas, plan another review lesson. Use the supplements suggested here, or create your own, but do not repeat skill book lessons. This is a good time to give extra reinforcement if S. needs it, but do not hold him back unnecessarily.

In the *Workbook for Skill Book 3*, the exercises for Lesson 15 may be done at this time.

In *Focus on Phonics-3*, Practice 15 may be used after Lesson 15. It reviews words with regular spellings for the long *i* sound.

If S. has trouble with fluent reading, you may want to try "duet reading." In duet reading, you sit next to S. and read aloud with him. Read at a fairly natural pace and with normal intonation, moving your finger beneath the line being read. Repeat the selection this way until S. is thoroughly familiar with it. Then let him read it aloud by himself. (For this activity, you can use stories 1 and 3, which S. did not read orally in this lesson, or other stories written in familiar vocabulary.)

In duet reading, you become the model for what fluent reading is like. This technique is useful for students whose phrasing is poor and those who hesitate frequently on words they can actually read because of timidity and overanalyzing.

If S. reads word by word, make a very large slip strip, with a "window" wide enough to show a whole phrase. (You can use phrases from today's stories, such as: *in my life, a fine husband, standing in line.*) Pull the slip of paper with the phrases on it through the window, a phrase at a time, allowing S. just enough time to grasp the phrase but not enough time to read it word by word.

LESSON 16 Skill Book 3 Pages 84-89

OBJECTIVES

To help your student:

- recognize the long sound for *o* as in the key word *go*
- recognize that *o* at the end of a syllable usually stands for the sound /ō/, as in *open*.
- recognize that *o* followed by *ld* usually stands for the sound /ō/, as in *old*.
- read words in which the sound /ō/ is represented by the letter *o*, at the end of a syllable or followed by the letters *ld*.
- distinguish between the long and short sounds for *o*.
- recall the sequence of events in a story.
- write a short summary of the story.
- read simple want ads for household furnishings.
- recognize the number of syllables in a word.
- recognize the new contraction *we'll* and review the contractions *that's, I'll, I'm, let's, didn't, wasn't*.
- write words and sentences, and a simple want ad from dictation.

INTRODUCTION

T: Today's lesson is about another long vowel sound. Look at Lesson 16, and find out what it is.

I. Reading

CHART: Page 84

Title and key word. Have S. read *Lesson 16* and tell what vowel sound the lesson is about.

T: Please read the key word. [S: go.] What is the vowel sound in *go?* [S: /ō/.] How is the sound /ō/ written in *go?* [S: The letter *o* by itself.]

Lines 1-4

T: Look at line 1, and read the word. [S: open.] How many syllables are there in *open?* (Point to column 3.) [S: Two.]

T: Remember, each syllable has a vowel sound. What is the vowel sound in the first syllable? [S: /ō/.] How is the sound /o/ written in *open*? [S: *o* by itself.]

T: Read the next three lines to yourself. Notice how many syllables are in each word and how the sound /ō/ is written.

After S. reads the words silently, have him read them aloud. Then have him tell the number of syllables in each word. Point out that *o* by itself at the end of a syllable is usually pronounced /ō/.

Lines 5-6. Have S. read these lines first to himself and then aloud. Ask him to tell the number of syllables in each word, the vowel sound, how /ō/ is written, and the names of the letters that come after *o*. Point out that when the letter *o* is followed by the letters *ld*, it is usually pronounced /ō/. Also, mention that *old* and *told* rhyme. Have S. think of other words that rhyme with them.

Review. Have S. read the words aloud again, including the key word. Go down the last column of the chart.

STORY: Pages 85-86 (The Door Was Open)

Have S. read the story title and new words first silently and then aloud. Ask him to tell which words have the sound /ō/ at the end of a syllable and which word has the letter *o* followed by *ld*. Call attention to the contraction *we'll* for *we will* and to the compound words *someone* and *anyone*.

Directed silent reading. Cover all but the first paragraph. Ask S. to read the first paragraph to himself. Then ask him what he thinks probably happened at Tony's apartment. [Someone broke in.]

Ask S. to read the rest of the story to himself to find out what happened. Tell him to be ready to summarize the story. His summary might be as follows:

> [Tony got home from work very late. The door to his apartment was open, and the lock was broken. Tony went next door and telephoned the police. Two police officers came. One officer went into Tony's apartment. The other stayed by the door. They didn't find anyone. They asked Tony to go in with them to see what was missing. Tony's sofa, color TV, clock radio, gold ring, and ten dollars were missing. The police officers told Tony they would try to find his things.]

Reading between the lines. Discuss these questions:

1. Why didn't Tony go into his apartment right away? What did he do instead? Do you think this was the right thing to do? Why or why not?
2. What information did Tony give the police when he telephoned?
3. Why wasn't a lot of money stolen from Tony?
4. Judging from things Tony said and did, which way of describing him do you think is better and why?
   a. Is Tony a careful person or a reckless one?
   b. In a crisis, can he remain coolheaded or does he become too upset to act sensibly?
   c. Is he sentimental or uncaring?
   d. Does he face problems with a sense of humor, or does he become completely downhearted?
5. Have you ever gone through a similar experience? What happened, and what was your reaction?
6. What can you do to protect your home from robbery or make it easier to recover what is stolen? (These can be mentioned: good locks, keeping doors and windows locked, neighborhood cooperation, keeping a list of serial numbers, engraved identification numbers.)

ō

go

ō

	open	ō pen	open
	broken	brō ken	broken
	stolen	stō len	stolen
	sofa	sō fu	sofa
	old	ōld	old
	told	tōld	told

The Door Was Open

Tony (Tō ny)	oh (ō)	door (dor)	we'll (wēl)	someone (some one)
Romano (Rō man ō)	so (sō)	both (bōth)	police (pu lēs)	anyone (any one)
		gold (gōld)	officer (of is er)	

Tony Romano lived in a big apartment building. One evening after work, Tony got back to his apartment very late. The door was open, and the lock was broken.

"Oh, no!" Tony said. "Someone has broken into my apartment. I'll go next door and telephone the police."

Tony told the police, "My name is Tony Romano. I live at 118 Valley Drive, Apartment 10-B. Someone has broken into my apartment. The door was open when I arrived from work. The door was open, and the lock was broken. I cannot tell if anyone is in there, so I didn't go in. I am telephoning from next door."

"You did the right thing," said the police officer. "We'll send a car right away."

Two police officers arrived very quickly. Both of them had guns. One officer went into Tony's apartment. The other one stayed at the door. They didn't find anyone, so both officers went next door to get Tony.

"Are you Tony Romano?" one officer asked.

"Yes, I am," Tony said. "Did you find anyone?"

"No one was there when I went in," said the other officer. "But someone has been there. Let's go and see what was stolen."

"Oh, my sofa!" said Tony. "My sofa was stolen! It was a gold sofa, and it wasn't very old." Tony looked here and there. "Both my color TV and my clock radio were stolen," he said.

Tony looked some more. "An old gold ring is missing," he told the police. "It was an old gold wedding ring. It was my mother's, so I loved it."

"Is any money missing?" asked one officer.

"Just ten dollars," Tony told her. "I never have much money in the apartment. But will I ever get my things back?"

"We'll work on it," said the police officer. "We'll see if anyone in the building can help us."

After the police left, Tony fixed his lock and went to bed. "I'm happy that my bed wasn't stolen," he said.

Story Checkup

Write Tony's story in four or five sentences.

____

____

____

____

____

____

____

____

____

____

Reading for Living

sale

After Tony Romano's sofa was stolen, he needed another one. Tony didn't have much money, so he looked at ads in the paper. He looked for an old sofa.

These are the ads that Tony looked at. Read them, and write short answers to the questions.

FOR SALE	FOR SALE
Green sofa with matching chair. 2 years old. $250 for both. 472-1653 after 5.	Gold sofa—$75, green curtains—$15, bed—$40, black and white TV—$30, 2 radios—$10 each, wedding dress—$75, tent—$20. 422-9121 any time.
Kitchen table and four chairs, painted white. Very nice. $50. 946 Second Street. Must sell this week.	Old clocks, dolls, glass plates, picture frames, quart jars. Old Red Barn, 3267 River Street. Open every day from 10 a.m. to 6 p.m.
Apartment sale: sofa, coffee table, large rug, chairs, dishes, pans. 205 Valley Drive. Saturday, 9 a.m. to 4 p.m.	Color TV—$140, gray sofa—cost $800, will sell for $400. 476-3986.

1. Are the green sofa and chair three years old? _______________

   What is the price of both? _______________

   What is the telephone number? _______________

2. What day is the apartment sale? _______________

   Does the ad tell the price of this sofa? _______________

   What is the address? _______________

3. What is the price of the gold sofa? _______________
4. What is the price of the gray sofa? _______________
5. Which is cheaper, the gray sofa or the gold one? _______________
6. Which is cheaper, the gold sofa or the green sofa and chair? _______________

Oral reading. Have S. read the part of Tony while you read the part of the police officers. Note his ability to read with expression and his observation of punctuation marks. If you have more than one student, you might like to have them dramatize the story.

STORY CHECKUP: Page 86

Have S. write a summary of the story in a few sentences. This summary does not need to be as long as the oral one. Encourage S. to use words he knows how to spell, but help him with any words that he needs and does not know how to spell.

READING FOR LIVING: Page 87

Have S. read the title of the page and the new word *sale*. Ask him to read the introductory paragraphs first silently and then aloud.

Ask S. what Tony's purpose was in looking at the ads [to find a sofa]. Explain that, when you are looking for a certain item, the fastest way to read the want ads is to skim through them, looking for that word. Ask S. to skim the ads, looking for the word *sofa*. He should circle the word *sofa* and any words that describe the sofa. When he comes to an ad that has a sofa, he can read the ad more carefully for details.

When S. has read the ads, ask how many he found for a sofa [four]. Then have him answer the questions. Give him help where needed. Cheeck his work, and help him find the correct answers for any items he has wrong.

Then, discuss the following points about all six ads:

1. Which ads give only a phone number? Which give only an address?
2. Which ads mention certain times that people can come or phone? (Point out that exact hours are usually written without zeros in ads, as *9 a.m.* instead of *9:00 a.m.*) What does "after 5" mean in the first ad?

II. Skills Practice

Have S. close his book before doing these exercises.

PRACTICE 1: Distinguishing the Long Sound for *o*

T: Which of these words has the long sound for *o:*

open, office?	*Tom, Tony?*	*sold, stop?*
color, cold?	*sofa, sock?*	*both, bath?*
broken, bring?	*got, gold?*	*fold, flop?*

PRACTICE 2: Long *o* before Ending Blend *ld*

T: (Write *old*, have S. read it.) What consonant blend does *old* end with? [S: *ld*.] When the letter *o* is followed by *ld*, it usually stands for the sound / ō / .

Write the words *told, gold, cold, fold, hold, sold* under *old*. Have S. read each word.

PRACTICE 3: Determining the Number of Syllables

Say each word below, and have S. tell how many syllables it has and in which syllable he hears the sound / ō / .

go	[1]	*zero*	[2]	*potato*	[3]
so	[1]	*radio*	[3]	*Lopez*	[2]
sofa	[2]	*over*	[2]	*Romano*	[3]
soda	[2]	*hero*	[2]	*October*	[3]
no	[1]	*going*	[2]	*program*	[2]

PRACTICE 4: Contractions

Write the contraction *we'll*. Remind S. that when one word and part of another word are put together, we call the new word a *contraction*. An apostrophe stands for the letter or letters that are left out in the contraction.

Have S. read *we'll*, tell what two words it is made from, and tell what letters are left out. Write *we will* next to *we'll*. Follow the same procedure with *I'll, I'm, that's, let's, didn't, wasn't*.

PRACTICE 5: Compound Words

Write the word *someone*. Remind S. that when two whole words are put together to make a new word, we call it a *compound word*.

Have S. read *someone* and tell what two words it is made from. Write *some* and *one* next to it. Follow the same procedure with *something, anyone, myself, yourself, timetable, payday, landlady*.

III. Writing

CHECK HOMEWORK (In Notebook)

Have S. read the sentences he wrote for *I, eye, by, buy, right, write, ate, eight*. If a word is not used with the correct meaning, discuss the meaning, and have S. think of and write another sentence.

WRITING LESSON (In Notebook)

Have S. write the titles *Lesson 16* and *Words* and then number from 1 to 14 in two columns.

Words. Give S. a few minutes to study the words *sofa, door, anyone, someone*. Then dictate the words below. Check his work, and have him correct any errors.

1. so	4. gold	8. Tony	11. broken
2. oh	5. told	9. door	12. stolen
3. both	6. old	10. open	13. someone
	7. sofa		14. anyone

Sentences. Have S. write the title *Sentences* and number from 1 to 6. Dictate these sentences for S. to write:

1. The door was open.
2. An old gold ring was stolen.
3. Someone has broken into my apartment.
4. Did you find anyone?
5. Is any money missing?

Practice

Read the sentence. Underline each word with the sound ō.

1. The door was open, and the lock was broken.
2. Both my clock radio and my color TV were stolen.
3. Tony's sofa was stolen.
4. An old gold ring is missing.
5. Let's go and see what was stolen.

Read the word. Write the two words that it comes from.

I'll ___I___ ___will___

1. that's ______ ______
2. we'll ______ ______
3. didn't ______ ______
4. I'm ______ ______

Fill in the right word: *we'll, I'm, that's, didn't.*

1. ____________ a nice sofa.
2. ____________ see you at the party.
3. ____________ tired of standing in line.
4. Tony ____________ go into his apartment by himself.

Homework

Answer each question with a sentence.

1. Did Tony Romano live in a big apartment building or a little one?

____

2. What was broken at Tony's apartment?

____

3. Where did Tony go to telephone the police?

____

4. Why did Tony love the gold ring that was stolen?

____

Say the word. Write the number of syllables.

1. someone ____
2. police ____
3. officer ____
4. broken ____
4. sofa ____
6. telephone ____
7. arrived ____
8. quickly ____
9. sale ____
10. missing ____

Check what S. has written. Have him correct any errors, including errors in punctuation and capitalization. Then have him write the title *Study* and any words that he missed in the word and sentence dictation.

Want ad. Dictate the want ad below for S. to write. Tell him where to put commas and periods between items, but do not tell him where to put the periods in *a.m.* and *p.m.*

> Yard sale. Sofa for $100, color TV for $50. Dishes, tables, rugs. Many other nice things. Cheap prices. 540 Main Street. Saturday, 9 a.m. to 3 p.m.

Check what S. has written for correct spelling and the correct form for writing the prices, the address, and the times of day.

PRACTICE: Page 88

Have S. read the directions for the first exercise to himself and then do the exercise. Check his work. If he missed any words, have him read the sentence aloud.

Go over the directions for both parts of the second exercise with S. Then have him do it by himself. When he is finished, have him read aloud each contraction and the words it is made from. Also, have him read the sentences. Help him correct any errors.

HOMEWORK: Page 89

Go over the directions for both exercises with S. Also, encourage him to read the story and the ads again.

CHECKING PROGRESS

Write the words below, and ask S. to read them. (In each pair of words, the first is known and the second is new.) Note how many of the new words S. is able to figure out by comparing them with the known words.

Tony	*sofa*	*told*	*broken*
pony	*soda*	*bold*	*spoken*

Also, note the student's progress in summarizing a story, recalling events in the order they happened, and interpreting the actions and feelings of the characters.

MEETING INDIVIDUAL NEEDS

If S. needs more help with comprehension skills, read a short story or paragraph to him. Ask questions with *who, what, where, when,* and *why*.

In the *Workbook for Skill Book 3*, the exercises for Lesson 16 may be done at this time.

In *Focus on Phonics-3*, Practices 16A-16B may be used after Lesson 16. They cover word families with *-o, -oe, -old, -olt,* and *-oll,* having the long sound for *o*.

LESSON 17 Skill Book 3 Pages 90-95

OBJECTIVES

To help your student:

- recognize that the letters *o* and *e* separated by one consonant (*o-e*) usually stand for the sound /ō/, as in the key word *home.*
- read words in which the sound /ō/ is spelled *o-e.*
- distinguish between the long and short sounds for *o.*
- predict the outcome in a story.
- recognize cause and effect in the story.
- recall the sequence of events in a story.
- read factual material to obtain information.
- recognize the new contraction *don't* and review other contractions.
- recognize the new compound words *anything* and *everyone* and review other compound words.
- recognize the number of syllables in a word.
- recognize rhyming words such as *woke, smoke.*
- review adding the endings *-ing* and *-ed.*
- recognize that verb forms ending in *en* are related to known verbs, as *broke, broken; stole, stolen.*
- write words and sentences from dictation.

INTRODUCTION

T: Today, you will learn another way that the long sound for *o* is written.

I. Reading

CHART: Page 90

Title and key word. Have S. read *Lesson 17*, the vowel sound and spelling, and the key word *home.*

Lines 1-6. Tell S. that most of the chart words are written the way they sound. Ask him to read them to himself and notice what consonant comes between *o* and *e.*

After S. has studied the chart silently, have him read each word aloud. Call attention to these points:

1. The sound /z/ for *s* in *nose.*
2. The consonant blend *sm* in *smoke.*
3. The use of *k* for the sound /k/ in *smoke* and *woke.* Review the rule that after a long vowel sound, the sound /k/ is written with *k.*
4. The sound /f/ for *ph* in *phone.*
5. The sound /u/ for *a* in *alone.*
6. The number of syllables in each word.
7. The rhyming words *woke, smoke* and *phone, alone.* Ask S. to think of a rhyming word for *woke* and for *phone.*

Review. Have S. read the words aloud again, including the key word. Go down the last column of the chart.

STORY: Pages 91-92 (A Fire at Home)

Have S. read the story title and new words. Call attention to the sound /ō/ and how it is written. Have S. tell which words have more than one syllable.

Directed silent reading. Cover all but the first paragraph. Ask S. to read the first paragraph to himself. Then ask him to tell, judging from the story title and first paragraph, what he thinks will probably happen in this story. [Joe will start a fire by smoking in bed.]

Ask S. to read the rest of the story to himself to find out what happens.

Reading between the lines. Discuss these questions.

1. What caused the fire?
2. What caused Joe to wake up?
3. Why do you think Joe phoned the fire department from next door instead of phoning from his own home?
4. What did Joe mean when he told his wife, "I have learned my lesson"?

STORY CHECKUP: Page 92

Go over the directions with S. Let him do the exercise by himself. Remind him to read all of the sentences before he writes any numbers. If he has the order wrong, refer him to the story, and have him correct the errors. Then have him read the sentences aloud in order.

Oral reading. Have S. read the parts that Joe said while you read the other parts. Then reverse roles.

READING FOR LIVING: Page 93

Have S. read the title and new words. Have him tell the two words from which the contraction *don't* is made and the two words that form each compound word.

T: This page gives some information that may help you in case of fire. There are three main subjects on this page. What is the first one? [S: Phoning for help.]

Phoning for help. Ask S. to read the first paragraph to himself to find out one of the most important things to do even before you need help. Have him tell the important thing and the reason for it. Point out that, if he doesn't have an emergency number, he can dial 0 (zero) for Operator, but this may waste time, as the Operator must pass along the information.

Have S. read the rest of this section to himself. Then have him tell what the four points are, recalling as many as possible without looking at the book.

What Joe said on the phone. Have S. read aloud the title and first paragraph of the second section. Ask him to read the rest of this section silently and tell whether Joe handled the emergency phone call well.

Then have S. read aloud the part of Joe while you read the part of the person at the fire department. Explain that this is written as dialog in a play. The name of the speaker is followed by a colon (:). Then his speech is given without quotation marks.

o—e = ō

home = hōm

o—e = ō

	robe	robe rōb	robe
	nose	noze nōz	nose
	woke	woke wōk	woke
	smoke	smoke smōk	smoke
	phone	fone fōn	phone
	alone	u lone u lōn	alone

A Fire at Home

Rose (Roze)	Joe (Jō)	smell	department (dē part ment)
Stone	cold (cōld)	fire	cigarette (sig u ret)
hope		glad	

It was late at night. Joe Stone was home alone. He had on his robe. He was smoking in bed while he watched TV. Joe never smoked in bed while his wife, Rose, was home. But he sometimes smoked in bed when he was alone.

Joe went to sleep with his cigarette in his hand. The cigarette didn't burn Joe's robe, but it did burn the bed covers. Smoke filled the air.

Joe was sleeping, so he did not smell the smoke. But Joe's puppy smelled the smoke. The puppy jumped on the bed and put its cold nose on Joe's face. The puppy's cold nose woke Joe up.

When Joe woke up, the bed was on fire. "I must phone the fire department, but not from here," he said. "I'll go next door to phone." Joe picked up the puppy and ran into the cold night. He ran next door and phoned the fire department.

The fire department worked fast. A fire truck arrived at Joe's home very quickly. Joe was standing in the street.

Men and women came on the fire truck. "Is anyone in there?" one of them asked Joe.

"No," Joe answered. "I was home alone. I'm glad that you are here. I hope that you can save my home."

The men and women started putting water on the fire. Joe watched them with the puppy in his arms. It was cold, so Joe put the puppy in his robe.

Rose Stone came home while the fire was burning. She ran to her husband. "Oh, Joe!" she said. "I'm glad that you are OK. We worked very hard to buy this home. I hope that they can save it."

Rose picked up the puppy and patted its nose. "I'm glad that you saved the puppy," she said.

"I didn't save him," said Joe. "He saved me. He smelled the smoke and woke me up. I was smoking in bed, but I have learned my lesson."

"I hope so," said Rose.

The people from the fire department saved the Stones' home. The Stones thanked the men and women for saving their home.

Story Checkup

Read these eight sentences.
What happened first? Put a number 1 by that sentence.
Put the right numbers by the other sentences.

_____ Joe went to sleep.

_____ Joe phoned the fire department.

_____ Joe was smoking in bed.

_____ Rose Stone came home.

_____ The cigarette burned the covers.

_____ The puppy smelled the smoke.

_____ A fire truck arrived at Joe's home.

_____ The puppy woke up Joe.

Reading for Living

don't (dōnt)	anything (any thing)	everyone (every one)

Phoning for help

Keep the numbers of the police and fire department by your telephone. If you need help, you can find the phone number quickly.

What do you say when you phone the fire department?

1. Give your name.
2. Give your street address.
   Add anything that will help them find you.
3. Tell what has happened.
4. Give the other person time to ask you more.

What Joe said on the phone

This is what Joe Stone told the fire department when he phoned. Did Joe say the right things?

Joe Stone: This is Joe Stone. There is a fire in my home. It's at 1428 Garden Drive. That's not far from Second Street. The fire started in a bed at the back of the building.

Fire department: Where are you?

Joe Stone: I'm phoning from next door.

Fire department: Is everyone away from the building?

Joe Stone: Yes, I was home alone.

Fire department: Fine. Don't go back home. Don't try to save anything.

If you have a fire

Here are some other things to think of if you have a fire.

1. Get everyone away from the burning building fast.
   Don't stop to telephone. Don't stop to take anything with you.
2. Phone the fire department from next door or from a pay phone.
3. Never go back into a burning building.

If you have a fire. Ask S. to read the title and all of the third section silently and then tell the three important points.

Discussion. Discuss these items with S.

1. Why did Joe tell what part of the house the fire started in? Why might it be important to give other directions besides your street address, such as the nearest cross street, as Joe did?
2. You may want to discuss the importance of having smoke detectors in houses and apartment buildings. (It's not safe to rely on family pets. Joe was lucky.)
3. Help S. find the phone numbers for the police, fire department, and ambulance. Have him write these on the inside back cover of his notebook.
4. You may want to role-play emergency phone calls. Have S. practice giving his name, address, other helpful directions, and information about the emergency.
5. Give S. an opportunity to share any experience he has had in regard to a fire.

II. Skills Practice

Have S. close his book before doing these exercises.

PRACTICE 1: Distinguishing the Long Sound for *o*

T: I will say three words. Listen to the words, and tell which one has the long sound for *o*.

rub, rob, robe	*not, night, note*
hip, hope, hop	*ham, home, hum*
red, rod, rode	*slope, slop, slap*

PRACTICE 2: Recognizing Rhyming Words

Write *nose, woke, phone, hope, Joe,* and have S. read them. Then say each word below, and have S. tell which of the words in the written list it rhymes with.

Stone	*Rose*	*toe*	*bone*	*toe*
broke	*rope*	*hose*	*cope*	*cone*

PRACTICE 3: Identifying the Number of Syllables

Say each of the words below, and have S. tell how many syllables it has.

saved	[1]	*quickly*	[2]	*department*	[3]
patted	[2]	*watched*	[1]	*cigarette*	[3]
phoned	[1]	*arrived*	[2]	*sometimes*	[2]
started	[2]	*smoking*	[2]	*anything*	[3]

PRACTICE 4: Compound Words

Review what a compound word is—a new word made of two whole words put together. Then write the compound words below. Have S. read each one and tell the two words it is made from. As he answers, write the two words.

anyone	*everyone*	*someone*	*sometimes*
anything	*everything*	*something*	

PRACTICE 5: Contractions

Write the contraction *don't*. Have S. read it and tell the two words it is made from. Write *do not* by *don't*.

Review what a contraction is—a new word formed when one word and part of another word are put together. Then read each sentence below. Have S. tell what contraction he hears and the two words it is made from. As he answers, write the contraction and the two words.

1. Joe's wife *wasn't* at home.
2. The cigarette *didn't* burn Joe's robe.
3. *I'll* go next door to phone.
4. Joe said, "*It's* at 1428 Garden Drive."
5. *That's* not far from Second Street.
6. *Don't* try to save anything.
7. *I'm* glad that you are OK.

PRACTICE 6: Adding Endings *-ing* and *-ed*

Write these short vowel words in a column: *hop, kick, smell, stop, pat.* Leave enough space to write their *-ing* and *-ed* forms. In another column, write these long vowel words: *hope, smoke, smile, phone, save.*

Have S. read *hop* and then tell what it would be with *-ing* and *-ed* and how to spell these forms. Write *hopping* and *hopped* as he answers. Review the rule that, after a short vowel sound, the final consonant is doubled before the ending, unless the root word ends in two consonants.

Have S. read *hope* and then tell what it would be with *-ing* and *-ed* and how to spell these forms. Write *hoping* and *hoped* as he answers. Review dropping final silent *e* before *-ing* and adding just *-d* when the root ends in *e*. Also, review the rule that the consonant is not doubled after a long vowel sound.

Follow the same procedure with *kick* and *smoke* and the other pairs of short and long vowel words. Finally have S. read all three forms of each word.

PRACTICE 7: Recognizing Verb Forms Ending in *en*

Write *stole, broke, spoke* in one column and *stolen, broken, spoken* in another. Ask S. to read both forms of each verb aloud.

Write out the exercise below, as shown. Have S. read the sample pair of sentences aloud. Then have him fill in the correct form of the verb in each blank. When he has finished, have him read each pair of sentences aloud.

I broke my arm.	My arm was broken.
1. Someone stole my TV.	My TV was ________.
2. Someone spoke my name.	My name was ________.
3. He broke his leg.	His leg was ________.

III. Writing

CHECK HOMEWORK: Page 89

Check this page with S. Have him correct any errors. In the sentence answers, note the punctuation and the number of

Practice

Read the sentences. Underline each word with the sound ō.

1. Joe Stone was home alone.
2. Joe was smoking in bed.
3. The puppy's cold nose woke up Joe.
4. I hope that you can save my home.
5. Joe put the puppy in his robe.
6. I will not phone from here.

Read the big word. Then write the two little words that you see in it.

anything ___any___ ___thing___

1. someone ________ ________
2. anyone ________ ________
3. everyone ________ ________
4. myself ________ ________
5. himself ________ ________
6. yourself ________ ________

Homework

Write a short *yes* or *no* answer.

1. Was Joe home alone? ________
2. Did the cigarette burn Joe's robe? ________
3. Did Joe phone from his home? ________
4. Did the puppy save Joe's life? ________
5. Did the fire department save the Stones' home? ________

Read each word. In List 1, write the word with *-ing*. In List 2, write the word with *-d* or *-ed*.

	List 1	List 2
smoke	smoking	smoked
1. phone		
2. save		
3. smell		
4. arrive		
5. answer		

sentences written correctly. Help S. make a complete sentence for any answers that are not complete. Refer him to the story for any answers that are wrong.

WRITING LESSON (In Notebook)

Have S. write the titles *Lesson 17* and *Words* and then number from 1 to 16 in two columns.

Words. Have S. study the words *phone, alone, don't.* Then dictate the words below for S. to write. For numbers 8 and 9, tell S. to write *Rose* and *Stone* as he would when they are used as names. When S. has finished, check his work, and have him correct any errors.

1. home	5. smoke	9. Stone	13. smell
2. robe	6. phone	10. hope	14. fire
3. nose	7. alone	11. Joe	15. glad
4. woke	8. Rose	12. cold	16. don't

Sentences. Have S. write the title *Sentences* and then number from 1 to 5. Dictate these sentences:

1. Rose Stone came home.
2. The puppy smelled the smoke.
3. The puppy's cold nose woke Joe up.
4. I'm phoning from next door.
5. Don't try to save anything.

Check his work, and have him correct any errors. Then have S. write the title *Study* and any words he missed in the word and sentence dictation.

PRACTICE: Page 94

Have S. read the directions and do the page by himself. Check his work. In the first exercise, have him read aloud any words he did not mark correctly. If he doesn't pronounce the vowel sound clearly, have him listen as you read the word. Note which vowel sounds he is confusing.

HOMEWORK: Page 95

Go over the directions with S. Have him write the answer to the first question so that he will remember the form that is expected [Yes, he was].

CHECKING PROGRESS

Write these as signs: *No Smoking, Fire Escape, Fire Alarm, Fire Hose, Keep Door Closed, No Fireworks.* Have S. read them. Note how well he can read new words.

Write *rob, hop, not, rod, con* in a column on a card. At the edge of another card, write *e*. Have S. read the short vowel words. Then have him place the *e* after each one and read the long vowel word thus formed.

MEETING INDIVIDUAL NEEDS

In the *Workbook for Skill Book 3*, the exercises for Lesson 17 may be used at this time.

In *Focus on Phonics-3*, Practices 17A-17D may be used after Lesson 17. They cover word families with *o-e*.

LESSON 18

Skill Book 3
Pages 96-101

OBJECTIVES

To help your student:

- recognize that the letters *oa* usually stand for the sound /ō/, as in the key word *boat*.
- read words in which the sound /ō/ is spelled *oa*.
- distinguish between the long and short sounds for *o*.
- recall the sequence of events in a story.
- scan a story to find specific details.
- read a simple road map.
- recognize rhyming words, such as *boat, coat*.
- recognize the ending blend *mp* as in *camp*.
- review the ending blends *nt, st, ft*.
- recognize the ending *-y* and how to add it to words.
- recognize the new compound word *weekend* and review other compound words.
- write a short summary of a story.
- write words and sentences from dictation.

INTRODUCTION

T: You have learned two ways that the sound for *o* is written. Today you will learn another way.

I. Reading

CHART: Page 96

Title and key word. Have S. read *Lesson 18,* the vowel sound and spelling, and the key word.

Lines 1-6. Tell S. that the other words in the chart have the sound /ō/ spelled *oa* and that they are all written the way they sound. Ask him to read the words to himself and notice which words rhyme.

After S. has studied the chart, have him read each word aloud. Ask him to tell the pairs of rhyming words, how many syllables are in each word, and whether the sound /ō/ comes in the middle or at the end of these words.

Review. Have S. read the words aloud again, including the key word. Go down the last column of the chart.

STORY: Pages 97-98 (Camping in October)

Have S. read the story title and new words. Call attention to the sound /ō/ and how it is written. Point out that *Oak* is written with a capital letter here because it is used as a name in the story; when *oak* is used to mean a kind of tree, it is written with a small letter. *October* is always written with a capital letter because it is the name of a month. Have S. tell which words have more than one syllable and which word is a compound word.

Directed silent reading. Ask S. to read the story to himself to find out who went camping and what things they did.

While S. is reading, write the sentences below on strips of paper. When S. has finished, have him tell who went camping and some of the things they did. Then, mix up the strips, and have S. arrange them in the order in which they happened.

Joan Oak and her mother plan to go camping.
Joan and Mrs. Oak load their truck.
They drive to the state park at Green Lake.
Mrs. Oak rents a boat.
The two women catch six fish.
Joan roasts the fish over a fire for dinner.
The women sleep in their sleeping bags.

Reading between the lines. Discuss these questions:

1. How many times did Joan and her mother go fishing? [Twice.] How many fish did they catch the first time? [Twelve.] Can we tell from the story if they caught any fish the second time? [No.]
2. About what age do you think Joan is? Why?
3. Do Joan and her mother seem to be experienced or inexperienced campers? Why?
4. Describe the kind of relationship the mother and daughter seem to have.
5. Why didn't Joan's father come with them? What clue in the story lets you know this? [He was probably out of town that weekend. Joan says, "Let's go camping again when Dad is home."]
6. Why didn't Joan and Mrs. Oak take any meat with them? [They planned to catch fish.] Do you think that was a wise thing to do?

STORY CHECKUP: Page 98

Have S. read the directions and do the exercise by himself. Tell him to try to remember as many answers as he can without looking at the story. For numbers 3 and 4, he should list as many things as he can from memory and then look back to add any he didn't remember.

When S. has finished, check his work, and have him correct any errors by looking back at the story.

Oral reading. Have S. read what Joan said while you read the parts Mrs. Oak said. Then reverse roles.

READING FOR LIVING: Page 99

Have S. read aloud the title, new words, and directions for the first exercise. Ask him to read each question first silently and then aloud. Have him find each place mentioned in the question on the map and then point to the part of the map that answers the question. Then have him write the answer.

oa = ō

boat = bōt

oa = ō

	coat	coat	coat
	road	road	road
	load	load	load
	loaf	loaf	loaf
	toast	toast	toast
	roast	roast	roast

Camping in October

Joan	lake	camp	shore (shor)	over (ō ver)
rain	made	end	clothes (clōz)	October (Oc tō ber)
Oak		weekend (week end)	wear (war)	heavy (hev y)

"Let's go camping this weekend," said Joan to her mother. "There is a state park at Green Lake. It's on Shore Road. We can rent a boat there."

"Fine," said Mrs. Oak. "I think that camping in October is fun. What shall we take to eat? Let's see, we'll need coffee, apples, cheese, eggs, and a loaf of bread. Shall we take any meat?"

"No, we'll go fishing," Joan told her mother. We can roast fish over a fire. Wear old clothes, and bring a heavy coat. It's cold at the lake in October, and sometimes it rains."

On Saturday, Joan and her mother loaded the back end of their truck. They loaded their tent and two sleeping bags into the truck. They loaded other things that they needed.

Mrs. Oak and Joan were on the road by seven o'clock. Mrs. Oak was wearing old clothes and her husband's heavy hunting coat. Joan was wearing old clothes and a heavy coat.

They got to Shore Road at eight o'clock. The state park was at the end of the road. After they put up their tent, Mrs. Oak went to rent a boat. Joan cut the loaf of bread and made cheese sandwiches.

The two women spent the day fishing on the lake. At the end of the day, they each had six fish.

When they got to the shore, Mrs. Oak made a fire and Joan cleaned the fish. Joan roasted the fish over the fire. While Joan was roasting the fish, Mrs. Oak made coffee and toast. She cut some bread from the loaf and toasted it over the fire.

After dinner, they watched the fire for a while. Then they got into their sleeping bags and went to sleep.

The next day, it rained for a while. After it stopped raining, the two women fished again. Then they went for a boat ride on the lake.

"This has been a nice weekend," said Joan. "Let's go camping again when Dad is home. Do you think that you and Dad can go next weekend?"

"Yes, I think so," said Mrs. Oak. "Your dad will like camping at this lake in October."

Story Checkup

Write short answers.

1. What month was it? ______________________
2. Where did Joan and her mother go camping?
____
3. What did they take with them to eat? ______________________
____
4. What other things did they take? ______________________
____
5. Why did they rent a boat? ______________________

Reading for Living

map way

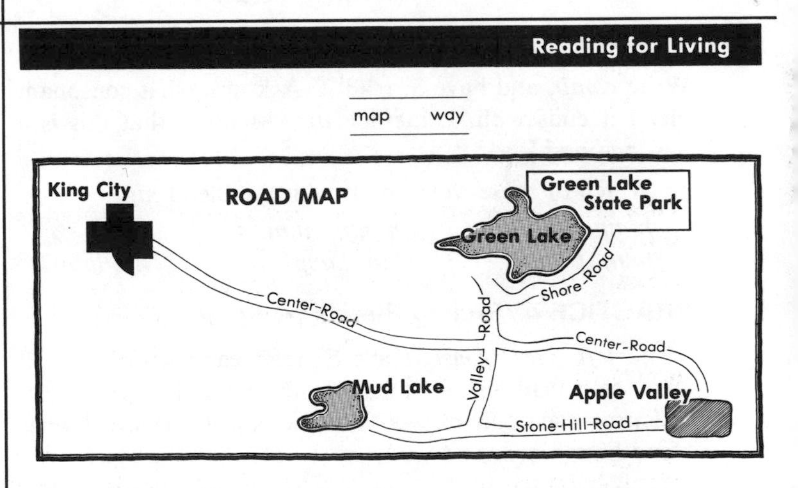

Write the answers. Find the answers by looking at the road map.

1. What road goes from King City to Apple Valley?
____
2. What is the best road to take from Apple Valley to Mud Lake?
____
3. The Oaks live in King City. Which roads do they take to the state park?
______________________ ______________________
____

Circle the right answers. Find the answers by looking at the map.

1. Mrs. Oak and Joan are on their way to the state park. They are on Center Road. When they get to Valley Road, which way do they turn? Left Right
2. They are on Valley Road. When they get to Shore Road, which way do they turn? Left Right

Have S. read the directions for the second exercise aloud. Ask him to read each question silently and then aloud. For number 1, ask S. where the Oaks are starting from, that is, where they live. If he doesn't remember, refer him to question 3 in the first exercise. Then have him trace the route described in the question and give the answer. Continue with this procedure for number 2.

II. Skills Practice

Have S. close his book before doing these exercises.

PRACTICE 1: Distinguishing the Long Sound for *o*

T: I will say three words. Listen to the words, and tell which one has the long sound for *o*.

cat, cot, coat — *rest, roast, rust*
read, road, rod — *boat, bottle, bat*
toast, fast, toss — *rock, ask, oak*

PRACTICE 2: Identifying Rhyming Words

Write *boat, road, toast, oak*, and have S. read them. Then say each word below, and have S. tell which of the words in the written list it rhymes with.

toad	*soak*	*boast*	*float*
goat	*load*	*croak*	*coast*

PRACTICE 3: Ending Consonant Blend *mp*

Write *camp*, and have S. read it. Ask him what consonant blend it ends with. Underline *mp*. Mention that this is a new ending blend.

T: Which of these words ends with the blend *mp:*

jump, just? — *hump, hum?* — *ramp, rap?*
bum, bump? — *lap, lamp?* — *lip, limp?*

PRACTICE 4: Ending Blends *ft, nt, st*

Write *left, tent, roast*. Have S. read each word and tell what consonant blend it ends with. Underline *ft, nt, st*. Then say each pair of words below, and have S. tell what blend both words end with.

coast, toast — *bent, sent* — *gift, raft*
lift, sift — *most, post* — *went, dent*

PRACTICE 5: Adjective Ending *-y*

Write *windy* and *funny*, and have S. read them. Ask him what the root word is for each. As he answers, write *wind* and *fun* under the words with the endings. Point out that, after a short vowel sound, the final consonant is doubled before the ending *-y*, unless the root word already ends in two consonants.

Write *rain*. Have S. read it and tell what it would be with the ending *-y* added. Write *rainy* over *rain*. Point out that the final consonant is not doubled after a long vowel sound.

Write *rock, sun, sleep*. Have S. read each one, tell what it would be with the ending *-y*, and tell how to spell the word with the ending. Write *rocky, sunny, sleepy*.

Finally, have S. read each pair of words. Have him tell how many syllables are in each word. Point out that the ending *-y* adds a syllable because it adds a vowel sound.

III. Writing

CHECK HOMEWORK: Page 95

Check this page with S. Have him correct any errors. If he had any difficulty with the exercise on endings, plan extra practice for the next session.

WRITING LESSON (In Notebook)

Have S. write the titles *Lesson 18* and *Words* and then number from 1 to 16 in two columns.

Words. Dictate the words below for S. to write. For number 8, tell him to write *Oak* as he would when it is used as a name. When he has finished, check his work, and have him correct any errors.

1. boat	5. loaf	9. rain	13. shore
2. coat	6. toast	10. lake	14. over
3. road	7. roast	11. made	15. October
4. load	8. Oak	12. end	16. camp

Sentences. Ask S. to write a short summary of the story in about five sentences. Check what he writes. Note the number of complete sentences, correct punctuation, and capitalization. Circle any words he misspelled.

If S. has difficulty writing a summary on his own, dictate the following for him to write:

> Joan Oak and her mother went camping one weekend in October. They went to the state park at Green Lake. They rented a boat. They spent the day fishing. Joan roasted fish for dinner. Mrs. Oak made coffee and toast. They went to sleep in their sleeping bags. They had a nice weekend.

Have S. write the title *Study* and any words he missed in the word dictation and summary.

PRACTICE: Page 100

Have S. read the directions for the first exercise and do it by himself. Check his work. Have him read aloud any words he did not mark correctly. If he doesn't pronounce the vowel sound clearly, have him listen as you read the word. Note which sounds he is confusing.

Go over the directions and samples for the second exercise. Then let S. do it by himself. Check his work, and have him correct any errors.

HOMEWORK: Page 101

Go over the directions and the sample items with S.

Practice

Say the words. Circle the words with the sound ō.

1.	Joan	John	Joe	Jason
2.	red	road	Rosa	robe
3.	bat	boat	both	box
4.	cold	cop	coat	come
5.	top	toast	roast	best
6.	left	love	load	loaf

Copy the word. Add the ending -y. Make a change in the word if you have to. Write one of the words in each sentence.

wind windy ______ fun funny ______

rain ______ sun ______

sleep ______ rock ______

1. It's fun to be at the shore on a ______ day.
2. It's not fun to be there on a ______ day.
3. Carla put her ______ child to bed.
4. Joan does not like to run on the ______ path.

100 Lesson 18

Homework

Answer with the name of a person in the story.

1. Who went to rent a boat? ______
2. Who made cheese sandwiches? ______
3. Who cleaned the fish? ______
4. Who roasted the fish? ______
5. Who made coffee and toast? ______

Read the big word. Then write the two little words that you see in it.

anyone any ______ one ______

1. weekend ______ ______
2. everyone ______ ______
3. homework ______ ______
4. cannot ______ ______
5. someone ______ ______
6. anything ______ ______
7. yourself ______ ______

Lesson 18 101

CHECKING PROGRESS

Write these as signs: *No Campfires, No Fishing Here, No Left Turn, Boats for Rent, Road Closed, Loading Zone, Green Lake—10 Miles.* Have S. read each sign. Give help where needed. Note how well S. can recognize old words in a new context, sound out new words—such as *zone*, and recognize the new compound word *campfire*.

Make flash cards for *cot, got, rod, sock* and *coat, goat, road, soak*. Put the short *o* words in one pile in this order; put the long *o* words in another pile in order. Have S. read the cards alternately from the two piles, telling which has the short sound and which has the long sound for *o*.

MEETING INDIVIDUAL NEEDS

If S. needs more practice with the sequence of events, make sentence strips from the review story "A Teenager Learns to Drive" in Lesson 15. Have S. arrange them in order.

If S. needs help with contractions, use the suggestions in Lesson 14, making up new sentences.

For practice with compound words, write these words on separate cards: *sailboat, weekend, campfire, overcoat, flashlight*. Bring scissors to class. Have S. cut apart the two small words in each compound word. Mix up the pieces, and have him put the compound words back together.

For more practice with verb endings, write the following words in a column in his notebook: *hope, smoke, phone, load, toast, stop, ask, watch*. Across the top of the page, write these headings: *-s* or *-es, -ing, -d* or *-ed*. Have S. read each root word, tell what it would be with the ending, tell how to spell it, and then write the word with the ending. Do all three endings for each root word before going on to the next root word. Review the rules for adding endings as necessary.

For more practice with the ending *-y*, make flash cards for the following pairs of words. Put the root word on one side of the card and the *-y* form on the other side.

smell, smelly	*bag, baggy*	*hair, hairy*
fish, fishy	*mud, muddy*	*sleep, sleepy*
run, runny	*rock, rocky*	*rain, rainy*
sun, sunny	*wind, windy*	*fun, funny*

Have S. read all of the words with *-y*. For each one, have him tell what the root word is and how to spell it. Then turn the cards over, and have him read the root words. For each one, have him tell what the word would be with *-y* and how to spell it.

In *Focus on Phonics-3,* Practices 18A-18B may be used after Lesson 18. They cover the word families with *oa*.

In the *Workbook for Skill Book 3*, the exercises for Lesson 18 may be used at this time.

LESSON 19 — Skill Book 3, Pages 102-107

OBJECTIVES

To help your student:

- recognize that the letters *ow* often stand for the sound /ō/.
- read words in which the sound /ō/ is spelled *ow*.
- review other regular spellings for the sound/ō/: *o-e, oa, o* followed by *ld*.
- distinguish between the long and short sounds for *o*.
- predict the outcome in a story.
- recognize cause and effect.
- recall the sequence of events in a story.
- read and interpret road signs.
- review the ending blend *nd* as in *sand*.
- recognize *you're* and review other contractions.
- add the ending *-y* to words ending in silent *e*, as *ice, icy*.
- recognize the ending *-ly* and how to add it to words.
- recognize the root word in words with the endings *-y, -ly, -ed, -ing*.
- write a short summary of a story.
- write words and sentences from dictation.

INTRODUCTION

Write *coat* and *boat*. Have S. read them and tell what two letters together stand for the sound /ō/.

T: In today's lesson, you will study another combination of letters that often stand for the sound /ō/.

I. Reading

CHART: Page 102

Title and key word. Have S. read *Lesson 19* and then look at the letters in the top right-hand corner.

T: What two letters together equal the sound /ō/? [S: *ow*.] What do you notice over the letter *o* in *ow*? [S: A line.] What does the line mean? [S: The sound for *o* is long.] The letters *ow* often stand for the sound /ō/, but not always. Later, you will learn another sound for *ow*. All of the words in this chart have the long *o* sound. The line over the *o* will help you know that in these words *ow* equals /ō/.

T: What is the key word? [S: snow.] What is the vowel sound? [S: /ō/.] What letters together stand for the sound /ō/? [S: *ow*.]

Lines 1-6. Tell S. that the other words in the chart have the sound /ō/ written with *ow*, and most words are written the way they sound. Ask him to read the words to himself and notice where the sound /ō/ comes in each word. Also, he should notice which words rhyme.

After S. has studied the chart, have him read each word aloud. Have him tell how many syllables are in each word and what beginning blend is in *blow* and *throw*. Ask him which words in the chart rhyme [all of them]. Point out that *ow* often comes at the end of words. Mention that when a word begins with *kn*, as in *know*, the *k* is silent.

Review. Have S. read the words aloud again, including the key word. Go down the last column of the chart.

STORY: Pages 103-104 (Stuck in the Snow)

Have S. read the story title and new words. Call attention to words with the sound /ō/ and how it is written. Call attention to the contraction *you're* and the two words it is made from. Have S. tell which words have more than one syllable.

Directed silent reading. Cover all but the first five paragraphs. Ask S. to read these to himself to find out how the story begins. When he has finished, ask him what he thinks will happen next. [His answer should indicate that the yellow car will go off the road, get stuck in the snow, or something similar.] Then have him finish the story and see if his prediction is right.

Reading between the lines. Discuss these questions:

1. About what age is Sam? What clues are in the story?
2. What shows that Sam is a responsible person?
3. What shows that the driver of the yellow car was not used to driving in snow?
4. What was Sam's reaction when he saw that the yellow car was stuck? Did you think Sam would help? Why?
5. Describe how Sam got the yellow car back on the road.
6. What was the actual temperature? What made it feel much colder? How cold did it feel?
7. Have you ever been stuck in snow, mud, or sand? How did you get out?

STORY CHECKUP: Page 104

Ask S. to think of the main events in the story and the order in which they happened. Give him a few minutes to review the story to himself. Then ask him to write a short summary. Have him read his summary aloud. If he omitted any important points or had them in the wrong order, have him scan the story and make corrections.

Oral reading. Have S. read aloud the paragraph that answers each of the following questions.

1. How cold was it? [Par. 1]
2. Why did Sam stop by the side of the road the first time? [Par. 3]
3. Where had Sam been? [Par. 2]
4. What did Sam see when he came to the turn in the road? [Par. 6]
5. What did Sam do with the sand? [Par. 8]
6. What did Sam show the man? [Par. 10]
7. What did the man say to Sam when the car was back on the road? [Par. 11]
8. How else did Sam offer to help the man? [Par. 12]

ōw = ō

snow = snō

ōw = ō

blow	blōw	blow
show	shōw	show
know	nōw	know
throw	thrōw	throw
window	win dōw	window
follow	fol ōw	follow

Stuck in the Snow

slowly (slōw ly)	below (bē lōw)	wind	side	you're (your)
yellow (yel ōw)	zero (zē rō)	sand	ice (ise)	onto (on to)
				ahead (u head)

It is snowing, and the wind is blowing. It is five below zero. The wind is blowing so hard that it feels much colder. It feels like forty below zero. There is snow and ice on the road.

Sam is on his way home from hockey practice. He is driving his father's car. Sam knows that he must drive slowly in the snow. It is snowing so hard that Sam cannot see the road. He follows the lights of the car ahead of him.

The wind blows snow onto Sam's car windows. Sam stops by the side of the road. He cleans the snow and ice from his windows.

A yellow car passes Sam. It is not going slowly. The yellow car throws more ice and snow onto Sam's windows.

Sam cleans his windows again. "He is driving very fast," Sam thinks. "He is going so fast that he will miss the turn up ahead."

Sam gets back in his car and drives slowly. When he comes to the turn in the road, he sees the yellow car again. It is on the side of the road. It is stuck in the snow and ice. Sam stops to help the driver.

The man says, "I'm stuck, and I don't know what to do."

"I have a bag of sand in my car," says Sam. "I'll throw some sand under your wheels." Sam throws sand under the wheels of the car.

Then Sam tells the man to rock the car. "Drive ahead a little. Then drive back," he says. "Then drive ahead a little more. Make a path in the snow." But the man does not know what to do.

"Here, let me show you," Sam says. He gets into the man's car on the driver's side. Sam shows him what to do. Sam rocks the car and gets it onto the road again.

The man says, "You're not very old, but you know a lot. Thanks for showing me. If this ever happens again, I'll know what to do."

Sam says, "It's no fun to get stuck when it's below zero. I was glad to help you. If you're going my way, you can follow me. Follow the lights of my car."

Story Checkup

Write the story in three or four sentences.

____

____

____

____

____

____

Reading for Living

Read these traffic signs.

speed limit (lim it)

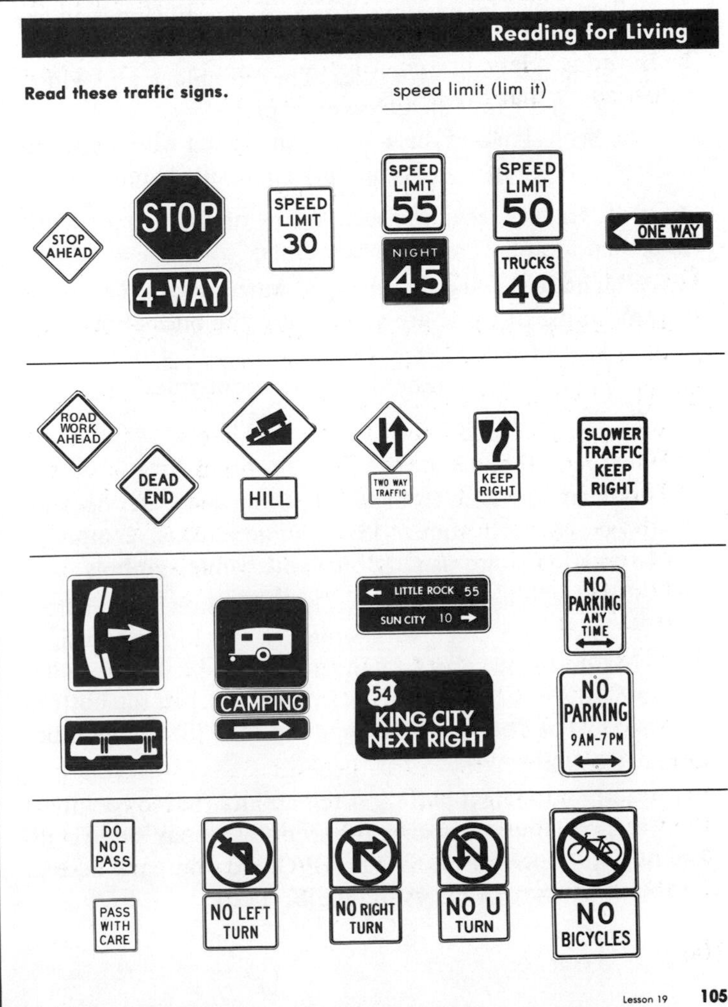

READING FOR LIVING: Page 105

Have S. read the title, the new words *speed limit*, and the directions.

Row 1

T: Look at the first three signs. What are all of them about? [S: Stopping.] What does the first sign warn you about? [S: That there is a Stop sign ahead.] The 4-Way sign is found below a Stop sign. What does the 4-Way sign mean? [S: Cars coming from all four directions must stop.]

T: Look at the next five signs. What are all of them about? [S: Speed limit.] What does the number on each sign mean? [S: How many miles an hour you can drive.] When two Speed Limit signs are placed together, the bottom one applies to special cases named on the sign. What is the speed limit at night shown here? [S: 45 miles an hour.] What is the daytime speed limit on this same road? [S: 55.] What is the speed limit shown here for trucks? [S: 40 miles an hour.] What is the speed limit for cars on the same road? [S: 50.]

T: What is the last sign in the first row? [S: One Way.] What does the arrow mean? [S: That's the direction you can go.]

Have S. read all of the signs in the first row aloud. Then call attention to these points:

1. Diamond-shaped signs are warning signs. They are yellow with black letters. The Stop Ahead sign is an example of a warning sign.
2. Rectangular signs give rules. They are black and white. The Speed Limit signs are examples.
3. The Stop sign and the 4-Way sign are red with white letters. The Stop sign is the *only* eight-sided sign.

Row 2. Have S. read the second row of signs first silently and then aloud. Discuss these points:

1. Which are the diamond-shaped warning signs? Mention that most of these are yellow, but the ones about road work are orange.
2. Which are the rectangular signs about rules?
3. What does the Dead End sign mean?

Row 3

T: Look at the first three signs. What three services do these signs tell about? [S: Telephone, bus, camping.] Service signs are usually blue with white symbols.

T: Look at the next two signs. They give directions. Direction signs are green with white letters. In the top sign, what do the numbers 55 and 10 mean? [S: It is 55 miles to Little Rock and 10 miles to Sun City.] In the bottom sign, what does the number stand for? [S: The number of the highway.]

T: What do the next two signs tell about? [S: No parking.] During what hours does the second sign say there is no parking? [S: 9 a.m. to 7 p.m.] Could you park here at eight o'clock in the evening? [S: Yes.]

Row 4. Have S. read the signs aloud. Ask him to explain the difference in meaning between the first two signs.

Point out that the circle-and-slash-mark symbol used on the last four signs is red on real signs. Ask him what he thinks this symbol means. Cover the part with the words on the last four signs, and have S. tell what each one means just by looking at the symbols.

II. Skills Practice

Have S. close his book before doing these exercises.

PRACTICE 1: Distinguishing the Long Sound for *o*

T: I will say three words. Listen to the words, and tell which one has the long sound for *o*.

row, ray, rot	*snow, stop, snail*
an, on, own	*sleep, slow, slop*
lot, low, lay	*shop, shy, show*

PRACTICE 2: Spellings of the Long *o* Sound

Write *nose, road, show, old.* Have S. read each word, tell how the sound /ō/ is written, and give another word in which the sound is written the same way.

PRACTICE 3: Ending Consonant Blend *nd*

Write *wind, sand.* Have S. read them and tell what consonant blend they end with. Underline *nd.*

T: I will say two words. Which one ends with the consonant blend *nd:*

sent, send?	*bed, bend?*	*win, wind?*
spend, spent?	*hand, had?*	*and, an?*

PRACTICE 4: Contractions

Write the contraction *you're.* Have S. read it and tell the two words it is made from. Write *you are* by *you're.* Review what a contraction is—a new word formed when one word and part of another word are put together. Then follow the same procedure with *we'll, that's, didn't, wasn't, it's, don't.*

PRACTICE 5: Adding *-y* to Words Ending in Silent *e*

Write *ice* and *icy*, and have S. read both words. Explain that, when the root word ends in silent *e*, the *e* is dropped before the ending *-y* is added. Write *smoke* and *stone* under *ice*. Have S. read each one, tell what it would be with the ending *-y*, and tell how to spell the word with *-y*. As he answers, write *smoky* and *stony*. Finally, have S. read both forms of each word.

PRACTICE 6: Adding the Ending *-ly*

Write *slowly*. Have S. read it and tell the root word. Underline *slow*. Ask S. what ending is added to *slow* to make *slowly* [*-ly*].

Practice

opy the word. Add the ending -y to each word.
the word ends with e, drop the e and then add -y.
rite one of the words in each sentence.

smoke ________ snow ________

ice ________ sand ________

. We camped on the ________ shore.

. The ________ air hurts my eyes.

. I will not drive on ________ roads.

Copy the word. Add the ending -ly.
Then write one of the words in each sentence.

quick ________ glad ________

slow ________ light ________

sad ________ cheap ________

. Sam drives ________ in the snow.

2. The boy looked at his dead puppy ________.

3. It was raining ________, but we went fishing.

4. If I work ________, I can finish by three o'clock.

106 Lesson 19

Homework

Write a short yes or no answer.

1. Does Sam drive slowly in the snow? ________
2. Does Sam's car get stuck? ________
3. Is it forty below zero? ________
4. Is Sam on his way to hockey practice? ________
5. Does Sam help the man in the yellow car? ________
6. Does Sam throw sand under the car wheels? ________

Drop the ending from each word. Write the word that is left.
Make a change in the word if you have to.

having have shopped shop

1. stopped ________ 6. rained ________
2. loaded ________ 7. quickly ________
3. windy ________ 8. slowly ________
4. icy ________ 9. sleeping ________
5. smoking ________ 10. running ________

Lesson 19 107

Write *glad, quick, light, safe* in a column. Have S. read each word and tell what it would be with the *-ly* ending. As he answers, write *gladly, quickly, lightly, safely* in a second column.

Have S. look at each pair of words and tell if any change is made in the root word before the ending is added. Explain that when *-ly* is added, usually *no* change is made in the root word.

Have S. tell how many syllables are in the root word and in the word with *-ly*. Point out that the *-ly* ending adds a syllable to the word.

III. Writing

CHECK HOMEWORK: Page 101

Check this page with S. Have him correct any wrong answers in the first exercise by referring to the story. Also, help him correct any errors in the exercise on compound words. Plan extra practice if needed.

WRITING LESSON (In Notebook)

Have S. write the titles *Lesson 19* and *Words* and then number from 1 to 16 in two columns.

Words. Dictate the words below for S. to write. For number 4, give a sentence using *know*. For number 14, give a sentence using *you're*. When S. has finished, check his work, and have him correct any errors.

1. snow	5. throw	9. slowly	13. ahead
2. blow	6. window	10. sand	14. you're
3. show	7. follow	11. side	15. speed
4. know	8. yellow	12. onto	16. limit

Sentences. Have S. write the title *Sentences.*

T: Today you will write a paragraph from the story. I'll dictate one sentence at a time. But instead of numbering the sentences and beginning each one on a new line, you will write the sentences in paragraph form. Remember to indent the first word of the paragraph.

Show S. where to begin. Then dictate the sentences in the first paragraph of the story on page 103. (Tell S. where to put the comma in the first sentence.) Have S. read aloud the paragraph he has written. Check his work. Have him correct any errors by looking at the paragraph in the book.

Explain that a comma is used in the first sentence because it is made up of two shorter sentences (*It is snowing. The wind is blowing.*) that are joined by *and*.

Have S. write the title *Study* and any words he missed in the word and sentence dictation.

PRACTICE: Page 106

Have S. read the directions and do each exercise by himself. Check his work after he finishes each exercise. Have him read aloud each root word and word with the ending and the sentences. Have him correct any errors.

HOMEWORK: Page 107

Go over the directions and sample items with S.

CHECKING PROGRESS

Applying phonics skills. Make a slip strip for the *ow* word family, following the directions in Lesson 3. For the beginning letters, use *b, l, m, r, sh, bl, fl, gl, cr, gr, thr, sl, sn, kn.* Note the number of words S. is able to read correctly. Do not give help or further practice at this time.

Applying word recognition skills. Make flash cards for these words: *driving, slower, sandy, sadly, follower, smoking, dropped, camper, dried, cleaner, icy, friendly.* Have S. read each word. If he needs help, ask him what the ending is and what the root word is. Note how many words he can read without help, how many he can read with some help, and how many he is unable to read. If needed, plan more practice for a later time.

Comprehension skills. Note the student's progress in summarizing a story, recalling events in sequence, interpreting the actions and feelings of the characters, and drawing inferences. Note which skill needs the most reinforcement and plan related practice exercises.

MEETING INDIVIDUAL NEEDS

If S. needs more practice on reading words with endings, you may find a word wheel helpful. You can make a word wheel from a 4-by-6-inch file card or other light cardboard, as follows:

1. Cut a large circle.
2. Choose 8 or 10 root words to which the ending that needs practice can be added. (The root words must be ones that are not changed before the ending. The word wheel cannot accommodate dropping final *e* or doubling the final consonant.)
3. Write the root words on the circle card, as "spokes" on the wheel. The words should begin at the edge of the circle and go in toward the center.
4. Cut a short arrow-shaped pointer from cardboard and attach it to the center of the circle with a paper fastener. Write the ending on the arrow end.

Have S. read the root words going around the wheel. Then have him place the pointer after each root word and read the word with the ending.

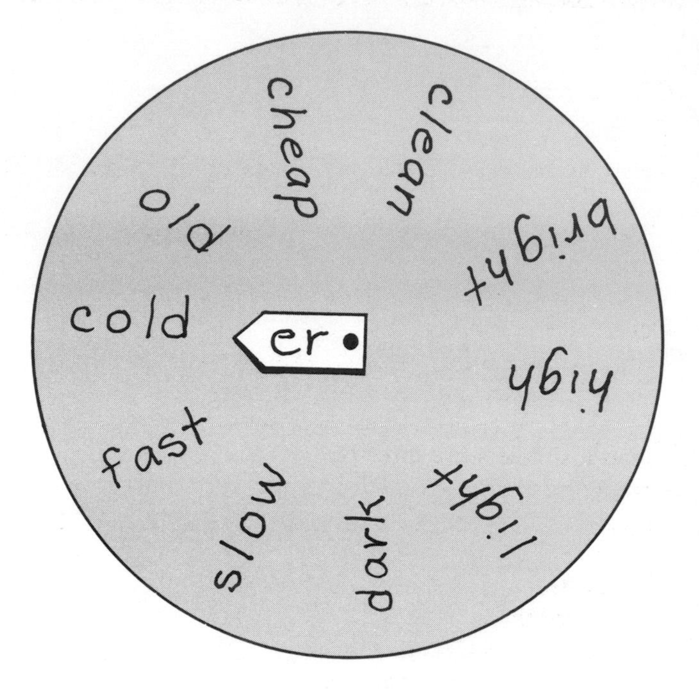

A sample wheel is shown here with root words to which the adjective ending *-er* can be added.

Words to which the ending *-y* can be added are: *rain, snow, wind, sand, rock, air, hair, sleep, fish, glass, hand, dress.*

Words to which the ending *-ly* can be added are: *slow, quick, sad, glad, bad, safe, nice, week, month, year.* You might also use *dead, hard, large, late,* although the meaning changes more when *-ly* is added to these.

In *Focus on Phonics-3,* Practices 19A-19B may be used after Lesson 19. They cover word families with *ow*, having the long sound for *o*.

In the *Workbook for Skill Book 3*, the exercises for Lesson 20 may be used at this time.

LESSON 20 Skill Book 3 Pages 108-113

OBJECTIVES

To help your student:
- recognize that the letters *or* and *ore* usually stand for the sound /or/, as in *York* and *store*.
- read words in which the sound /or/ is written with *or* and *ore*.
- distinguish the sound /or/ from /er/ and /ar/.
- predict the outcome in a story.
- recall the sequence of events in the story.
- recognize cause and effect in the story.
- relate the story to his own experiences.
- read a simple store directory.
- recognize rhyming words, such as *tore, store*.
- recognize the new compound word *salesperson* and review other compound words.
- review the ending consonant blends *nt, st*.
- recognize the adjective endings *-er* and *-est*, and how to add them to words.
- review the endings *-ing, -ed, -y, -ly*.
- alphabetize words by the first letter.
- write words and sentences from dictation.

INTRODUCTION

T: In today's lesson, you will study a sound represented by a vowel and a consonant together.

I. Reading

CHART: Page 108

Note: The sound for *or* has regional variations. Let S. make the sound the way he normally pronounces it in words like *York*. If your pronunciation is different, explain that people in different parts of the country pronounce *or* in different ways.

If S. asks whether /or/ is a long *o* sound, explain that it is usually considered a different sound because the *r* changes the vowel sound. If he doesn't ask, don't bring up this point. Just treat /or/ as a separate sound.

Title and key words. Have S. read *Lesson 20*.

T: What are the first two letters that you see in the top right-hand corner? [S: *or*.] Read the first key word. [S: York.] What is the sound for *or* in *York*? [S: /or/.]

T: Look at the next group of letters in the top right-hand corner. What is another way that the sound /or/ can be written? [S: *ore*.] Read the second key word. [S: store.] How is the sound /or/ written in *store*? [S: *ore*.]

T: Usually when the sound /or/ is followed by a consonant, it is written *or*. When the sound /or/ comes at the end of a word, it is usually written *ore*.

Lines 1-5. Ask S. to study the chart and notice which words have the sound /or/ written *or* and which have the sound /or/ written *ore*. Also, ask him to notice whether the sound /or/ comes in the middle of the word or at the end.

After S. has studied the chart silently, have him read each word aloud. Ask him to tell where the sound /or/ comes in the word and how the sound is spelled. Also, have him tell which words rhyme with *store*.

Review. Have S. read the words aloud again, including the key words. Go down the last column of the chart.

STORY: Pages 109-110 (At the Department Store)

Have S. read the story title and new words. Call attention to words with the sound /or/ and how it is written. Call attention to the contraction *what's* for *what is*. Have S. tell which words have more than one syllable and which word is a compound word [*salesperson*].

Directed silent reading. Ask S. to read page 109 and the first paragraph on page 110 to himself. (Have him mark the place where he is to stop reading.) Ask him to find out why Steve was hurrying and what he planned to buy.

When S. has read up to the place he marked, have him answer the questions. Then discuss these questions:

1. Why was Steve planning to buy a shirt for his brother?
2. Do you think this was the right thing for him to do? Why or why not?
3. What did Steve's friend David tell him about a similar experience he had?
4. Which shirt do you think Steve will buy? Why do you think that? What could keep him from buying that shirt?

Have S. finish the story to see if Steve bought the shirt that S. thought he would. Discuss the lesson that Steve learned. Ask S. if he has had any similar experience. Let S. tell what he thinks will happen when Steve gives the new shirt to his brother.

STORY CHECKUP: Page 110

Go over the directions with S. Then let him work independently. Check his answers. Have him scan the story to make any needed corrections.

Oral reading. Have S. read the part that Steve says while you read the parts of David and the salesperson. If you have several students, they might like to dramatize the story, adding their own ending to show what happens when Steve gives the shirt to his brother.

READING FOR LIVING: Page 111

Have S. read the title and new words. Explain that the symbol *&* stands for the word *and*. The *and* symbol is often used on signs and in ads. It is used in the names of some companies. (Mention some local examples.)

Have S. read the introductory section that explains what a store directory is.

T: Look at the store directory. How is it arranged to make it easier for customers to find things? [S: By floors.] How many floors are there? [S: Four.] This is not a complete directory of everything in the store. But it gives some of the main things. What kinds of things are on the second floor? [S: Clothing for women and children.] What departments are on the fourth floor? [S: Men's and sports.]

Have S. do the exercise by himself. Check his work, and help him find the correct answers for any he had wrong.

II. Skills Practice

Have S. close his book before doing these exercises.

PRACTICE 1: Distinguishing the Sound /or/

T: I will say two words. Tell me which one has the sound /or/ as in *York* and *store*.

wore, were	*start, short*	*form, farm*
fur, for	*born, barn*	*shirt, short*
sore, sir	*sport, spurt*	*store, star*

PRACTICE 2: Identifying Rhyming Words

Write *store*, and have S. read it. Say each pair of words below, and have S. tell which one rhymes with *store*.

more, mare	*wear, wore*	*shore, sheer*
four, fire	*bore, bare*	*wire, wore*

Write *short*, and have S. read it. Say each pair of words below, and have S. tell which one rhymes with *short*.

sport, spark	*snort, snore*	*part, port*
first, fort	*court, cart*	*sort, sore*

PRACTICE 3: Compound Words

Write these words in a column: *salesperson, timetable, weekend, everyone, highway, raincoat*. Ask S. to read each compound word and tell what two words it is made from. As he answers, write the two words. (The last two words here are new, so he may need help with them.)

PRACTICE 4: Ending Blends *nt* and *st*

Write *want* and *most*. Have S. read each word and tell what consonant blend it ends with. Underline *nt* and *st*.

T: Which of these words ends with the *nt* blend:
send, sent? *hunt, hand?* *mint, mind?*

T: Which of these words ends with the *st* blend:
coat, coast? *less, least?* *best, Bess?*

PRACTICE 5: Adjective Endings *-er* and *-est*

Write *cheap*, and have S. read it. Next to it, write *cheaper*. Have S. read the word and tell what ending has been added. Underline *-er*. Next, write *cheapest*, and have S. tell what ending has been added. Underline *-est*.

T: You have had practice with the *-er* ending. The *-est* ending is new. We use *-er* when we are comparing two things. We use *-est* when we are comparing more than two things. Remember, in the story, Steve was comparing the prices of the three shirts. He said, "The green shirt is cheaper than the yellow one, and the red shirt is the cheapest."

Write *slow, short, old* under *cheap*. Have S. read each root word and tell what it would be with the *-er* ending and with the *-est* ending. As he answers, write the *-er* and *-est* forms next to the root word. When you have done this, have S. read all three forms of each word.

Write out the exercise below. Have S. read the first three-sentence paragraph. Then tell him to write the correct form of *old* in the blanks. When he has done this, have him read the completed sentences aloud. Do the second part of the exercise the same way.

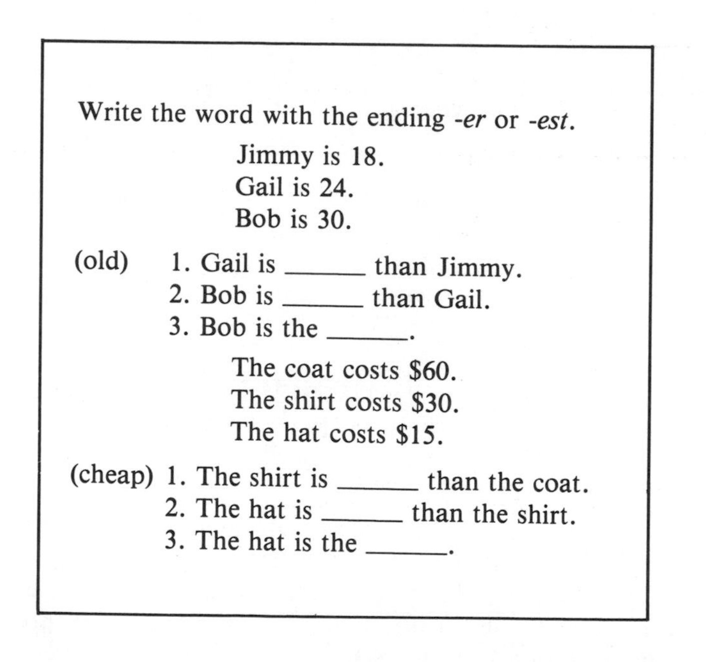

Write the word with the ending *-er* or *-est*.

Jimmy is 18.
Gail is 24.
Bob is 30.

(old) 1. Gail is ______ than Jimmy.
2. Bob is ______ than Gail.
3. Bob is the ______.

The coat costs $60.
The shirt costs $30.
The hat costs $15.

(cheap) 1. The shirt is ______ than the coat.
2. The hat is ______ than the shirt.
3. The hat is the ______.

PRACTICE 6: Alphabetical Order

T: Many lists are made in alphabetical order. Words in a dictionary are listed in alphabetical order. Names in the phone book are in alphabetical order. The words listed in the back of your skill book are in alphabetical order. It is helpful to know the letters of the alphabet in order so that you can find things easily in an alphabetical list.

Ask S. to say the letters of the alphabet in order. If he has any difficulty, have him write the letters in order. Let him keep the list in front of him at all times during the rest of this exercise.

York
or

or

ore = or

store
ore = or

40	forty	for ty	forty
	short	short	short
	corner	cor ner	corner
	tore	tore	tore
	before	bē fore	before

At the Department Store

wore	fourth (forth)	than	what's
sport	floor (flor)	want (wont)	cheapest (cheap est)
shirt	Porter (Port er)	most (mōst)	salesperson (sales person)
sleeve		close (cloze)	

Steve was hurrying up York Street. He was on his way to Porter's Department Store. Porter's was on the corner of York Street and Fourth Street.

Steve's friend David was at the corner. "What's the hurry?" David asked.

"I have to buy a sport shirt before the store closes," Steve said. "I wore my brother's best sport shirt last night, and I tore it. I tore the sleeve on the car door."

"One time, I wore my father's shirt and tore it," David said. "He's still angry that I wore his shirt."

"I want to buy another shirt like my brother's before he gets home," said Steve. "I'm in a hurry. See you later."

Steve looked at a sign on the first floor. It said that men's clothes were on the fourth floor. Steve hurried up to the fourth floor. He went to the men's department. "I want a yellow shirt with short sleeves," he told the salesperson.

"The shirts with short sleeves are over there," said the salesperson.

Steve picked up a red shirt with short sleeves. It cost fourteen dollars. A green shirt cost twenty dollars. "That one costs more than the red one, but it's a better shirt," said the salesperson. "And this yellow one is Porter's best sport shirt," he added.

Steve was thinking, "The best shirt will cost the most." And he was right. The yellow shirt did cost the most. It cost thirty dollars.

"I have forty dollars," Steve was thinking. "The green shirt is cheaper than the yellow one, and the red shirt is the cheapest. But I will have to buy the one that costs the most. The yellow shirt is like my brother's."

"The store is going to close," the salesperson said. "Do you want to buy anything before it closes?"

"Yes," said Steve, "I'll take the thirty-dollar shirt. Here is forty dollars."

Steve got back some change from his forty dollars. He picked up the shirt and hurried to the corner. On the bus, he was thinking, "It cost me thirty dollars to wear a shirt one time! I'll never wear my brother's clothes again."

Story Checkup

order (or der)

In what order did these things happen?
Put a number by each sentence to show the right order.
If you don't know the order, please read the story again.

_____ Steve was hurrying up York Street.

_____ Steve tore his brother's shirt.

_____ Steve looked at a sign on the first floor.

_____ The salesperson showed Steve the best shirt in the store.

_____ Steve got back some change.

_____ Steve gave the salesperson forty dollars.

Reading for Living

& (and) directory (di rec tor y)

Porter's Department Store			
FIRST FLOOR	SECOND FLOOR	THIRD FLOOR	FOURTH FLOOR
Garden Shop Bake Shop Clocks & Watches Coffee Shop Paper	***Women's Clothes*** Skirts, Shirts Dresses, Hats ***Children's Department*** Children's Clothes Baby Clothes	***For the Home*** Beds Sofas & Chairs Dishes Curtains Radios & TVs	***Men's Department*** Coats Shirts ***Sports Department*** Bicycles Tents Boats

This is a store directory. A store directory is a sign. It tells where to find things in the store. The directory is on the first floor. Some stores have a directory on every floor.

Look at this store directory, and answer the questions below.

1. On which floor can you find men's coats? _____
2. On which floor can you find a dress for a baby? _____
3. On which floor can you buy a radio? _____
4. On which floor can you get something to eat? _____
5. Where is the sports department? _____
6. Which floor has things for camping? _____
7. In which shop can you get a loaf of bread? _____
8. Which floor has things for the kitchen? _____

Write each of these words on a separate card: *ad, baby, coat, door, end, fire, gold, home*. Mix up the cards. Ask S. to arrange the words in alphabetical order according to the first letter in each word. Check his work, and help him correct any errors.

Next, write these names on cards: *Chan, Fisher, Green, Hunt, King, Lopez, Mason, Oak, Romano, Stone, White, York*. Mix up the cards. Tell S. that the cards in this set have people's last names on them. Ask him to arrange them in alphabetical order. Tell him to say each letter of the alphabet and look to see if there is a name beginning with that letter. If there isn't, he should go on to the next letter. If S. has difficulty, work with him until he has two or three names in order, and then let him finish by himself. Check his work, and help him correct any errors.

III. Writing

CHECK HOMEWORK: Page 107

Check this page with S. Have him correct any errors in the first exercise by referring back to the story. In the second exercise, have him read aloud each word with an ending and its root word. Check his work for correct spelling, and have him correct any errors.

WRITING LESSON (In Notebook)

Have S. write the titles *Lesson 20* and *Words* and then number from 1 to 20 in two columns.

Words. Give S. time to study the chart and story words. Then dictate these words for him to write. For number 17, give this sentence for the verb *close: The store will close at nine.* When S. has finished, check his work, and have him correct any errors.

1. tore	6. York	11. door	16. want
2. wore	7. short	12. floor	17. close
3. more	8. sport	13. fourth	18. most
4. store	9. forty	14. shirt	19. cheapest
5. before	10. corner	15. sleeves	20. than

Sentences. Dictate the following paragraph, one sentence at a time. Ask S. to write it in paragraph form and to spell out all the numbers.

Steve wore his brother's best sport shirt and tore it. Steve went to Porter's Department Store to get another shirt. He looked at the shirts on the fourth floor. The shirt that cost the most was like his brother's. It was a yellow shirt with short sleeves. It cost thirty dollars. Steve had forty dollars. He got the yellow shirt for his brother. It cost Steve thirty dollars to wear a shirt one time.

Check what S. wrote. Have him correct any errors in spelling, punctuation, or capitalization. Then have S. write the title *Study* and any words he missed in the word and sentence dictation.

The *and* symbol. Show S. how to make the form of the *and* symbol that we use when writing, as below:

Let him practice making the symbol. Then have him write this sign, such as one he might put up on a bulletin board. Have him use his own phone number.

For Sale
Radio & TV
Phone: ___________

Remind S. that we use the *and* symbol in signs and ads. Otherwise, we usually spell out the word *and*.

PRACTICE: Page 112

Have S. read the directions for the first exercise and do it by himself. Check his answers. If he has an error, read the whole row of words to him and have him listen for the ones with the sound /or/.

Go over the directions and sample item for the second exercise with S. Let him complete it by himself. Check his work, and have him correct any errors.

HOMEWORK: Page 113

Go over the directions with S. Also, ask him to observe the store directory the next time he is in a department store and to look for a building directory when he is in an office building.

CHECKING PROGRESS

Applying phonics skills. Make slip strips for the word families and beginning letters listed below, following the directions in Lesson 3.

-orn family: *b, c, h, t, w, th*
-ore family: *b, c, m, s, t, w, ch, sh, st, sn, sc*

Note the number of words on each strip that S. is able to read correctly. Do not give help or further practice at this time.

Word recognition skills. Check your student's progress in the use of word endings by noting his performance on the homework assignment in Lesson 19 and the Practice on page 112 of this lesson. Plan extra practice on any endings that he had trouble with.

Comprehension skills. The Story Checkup in this lesson will help you check your student's progress in recalling the sequence of events in a story. The oral discussion of the story will help you check other comprehension skills listed in the objectives for this lesson.

Practice

Say the words. Circle the words with the sound or.

1.	shirt	short	hurt	shore
2.	tore	wore	are	fire
3.	brother	order	corner	burn
4.	sport	start	floor	door
5.	turn	store	wear	York

Add *-er* to each word, and write the *-er* word in List 1.
Add *-est* to each word, and write the *-est* word in List 2.

	List 1	List 2
cheap	cheaper	cheapest
1. slow	______	______
2. fast	______	______
3. short	______	______
4. high	______	______
5. light	______	______
6. bright	______	______
7. clean	______	______

Homework

Write the missing number word.

first, third, thirty, fourth, fourteen, forty

1. Steve looked at a sign on the ______ floor.
2. He looked at sport shirts on the ______ floor.
3. The cheapest shirt cost ______ dollars.
4. The best shirt cost ______ dollars.
5. Steve gave the salesperson ______ dollars.

Write the missing endings: *-ing*, *-ed*, *-y*, *-ly*, *-er*, *-est*.

1. Sam drives the car very slow___.
2. Steve looks at three shirts, but he doesn't buy the cheap___ one.
3. Kitty lives in a wind___ city.
4. Steve was hurry___ up York Street.
5. Mrs. Oak toast___ the bread over the fire.
6. I am short___ than my brother.

MEETING INDIVIDUAL NEEDS

The next lesson will be a review lesson. Note the skills in which S. needs reinforcement and plan extra practice on them. It will be helpful to have at hand any of the following items that you may need:

- —flash cards for all chart words in Lessons 16-20
- —flash cards for all contractions and compound words in those lessons
- —slip strips and word wheels that you have used in previous lessons or new ones to cover other endings or other word families with vowel sounds that need practice.

In *Focus on Phonics-3*, Practices 20A-20D may be used after Lesson 20. They cover word families with *or, ore*, and *oar,* having the sound /or/.

In the *Workbook for Skill Book 3*, the exercises for Lesson 20 may be used at this time.

LESSON 21

Skill Book 3
Pages 114-117

OBJECTIVES

To help your student:

- review the sound /ō/ and its most regular spellings: *o-e, oa, ow*.
- review the sound /or/ and its regular spellings *or* and *ore*.
- read short stories that review words introduced in Lessons 16-20, especially those with the sounds /ō/ and /or/.
- recognize the sequence of events in a story.
- make inferences from clues in the stories.
- recognize cause and effect.
- interpret feelings of characters in the stories.
- develop further skill in reading practical material such as signs and ads.
- distinguish between the long and short sounds for *o*.
- distinguish the sound /or/ from /ar/ and /er/.
- review the ending blends *ft, mp, nd, nt, st*.
- review long *o* before the ending blend *ld*, as in *old*.
- recognize the contraction *won't* and review other contractions.
- review adding *-y, -ly, -er,* and *-est* to words.
- determine the number of syllables in a word.
- alphabetize words by the first and second letters.
- develop further skill in writing words, sentences, and questions.

INTRODUCTION

T: In today's lesson you will review the sounds /ā/, /ē/, /ī/, /ō/, /or/, and the main ways they are written. You will read four short stories that have many words with the sounds /ō/ and /or/. We'll also go over some of the other things that you have studied in the last five lessons.

I. Reading

CHART: Page 114

Have S. read *Lesson 21* and the lesson title *More Reading with ā, ē, ī, ō, or.*

For each vowel sound, have S. read each key word and tell what the vowel sound is and how it is written.

STORIES: Pages 115-117

T: In these stories, you will find out what happened to some of the people you read about in Lessons 16 through 20.

Story 1: The Ring That Was Stolen. Have S. read the new words *broke* and *stole.*

T: Remember the story about the break-in at Tony Romano's apartment? What were some of the things that were stolen? [S. may give these answers: sofa, gold ring, color TV, $10. If he doesn't remember any of these, have him scan the story in Lesson 16.] Why did the gold ring that was stolen have special meaning for Tony? [S: It was his mother's wedding ring.]

Silent reading. Ask S. to read the whole story to himself and find out if Tony got back any of his things. When he has finished, discuss these questions:

1. Was the police officer who called Tony a man or a woman? How do you know?
2. What might have made it possible for the police to identify Tony's ring? [An inscription inside.]
3. Was Tony more concerned about getting back the ring or his furniture? What shows this?
4. How do you think Tony felt when he got his ring back? How do you think he felt about *not* getting back any of his other things?
5. Have you ever gotten back anything of yours that was lost or stolen? How did you get it back?

Oral reading. Have S. read the story aloud. Notice whether he observes punctuation marks and reads with expression.

Story 2: Joe Quit Smoking

T: Remember the story about the fire at the home of Joe and Rose Stone? How did the fire start? [S: Joe went to sleep with a cigarette in his hand.] Story 2 will tell you what effect the fire had on Joe. In fact, the title will tell you what the effect was.

Have S. read the story title and new words. Call attention to the contraction *won't*, and explain that it stands for *will not*.

Silent reading. Ask S. to read the whole story to himself to find out how Joe was able to quit smoking. When he is finished, discuss these questions.

1. Why did Joe decide to quit smoking?
2. Why was his wife glad that he wanted to quit?
3. Why was it hard for Joe to quit?
4. What were the times that he most wanted to smoke? How was he able to keep from smoking at those times?
5. Have you ever known anyone who quit smoking or gave up some habit? What helped that person to succeed? How might family members or friends be helpful? What are the *worst* things they could do?

Oral reading. Have S. read the story aloud. Note whether he observes punctuation marks and reads with expression. List any words that he misses.

More Reading with ā, ē, ī, ō, or

paper ā	cake a–e	paint ai		day ay
we ē	Pete e–e	eat ea	see ee	key ey
I ī	time i–e	tie ie	night igh	my y
go ō	home o–e	boat oa	show ōw	
York or	store ore			

1. The Ring That Was Stolen

broke stole

One day in October, a police officer phoned Tony Romano. "This is Officer Roberts," she said. "I came to your home when someone broke into it. We think that two men stole your things. We think that we have both men."

Tony said, "Did you find my old gold ring? I hope so."

The officer told him, "Come to the police department, and we'll show you a ring. We think that it is yours."

Tony asked, "Did you find my sofa and other things?"

The officer said, "No, we don't have them yet. If we find anything, we'll let you know."

After a while, Tony got his gold ring back. But he never got back the other things that were stolen.

2. Joe Quit Smoking

quit	morning (morn ing)
won't (wōnt)	instead (in sted)

The morning after the fire, Joe Stone quit smoking. "I'm throwing my cigarettes away," he said. "I won't start another fire in my home."

His wife Rose was glad. She wanted Joe to live many more years. She didn't like smoke in her eyes and nose. She didn't like the smell of smoke in her clothes.

But it was hard for Joe to quit. "I have been smoking for forty years," he said. "If I quit, I won't have anything to do with my hands."

Every morning, Joe wanted a cigarette when he woke up. But he got up and made toast instead. He wanted to smoke when he was home alone. But he painted his boat instead. Joe wanted a cigarette every night before he went to sleep. But he kissed Rose instead.

One morning, Joe told Rose, "I have not smoked for four months. I won't ever smoke again."

3. The End of a Cold Night

forget (for get) young (yung) Jones (Jōnz)

When Bob Jones got stuck in the snow and ice, Sam helped him get his car onto the road again. Then Mr. Jones followed Sam's car. At the corner of Oak and Shore Roads, both cars stopped. Sam opened his window and yelled, "I'm turning here. Can you find your way alone? Your brother's home is two miles ahead. It's at the end of the road. Don't forget to drive slowly."

Mr. Jones yelled back, "I won't forget. Thanks a lot. You're a fine young man."

At his brother's home, Mr. Jones told his story. "I was stuck in the snow. The wind was blowing hard, and it was below zero. A young man stopped to help me. I will never forget that young man. He saved my life."

4. A Shirt Story

"Where is my yellow sport shirt?" Tom asked his brother.

Steve said, "I wore it last night, and I tore it on the car door."

"What?" said Tom. "You tore my best shirt! I wanted to wear it tonight."

"Don't be angry," said Steve. "I got you another one at Porter's Department Store. See, it's yellow, and it has short sleeves just like yours. It cost me thirty dollars."

"Oh," said Tom. "I got my shirt on sale. It was cheaper than this one. You're not a bad brother. You can wear my sport coat if you want to."

"No, thanks," said Steve. "I'm going to a party this weekend, but I'll wear my old coat."

Story 3: The End of a Cold Night

Note: It will help to have a copy of this story that you can mark as S. reads aloud. Also, in the first printing of *Skill Book 3*, a sentence was left out of the first paragraph of this story. After the sentence *Can you find your way alone?* there should be this sentence: *Your brother's home is two miles ahead.* If it is missing in your student's book, write it in the margin and draw an arrow to the point where it is to be inserted.

T: Remember the story in which a young man named Sam stopped to help a man whose car was stuck in the snow? Do you recall how Sam helped him? [S: Sam got the car out for him by rocking it.] What was the last thing Sam suggested that would help the man to find his way through the snowstorm? [S: To follow his car.] (If S. doesn't remember this, have him look at the last paragraph of the story in Lesson 19.)

T: In this story, you'll find out where the man was going and whether he got there safely.

Oral reading. Have S. read the title, new words, and then the whole story orally. As he reads aloud, mark your copy of the story as suggested below. Later, you can use this record to plan extra practice.

1. Underline any place where S. hesitates.
2. Mark through a word if S. says the wrong word. If you have time, write the word that he substitutes.
3. Mark through any ending that is omitted or wrong.
4. Circle any words that are omitted or any punctuation marks not observed.
5. Note his ability to read fluently and with expression.

Discussion. Discuss the following questions.

1. Which way of describing Sam is more accurate? Why?
   a. Would you say that Sam is helpful or unconcerned?
   b. Would you say that he is considerate or rude?
2. Where was Mr. Jones going? Does it seem that he has been there before or not? How can you tell?
3. Why did Mr. Jones think Sam was a fine young man?
4. Why did Mr. Jones say about Sam "He saved my life"? Do you think that was true? Why or why not? What might have happened if Sam had not stopped?
5. Do you think Sam did the right thing in stopping to help Mr. Jones? Why do you think that? Do you think we should always stop to help someone who is having car trouble? Why or why not?
6. Is "The End of a Cold Night" a good title for this story? What other title can you suggest?

Story 4: A Shirt Story

Note: It will be helpful to have a copy of this story that you can mark as S. reads aloud. The procedure for teaching it will be the same as for story 3.

T: Remember the story about Steve? Why was he buying a shirt for his brother? [S: He had worn his brother's shirt and torn it.] In this story, we'll find out what happens when Steve's brother looks for his shirt.

Oral reading. Have S. read the title and the whole story without reading it to himself first. As he reads, make notes as suggested for story 3.

Discussion. Discuss these questions:

1. Does it seem that Steve wore his brother's shirt with or without his brother's permission? What makes you think so?
2. Why did it cost Steve more to replace his brother's shirt than his brother paid in the first place?
3. Why do you think Tom offered to let Steve wear his sport coat?
4. Why do you think Steve turned down Tom's offer?
5. Do you think Steve will wear any of his brother's clothes again any time soon? Why do you think that?
6. Do you think it is a good idea for family members to wear one another's clothes? Why or why not?

READING FOR LIVING (Supplementary Materials)

Use whichever of the following activities will fit comfortably within your lesson period and seem most appropriate to your student's abilities and interests. In each group below, the first activity is for students who need more practice with words that have been introduced. The other activities are for students who are ready for more of a challenge.

Ads. Have S. reread the ads on page 87. Ask different questions from those on the page. Let S. answer orally.

Find or make ads for furniture or other home furnishings. (Look at both want ads and store ads in newspapers.) Try to collect samples with vocabulary that S. has learned or can sound out. Mark the parts you expect S. to read.

Traffic signs. Some of the traffic signs from Lesson 19 can be put on flash cards for extra practice.

Additional flash cards can be made for these traffic signs, some of which have new words.

Road Closed
10 Miles Ahead

Left Lane
Must Turn Left

Right Lane Closed

No Passing Zone

Roadside Park

Texas State Line

Next Exit
3 Miles

Exit 44
Next Right

No Parking
Tow-Away Zone

Phone—Gas—Camping
Next Right

No Dumping

Do Not Throw Litter

Right Lane Ends

One-Lane Road

Street names. Make a few flash cards of street names, using known words. A few examples are: *Shore Road, Oak Street, York Street, Valley Drive.*

Using a local map, find street names made up of words that S. has learned or can sound out. These might end with any of these words: *Street, Drive, Road, Circle, Place, Lane, Highway, Turnpike.* List several of these or put them on flash cards for S. to read.

Store signs. Have S. skim the store directory in Lesson 20. Ask questions different from those in the lesson, and let S. answer orally.

Make flash cards for names of well-known local stores and businesses. Choose names made up of known words or words that S. can sound out.

Make up a simple building directory for an office building. Or, use the one in Lesson 20 of the *Workbook for Skill Book 3* if you have not done so yet.

II. Skills Practice

T: Now we'll review some of the sounds and endings that you have had in the last five lessons.

PRACTICE 1: Distinguishing the Long Sound for *o*

T: I will say three words. Listen and tell which one has the long sound for *o* as in *go:*

snow, snack, stop	*job, Joe, Jay*
gold, God, gulf	*over, ever, offer*

Write the following pairs of words. Have S. read each pair and tell which word has the short sound for *o* and which has the long sound.

rob	*robe*	*cot*	*coat*	*on*	*own*
hop	*hope*	*got*	*goat*		
not	*note*	*rod*	*road*		

PRACTICE 2: Distinguishing the Sound /or/

T: I will say three words. Listen and tell which one has the sound /or/ as in *York* and *store.*

born, barn, burn	*corn, curl, card*
firm, form, farm	*turn, torn, tar*
hurt, hard, horn	*stir, star, storm*
bore, bar, bird	*for, fur, far*

PRACTICE 3: Review Ending Consonant Blends

Write *left, camp, wind, want, toast.* Have S. read each word and tell what consonant blend it ends with. As he answers, underline *ft, mp, nd, nt, st.*

T: I will say two words that end with the same consonant blend. Which of these blends do they end with?

sand, find	*damp, stamp*	*spent, tent*
gift, craft	*roast, most*	*lamp, dump*

PRACTICE 4: Long *o* before Ending Blend *ld*

Write *old, gold, cold, told, sold* in a column. Have S. read *old,* tell what blend it ends with, and tell what the vowel sound is. Point out that, when the letter *o* is followed by the blend *ld,* it usually stands for the sound /ō/. Have S. read the other words in the column.

PRACTICE 5: Contractions

Write the contraction *won't.* Have S. read it and tell the two words it stands for. Write *will not* by *won't.*

Then read each sentence below. Have S. tell what contraction he hears and the two words it is made from. As he answers, write the contraction and the two words.

1. If we find anything, *we'll* let you know.
2. *I'm* throwing my cigarettes away.
3. Rose *didn't* like the smell of smoke.
4. *Don't* be angry.
5. Tom said, "*You're* not a bad brother."
6. *It's* at the end of the road.
7. *I'll* wear my old coat.
8. I *won't* ever smoke again.
9. *That's* a nice shirt.
10. Rose *wasn't* at home when the fire started.

PRACTICE 6: Adjective Ending *-y*

Write these words in a column: *sand, wind, snow, sleep, rain, ice, sun, smoke.* Have S. read each word. Then have him tell what the word would be with *-y* added and how to spell it. Write the new word by the root word. Have S. tell what change, if any, is made in the root word before *-y* is added.

PRACTICE 7: Endings *-ly, -er, -est*

Write these words in a column: *slow, cheap, quick, high, light.* Follow the same procedure as for adding *-y,* but this time have S. add *-ly* to each word. Then have him add the endings *-er* and *-est* to the same root words.

PRACTICE 8: Identifying the Number of Syllables.

Say each word below, and have S. tell the number of syllables.

sandy	*sadly*	*brighter*	*morning*
smoked	*highest*	*department*	*October*

PRACTICE 9: Alphabetical Order

Note: If S. had any difficulty saying the letters in order last time, have him say the letters of the alphabet in order before you begin this exercise. Also, let him refer to a written alphabet during the exercise.

T: In the last lesson, you put some words in alphabetical order according to the first letter. In this exercise, you will learn how to alphabetize words that have the same first letter.

Write *bat, bed, big, boat, bus* on separate cards. Mix up the cards, and ask S. to arrange them in alphabetical order. Explain that, since the first letter is the same, we put them in order according to the *second* letter in each word.

When S. has the five words in order, give him cards for *blow, bright, by,* one at a time. Have him insert each one in alphabetical order. Then have him read all eight of the *b* words in order.

Make another set of cards for these words: *apples, beans, bread, butter, cheese, coffee, eggs, hamburger, matches, milk, potatoes, tea.* Mix up the cards. Ask S. to arrange them in alphabetical order. Tell him to say each letter of the alphabet and look to see if there are any words beginning with that letter. If there are two or more words with the same first letter, he should look at the second letter in each one.

III. Writing

CHECK HOMEWORK: Page 113

Check this page with S. Have him correct any errors. Note which endings, if any, were not added correctly. Plan additional practice on those endings.

WRITING LESSON (In Notebook)

Words. Have S. write the titles *Lesson 21* and *Words* and number from 1 to 20 in two columns. Give S. a chance to study the new words in this lesson. Then dictate the words below for him to write. (You may substitute words from his "Study" list in the last few lessons.) Check his work, and have him correct any errors.

1. broke	6. Jones	11. forty	16. don't
2. stole	7. won't	12. broken	17. over
3. forget	8. quit	13. fire	18. show
4. instead	9. young	14. door	19. store
5. morning	10. fourth	15. we'll	20. order

Sentences. Have S. write *Sentences* and number from 1 to 5. Dictate the following sentences.

1. Did you find my gold ring?
2. Where is my yellow sport shirt?
3. Don't forget to drive slowly.
4. Joe Stone quit smoking.
5. Mr. Jones followed Sam's car.

Check your student's work. Have him correct any errors. Then have him write the title *Study* and any words he missed in the word and sentence dictation.

REVIEW PRACTICE

Write out the exercise shown at the right. Go over the directions with S. Then let him do the page by himself. When he has finished, have him read aloud each sentence in the first exercise. If he circled a wrong word, have him read all three words aloud. Check his answers for the second exercise. If he has any item wrong, have him find the correct answer by referring to the "story."

HOMEWORK (In Notebook)

Explain to S. that the homework is to be done in his notebook. Have him copy these contractions: *we'll, don't, you're, won't, I'm*. Have him read each one aloud and tell the two words it is made from. For homework, he is to write a sentence for each contraction.

Have S. copy these words: *no, know, close, clothes.* Have him read each word aloud and tell what it means. For homework, he is to write a sentence for each word.

Encourage S. to read the stories in the lesson again and to study any words he missed in the dictation.

CHECKING PROGRESS

Comprehension. Note your student's progress in the following areas, as shown in the reading of the stories in this lesson. Plan reinforcement activities for the skills with which he needs the most help.

1. Scanning a story to find certain information.
2. Recognizing the sequence of events.
3. Interpreting the feelings of characters.
4. Making inferences from clues in the story.
5. Recognizing cause and effect.
6. Relating the story to his own experiences.

Word recognition. In the oral reading of stories 3-4, if S. missed five words or less per story, he is doing well. If he missed more, note the types of errors. If they are similar, plan extra practice in the skill needed.

Recording progress. Follow the suggestions in Lesson 6 for recording progress in comprehension and phonics skills. Also, record the number of words and sentences he wrote correctly in the dictation. Note which punctuation marks S. uses correctly.

MEETING INDIVIDUAL NEEDS

If S. did fairly well in this lesson, let him go on to Lesson 22. If he is having much difficulty, plan a supplementary lesson.

In *Focus on Phonics-3*, Practice 21 may be used after Lesson 21. It reviews words with long *o*.

In the *Workbook for Skill Book 3*, the exercises for Lesson 21 may be used at this time.

Circle the right word.

1. Bob's car was stuck in the	show	slow	snow
2. The police didn't find Tony's	sale	sofa	smoke
3. Last night it was five below	zero	zip	York
4. Steve tore his brother's	short	shore	shirt
5. I'll wear my old	cold	coat	boat

Read the story. Write short answers to the questions.

Joan and her mother went to Porter's Department Store. They looked at the store directory to find camping things. The sports department was on the fourth floor. The salesperson helped them find a sleeping bag. Joan's mother paid for it.

1. What was the name of the store? ____________
2. On what floor were the camping things? ____________
3. What did Joan and her mother buy? ____________
4. Who paid for it? ____________

LESSON 22-A

Skill Book 3
Pages 118-122

OBJECTIVES

To help your student:

- recognize the long sound for *u* as in the key word *music.*
- recognize that *u* at the end of a syllable or by itself in a syllable usually stands for the sound /ū/, as in *music* and *menu*.
- read words in which the sound /ū/ at the end of a syllable is represented by *u*.
- distinguish between the long and short sounds for *u*.
- scan a story to find specific information.
- distinguish between fact and fiction.
- read a simple map of North America.
- read factual material to obtain information.
- add the endings *-er* and *-est* to words, doubling the final consonant after a short vowel and adding just *-r* and *-st* when the root word ends in *-e*.
- review changing *y* to *i* before the ending *-es*.
- recognize the root word to which the ending *-ed, -er,* or *-est* has been added.
- determine the number of syllables in a word.
- alphabetize words to the third letter and locate words in an alphabetical list.
- write words and sentences from dictation.

INTRODUCTION

T: You have just one more long vowel sound to study. Please turn to Lesson 22, and find out what it is.

I. Reading

CHART: Page 118

Title and key word. Have S. read *Lesson 22* and tell what vowel sound the lesson is about.

T: Please read the key word. [S: *music*.] How is the sound /ū/ written in *music*? [S: The letter *u*.] How many syllables are in the word *music*? [S: Two.] In the word *music*, the sound /ū/ comes at the end of the first syllable. When the letter *u* comes at the end of a syllable or is by itself in a syllable, it usually stands for the sound /ū/.

Lines 1-6

T: All of the words in the chart have the sound /ū/ written with the letter *u*. Read the words to yourself. Notice how many syllables are in each word. Notice whether the sound /ū/ comes at the end of a syllable or by itself in a syllable.

After S. has studied the chart silently, have him read each word aloud. Call attention to these points:

1. The number of syllables in each word.
2. Which syllable the sound /ū/ is in and whether /ū/ is at the end of the syllable or by itself.
3. The sound /u/ for *a* in *Cuba*.
4. The pronunciation of *ture* in *future*. Remind S. of the same spelling and pronunciation in *picture*.
5. The sound /j/ for *g* in *refugees*.

Review. Have S. read the words aloud again, including the key word. Go down the last column of the chart.

STORY: Pages 119-120 (A Family from Cuba)

Have S. read the title and new words. Ask him to tell which words have the sound /ū/ and where it comes in its syllable. Point out that in *union*, the sound /ū/ does not come at the end of the syllable, but this is very rare. Call attention to the abbreviation *U.S.* and what it means. Ask S. to read each word aloud and tell the number of syllables in the word.

Directed silent reading. Ask S. to read the first three paragraphs to himself and find out who the family is, how they came to the United States and why they came. After S. has answered these questions, discuss the meaning of *refugee*. Explain that all people who move into a new country for any reason are called *immigrants*, but *refugees* refers just to people who are escaping from danger or cruel treatment in their own country.

Ask S. to finish reading the story silently and find out whether the Garcias' life in the United States did turn out well. Have S. give reasons for his answer.

Reading between the lines. Discuss these questions:

1. How many people were there in the Garcia family?
2. Where did the Garcias stay before they found a permanent place to live? Who helped them get settled?
3. At first, was Hugo able to find a job as good as the one he had had in Cuba? Why not? How did getting into a union help Hugo?
4. Why wasn't Rosa able to wait on tables at the snack shop at first? What did she do to become a waitress? Why did she enjoy the job?
5. How was the Garcias' son able to get a university education?
6. How long is the waiting period for immigrants to the United States before they can become U.S. citizens?
7. Is this story fact or fiction?
8. Even though this story is fiction, do you think it is true to life? That is, does it seem like the way things happen in real life? Why or why not?

STORY CHECKUP: Page 120

Go over the directions with S. Then let him work independently. Check his work. If he has any item wrong, have him find the part in the story that gives the answer.

Oral reading. Have S. read the whole story orally. Note his observation of punctuation marks and his ability to read smoothly and with expression.

READING FOR LIVING: Page 121

Have S. read the title of the page and the new words. Have him tell the number of syllables in each word. Point out that the final *y* in *country* is changed to *i* before the ending *-es* in *countries*.

Ask S. to read the first paragraph silently. Then have him locate on the map each country that was mentioned.

Have S. read the second paragraph silently and then locate the states of Texas and Florida on the map. Also, point out the location of the state you live in. (You may want to label it and draw an arrow to it.)

Then explain the directions on the map: north is at the top; south is at the bottom; east is at the right; west is at the left. Label each part of the map with a large letter *N, S, E,* or *W* as you explain. Then ask questions such as the following to be sure S. understands:

1. Is Mexico south of the United States?
2. Is the United States north or south of Mexico?
3. Is Cuba east of Florida?
4. Is our state north of Texas?

Have S. read the last paragraph aloud. Then have him write the answers to the questions. Check his work. Help him correct any errors by referring to the map.

II. Skills Practice

Have S. close his book before doing these exercises.

PRACTICE 1: Distinguishing the Long Sound for *u*

T: Which of these words has the long sound for *u*:

human, hundred?	*fuse, fuss?*	*cube, cub?*
butter, beauty?	*cut, cute?*	*humor, humming?*
union, onion?	*fill, fuel?*	*use, us?*

PRACTICE 2: Determining the Number of Syllables

Say each word below, and have S. tell how many syllables it has.

band	[1]	*Florida*	[3]	*country*	[2]
became	[2]	*forward*	[2]	*biggest*	[2]
menu	[2]	*university*	[5]	*united*	[3]
later	[2]	*countries*	[2]	*refugee*	[3]

PRACTICE 3: Adjective Endings *-er* and *-est*

Write *old, older, oldest* at the head of three columns. Have S. read all three forms. Write *young* in column 1. Have S. tell what it would be with the endings *-er* and *-est* and how to spell these forms. Write *younger* and *youngest* in columns 2 and 3.

Write *big, bigger, biggest*. Have S. read each one. Review doubling the final consonant when the root word ends in a short vowel and one consonant. Add *hot* and *sad* to column 1. Have S. read each one, tell what it would be with the endings *-er* and *-est*, and tell how to spell these forms. Write the words.

Write *fine, finer, finest*. Have S. read each one. Review adding just *-r* or just *-st* when the root word ends in *e*. Add *nice, late, large* to column 1. Have S. read each one, tell what it would be with the endings *-er* and *-est*, and tell how to spell these forms. Write the words.

PRACTICE 4: Changing *y* to *i* before *-es*

Write *story, day, country, key, party, play, lady* in a column. Have S. read each word and tell what it would be with the ending *-s* or *-es*. Have him spell the word with the ending as you write it next to the root word. If necessary, review the rule that after a consonant, final *y* is changed to *i* before adding *-es*. But, *y* is not changed when it comes after a vowel.

PRACTICE 5: Recognizing the Root Word

Write *bigger, biggest, nearer, nearest, studied, played* in column 1. Have S. read each word with the ending and tell its root word. Write the root word in column 2.

Ask S. which root words were changed when the ending was added. Underline *big* and *study* in column 2. Have S. tell what change was made in *big* before the endings *-er* and *-est* were added and why. Have him tell what change was made in *study* before *-ed* was added.

PRACTICE 6: Alphabetical Order

T: In the last lesson, you learned how to alphabetize words that have the same first letter. In this exercise, you'll learn how to alphabetize words that have the same first and second letter.

Write *what, when, which, who, why* on separate cards. Mix up the cards, and ask S. to arrange them in alphabetical order. Explain that, when the first two letters are the same, we put the words in order according to the *third* letter in each word. When S. has finished, check his work and help him correct any errors.

Make another set of cards for these words: *coat, coffee, cold, corner, cost, country*. Follow the same procedure.

III. Writing

CHECK HOMEWORK (In Notebook)

Check the sentences that S. was to write for homework. Note the correct usage of the assigned words, spelling, and punctuation. Have S. make any needed corrections. If he did not do the assignment, have him do some of it in class, and encourage him to finish it at home.

Ū

music

ū

	United States	Ū nīt ed	United States
	Cuba	Cū bu	Cuba
	menu	men ū	menu
	university	ū ni ver si ty	university
	refugees	ref ū jeez	refugees
	future	fū cher	future

A Family from Cuba

Hugo (Hū gō)	Garcia (Gar sē u)	studied (stud yd)	speak
Cuban (Cū bun)	citizen (sit i zen)	forward (for werd)	wait
union (ūn yun)	Florida (Flor i du)	became (bē came)	band
			U.S.

Hugo and Rosa Garcia came from Cuba with their three sons. The Garcia family came to the United States with other Cuban refugees.

The Cuban refugees came to the United States for a better future. They looked forward to a better future for their children. They wanted to be United States citizens.

The refugees came from Cuba on a boat. They came to Florida. At first, they lived in a refugee camp.

A family in Union Park, Florida, became friends with the Garcias. They helped the Garcias find a place to live in Union Park. They helped Hugo and Rosa find jobs.

Hugo was a music teacher in Cuba. He wanted to teach in the United States. But he didn't speak English very well. So Hugo got a job in a band. The band played on weekends. In the mornings, he cut grass and cleaned buildings at a university.

Rosa got a job in a snack shop. At first, she didn't know the words on the menu. So she had to work in the kitchen.

The Garcias had to work very hard. But they looked forward to a better future.

Rosa studied the words and prices on the menu. When she learned to read the menu, she got a better job. She waited on tables at the snack shop. Rosa liked to wait on tables. She liked to speak English with the people that came in.

Hugo got into a union. In the union, he got more money than he did before. He played in a bigger band.

The Garcias' sons looked forward to going to a university. They worked part time and saved their money. Later, each of them studied at a university in Florida.

The Garcias had to wait five years before they became U.S. citizens. They became fine citizens.

Story Checkup

Write a short answer to each question.

1. Where did the Garcias live before they came to the United States? ______________________

2. What state did they come to in the United States? ______________________

3. What city did they live in? ______________________

4. Where did Rosa work? ______________________

5. What job did Hugo have on weekends? ______________________

Reading for Living

country (cun try)	America (U mār i cu)	near
countries (cun tryz)	Mexico (Mex i cō)	north
		biggest (big est)

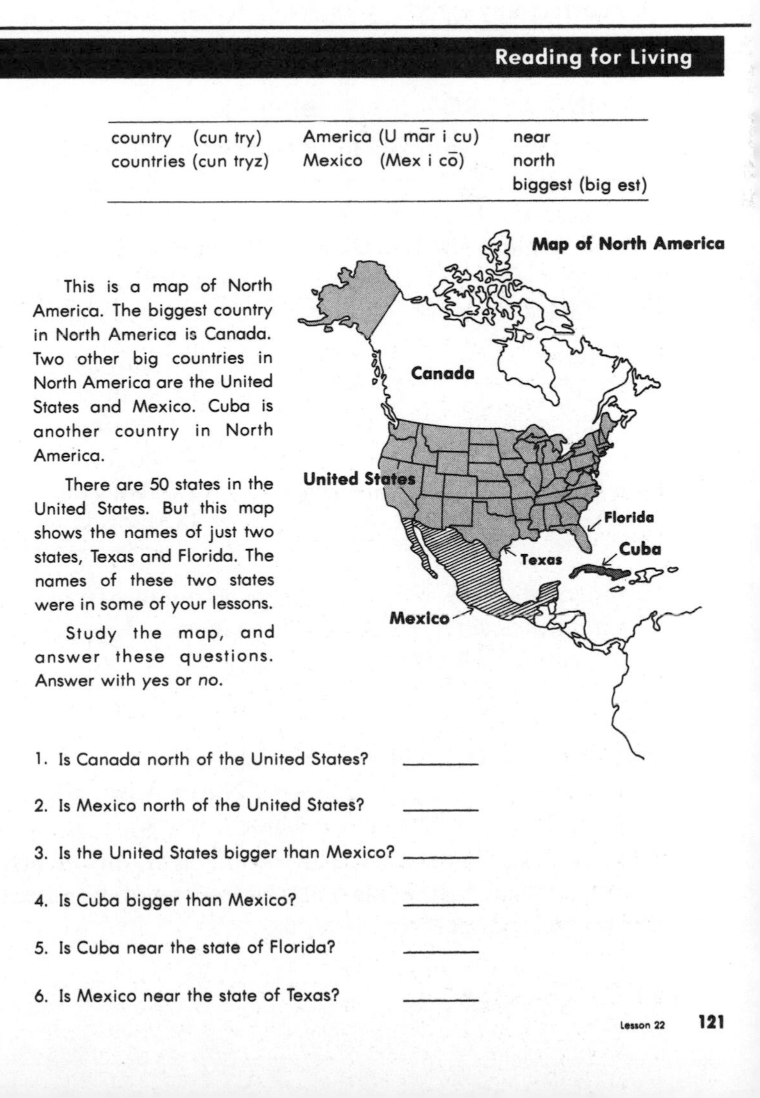

This is a map of North America. The biggest country in North America is Canada. Two other big countries in North America are the United States and Mexico. Cuba is another country in North America.

There are 50 states in the United States. But this map shows the names of just two states, Texas and Florida. The names of these two states were in some of your lessons.

Study the map, and answer these questions. Answer with *yes* or *no*.

1. Is Canada north of the United States? ________
2. Is Mexico north of the United States? ________
3. Is the United States bigger than Mexico? ________
4. Is Cuba bigger than Mexico? ________
5. Is Cuba near the state of Florida? ________
6. Is Mexico near the state of Texas? ________

Practice

Say the words. Circle the words with the sound ū.

1. Hugo	hunt	union	hurt
2. cut	Cuba	church	Cuban
3. future	United	funny	under
4. music	men	checkup	menu
5. young	you	studied	York

Homework

Circle *yes* or *no* to answer the question.

1. Did the Cuban refugees come to Florida on a boat?	Yes	No
2. Did Hugo teach at a university in Florida?	Yes	No
3. Did Rosa learn to speak English?	Yes	No
4. Did the Garcias become citizens in three years?	Yes	No
5. Did the Garcias' sons go to a university in Florida?	Yes	No

122 Lesson 22

WRITING LESSON (In Notebook)

Words. Have S. write the titles *Lesson 22* and *Words* and number from 1 to 18 in two columns. Give S. a chance to study these words: *refugee, future, union, America, Cuba, Florida*. Remind him that *a* stands for the sound /u/ in the last three words. Then, dictate the words below for S. to write. Check his work, and have him correct any errors.

1. music	7. speak	13. university
2. menu	8. wait	14. United States
3. union	9. near	15. became
4. future	10. north	16. country
5. Cuba	11. citizen	17. America
6. refugee	12. Mexico	18. Florida

Sentences. Have S. write *Sentences* and number from 1 to 5. Dictate the sentences below. For sentence 5, ask S. to use the number 60 rather than spelling out the word.

1. The refugees came from Cuba on a boat.
2. Hugo got a job in a band.
3. Rosa and Hugo became U.S. citizens.
4. What is the biggest country in North America?
5. Are there 60 states in the United States?

Check your student's work. Have him correct any errors. Then have him write the title *Study* and any words he missed in the word and sentence dictation.

PRACTICE: Page 122

Have S. read the directions and do the exercise independently. Check his work. If he circled a wrong word, have him read the whole line of words aloud. If he doesn't pronounce the vowel sounds clearly, have him listen as you read the words. Note which sounds he confuses.

HOMEWORK: Page 122

Go over the directions with S. Suggest that he answer the questions without looking at the story and check his answers by referring to the story. Also, suggest that he may want to reread some of the stories in *Skill Book 3* that he especially liked.

CHECKING PROGRESS

Look over the list of skills given in the Introduction to Skill Book 3 in this manual. Note those in which S. will need more practice before going on to *Skill Book 4*, particularly in the areas of phonics, word recognition, spelling, and the fundamental comprehension skills, such as understanding the main idea and recalling facts. Plan to give extra practice in these skills in the remaining lesson periods at this level of instruction. (There will be additional practice on such comprehension skills as sequence of events, cause and effect, and predicting outcomes in *Skill Book 4*. so it is not necessary to give extensive practice in those areas before going on to *Skill Book 4*.)

MEETING INDIVIDUAL NEEDS

If S. needs more review, use any of the suggestions in this manual that would be helpful. For variety, you may want to devise a card game of Concentration, in which pairs of words are matched. For example, you may want to have S. match singular and plural forms of nouns. Write the following words on separate cards: *baby, babies, lady, ladies, city, cities, story, stories, country, countries, university, universities, man, men, woman, women, child, children.*

Mix the cards and spread them out face down. The first player turns up two cards and reads them. If they match, he keeps them and takes another turn. If they do not match, he puts them back face down. The player with the most cards at the end of the game wins.

Concentration might also be played with pairs of words that begin with the same blend, word families such as *pay* and *day*, contractions and their meanings, opposites, or words that sound the same but have different meanings, such as *no* and *know*.

In the *Workbook for Skill Book 3,* the exercises for Lesson 22 may be used at this time.

In *Focus on Phonics-3,* the last section of the workbook (Practices 22-26) deals with irregular spellings for long vowel sounds. You may begin using these exercises now. Or, you may decide it would be less confusing for your particular student if you used them at a later time.

LESSON 22-B

CURSIVE WRITING WORKBOOK: Lesson 1

For students who need cursive writing. Instruction in cursive writing should begin at this point for students who have not already learned this skill. First, complete Lesson 22 of *Skill Book 3* in one lesson period. At the next lesson period, check the homework from Lesson 22. Then, devote the rest of the lesson period to Lesson 1 in the workbook titled *Laubach Way to Cursive Writing*. (Instructions for teaching this workbook are found in the *Cursive Writing Teacher's Guide*.)

In the remaining lessons covering *Skill Book 3* and its correlated reader *Changes*, instruction in cursive writing is recommended—for those who need it—in place of the lesson section heretofore called Writing Lesson. The chart below shows which components needed for this level of instruction are to be used in each of the remaining lesson periods.

Students who are learning cursive writing should, however, continue to use manuscript writing for written exercises in *Skill Book 3* and *Checkups for Skill Book 3*. They should not be expected to use cursive writing for all their writing until they have completed Lessons 1-9 in the *Cursive Writing* workbook.

For students who know cursive writing. Students who have already mastered cursive writing may proceed directly to Lesson 23-A. The material in this manual for each remaining lesson period will include an Alternative Writing Lesson for use with these students.

Lesson 22-A:	Lesson 22 in *Skill Book 3*
Lesson 22-B:	*Cursive Writing* workbook, Lesson 1
Lesson 23-A:	Story 1 in the correlated reader *Changes* Study Helps for story 1 in *Skill Book 3*, Lesson 23 *Cursive Writing* workbook, Lesson 2
Lesson 23-B	Story 2 in the correlated reader *Changes* Study Helps for story 2 in *Skill Book 3,* Lesson 23 *Cursive Writing* workbook, Lesson 3
Lesson 24-A:	Story 3 in the correlated reader *Changes* Study Helps for story 3 in *Skill Book 3,* Lesson 24 *Cursive Writing* workbook, Lesson 4
Lesson 24-B:	Story 4 in the correlated reader *Changes* Study Helps for story 4 in *Skill Book 3,* Lesson 24 *Cursive Writing* workbook, Lesson 5
Checkups for Skill Book 3:	An evaluation of the student's progress, using the 8-page booklet *Checkups for Skill Book 3*
Complete Cursive Writing:	Complete Lessons 6-9 in the *Cursive Writing* workbook in about four lesson periods before beginning *Skill Book 4*. Part of each period should be spent reviewing reading skills that need reinforcement, as revealed by the student's performance in the *Checkups for Skill Book 3*. Supplementary reading materials are needed for these lesson periods; see page 139 for suggestions, and begin now to make preparations.

LESSON 23-A

Changes, Story 1
Skill Book 3, Page 123
Cursive Writing, Lesson 2

In this lesson, S. begins reading the correlated reader *Changes*. Be sure that it is available at this time. No pages from *Changes* are reproduced here.

OBJECTIVES

To help your student:
- use a table of contents.
- read story 1 in *Changes* independently, understanding the main ideas.
- increase the speed of silent reading.
- interpret the feelings of characters in the story.
- recognize cause and effect.
- predict outcomes.
- relate the story to personal experience and values.
- scan the story to locate specific details.
- review words learned in *Skill Book 3* by recognizing them in a new book.
- apply phonics skills in reading new words independently.
- recognize the new contractions *can't* and *we're* and review other contractions.
- recognize the new compound words *anyway, herself, everything, paycheck,* and review other compound words.
- review alphabetical order.
- study Lesson 2 in the *Cursive Writing* workbook, or if S. has already mastered this skill, write words and sentences from dictation.

INTRODUCTION

T: Today you will begin a new book. It is a series of stories that you can read by yourself. Today, you will read the first story. After you finish it, you will read and answer some questions to see if you understood what you read. The questions are in your skill book.

I. Reading in *Changes*

Give S. his copy of *Changes*. Have S. read the title on the cover and again on the title page. Then ask him to turn to page 3. Ask what this page is called [Contents] and what kind of information it gives [title of each story and page number it begins on]. Ask S. to read the title of story 1, tell what page it begins on, and turn to that page.

STORY 1: A Baby Brings Changes

Silent reading (pages 5-9 in *Changes*). Have S. read aloud the story title and new words on pages 5 and 6. Point out that the new words on each page are listed in alphabetical order.

T: In the skill book, you read about Gail and Jason's wedding. This story takes place some time later. Read the first two pages to yourself. Find out what changes Gail and Jason thought having a baby might bring in their way of life. Read the pages quickly and carefully. Let me know when you have finished page 6.

Time your student's reading. Try to do this without his noticing. He should be able to finish in three minutes or less. Make a note of the time, but don't comment on it.

When S. has finished pages 5-6, ask him what things Gail and Jason were worried about. Then ask him to finish the story to find out if the changes they expected did happen. Remind S. to read any new words at the top of the page before reading that page.

S. should be able to finish the story in five or six minutes. Time his reading, and record the time. When S. finishes, have him give a brief answer to the question you asked, but don't go into detail at this time.

Study helps (page 123 in *Skill Book 3*). Have S. read aloud the titles *Lesson 23* and *Study Helps for Changes*.

Also have S. read aloud the heading *A Baby Brings Changes* and the directions for the first set of questions. Have him read each question silently and then aloud. Then have him give his answer. Let him look back at the story if he needs to. (Answers to the second part of numbers 1 and 2 may vary somewhat. The answer to number 6 will depend on the student's own values and experience.)

Let S. do the second exercise by himself. Let him refer to the story if he needs to. Check the answers he wrote, and have him correct any errors.

Oral reading. Have S. read pages 5-6 of the story aloud. Notice his phrasing, intonation, and expression in oral reading. After class, make a written record of your evaluation, but do not comment on it now to S. except to compliment him in some way on his reading.

II. Skills Practice

PRACTICE 1: Contractions

Write *we're* and *can't*. Ask S. to read each contraction and tell the two words it is made from. As he answers, write *we are* and *cannot*. Point out that *cannot* is made up of two words, but they are written together as one word.

Follow the same procedure with these contractions: *you're, don't, won't, wasn't, didn't, we'll, what's.*

PRACTICE 2: *It's* and *its*

Write these two sentences: *It's hard for me to change. The puppy put its cold nose on Joe.* Have S. read each sentence. Underline *It's* and *its*. Explain that *it's* with an apostrophe is a contraction for *it is*. Without an apostrophe, *its* means *belonging to it*. Say each sentence below. Have S. tell what /its/ means and whether it should be written with or without an apostrophe.

1. It's time to go.
2. The cat is sleeping in its box.
3. I think it's raining.
4. The shirt has a spot on its sleeve.
5. The store has many signs in its windows.
6. It's ten below zero.

PRACTICE 3: Compound Words

Write these words: *anyway, herself, everything, paycheck, weekend.* Ask S. to read each compound word and tell the two words that it is made from. As he answers, write the two words next to the compound word.

PRACTICE 4: Alphabetical Order

Write these words on separate cards: *afford, anyway, born, can't, matter, parent, we're.* Mix up the cards and ask S. to put them in alphabetical order. Have him check his own work by looking at the alphabetical list on page 5 of *Changes.* Ask S. to explain why *afford* comes before *anyway* in alphabetical order.

Lesson 23 **Study Helps for *Changes***

A Baby Brings Changes

Tell your answer to each question.

1. What changes in Jason's way of life did the baby bring? Which change do you think upset Jason the most?
2. What changes in Gail's way of life did the baby bring? Which change do you think upset her the most?
3. Why did Gail want to go back to work after the baby came?
4. Why didn't Jason want Gail to work?
5. What plan did Gail and Jason agree to try?
6. What do you think of their plan?

Write a short answer to each question.

1. What was the baby's name? ______________________
2. Where did Jason go one Saturday? ______________________
3. What two things do Gail and Mary plan to share?

____

Is Love Enough?

Tell your answer to each question.

1. Did Maria like to be a migrant? Why or why not?
2. What did Maria tell Carlos the first time he asked her to marry him?
3. In what ways do you think that love changed Carlos and Maria?
4. Do you like the name of the story? What other name can you think of for the story?

Lesson 23 **123**

III. Writing

CURSIVE WRITING WORKBOOK: Lesson 2

If S. is learning cursive writing, check his homework from Lesson 1 in the *Cursive Writing* workbook and do Lesson 2. His only homework for this time will be the homework for Lesson 2 in the *Cursive Writing* workbook.

ALTERNATIVE WRITING LESSON (In Notebook)

If S. has already mastered cursive writing, give the following dictation exercise.

Words. Have S. write the titles *Lesson 23, Story 1,* and *Words.* Have him number from 1 to 20 in two columns. Give S. a chance to study the new words in story 1. Call attention to the hyphen in *baby-sit*, and explain that the hyphen is sometimes used to join two words that are used together as one word. Dictate the words below for S. to write. Check his work. Have him correct any errors.

1. can't	6. we're	11. wonder	16. anyway
2. born	7. Mary	12. matter	17. paycheck
3. kind	8. share	13. agree	18. herself
4. Jay	9. spend	14. parents	19. everything
5. stay	10. upset	15. afford	20. baby-sit

Sentences. Have S. write *Sentences* and number 1 to 8. Dictate the following sentences for him to write:

1. What's the matter?
2. We're going to be parents.
3. Why was Jason upset?
4. We can't afford everything we want.
5. When was Jay born?
6. We need two paychecks.
7. Gail and Mary agreed to share a job.
8. What kind of person is Mary?

Check your student's work. Have him correct any errors. Then have him write the title *Study* and any words he missed in the word and sentence dictation.

If S. is not studying cursive writing, ask him to write the 20 words in his writing lesson in an alphabetical list in his notebook as homework.

MEETING INDIVIDUAL NEEDS

If time remains in the lesson period, spend it on oral reading. Let S. finish reading story 1 aloud. Or, let S. read the part of Jason or Gail while you read the other part. Then reverse roles.

If it took S. much longer to read the story silently than the time that was suggested here, you may want to read the story aloud *with* him, using the duet reading method described in Lesson 15.

LESSON 23-B

Changes, Story 2

Skill Book 3, pages 123-124

Cursive Writing, Lesson 3

OBJECTIVES

To help your student:

- use a table of contents.
- read story 2 in *Changes* independently, understanding the main ideas.
- increase the speed of silent reading.
- interpret the feelings of characters in the story.
- recognize cause and effect.
- predict outcomes.
- relate the story to personal experience and values.
- scan the story to locate specific details.
- review words learned in *Skill Book 3* by recognizing them in a new book.
- apply phonics skills in reading new words independently.
- review the noun ending *-er* as in *worker*, the adjective endings *-er* and *-est*, and the ending *-ly*.
- review contractions.
- study *Lesson 3* in the *Cursive Writing* workbook, or if S. has mastered this skill, write words from dictation and write a short letter based on information in the story.

INTRODUCTION

T: Today you will read another story in *Changes* and discuss the study questions in the skill book. Look at the table of contents in *Changes*. Find the page number for story 2, and then turn to that page.

I. Reading in *Changes*

STORY 2: Is Love Enough?

Silent reading (pages 10-16 in *Changes*). Have S. read the story title aloud. Have him read the new words on page 10 first silently and then aloud.

Ask S. to read the whole story silently to find out the main things that happened and why the story has this title. Remind S. to read any new words at the top of a page before reading that page. Ask S. to let you know when he has finished page 16. Time his reading. He will probably finish in about 10 minutes. When he finishes, have him summarize the story. If he misses any of the main points, refer him back to the story.

Study helps (pages 123-124 in *Skill Book 3*). At the bottom of page 123, have S. read the directions for the set of questions. Have him read each question silently and then aloud. Then have him give his answer. Let him look back at the story if he needs to. The answers to numbers 3 and 4 will depend on the student's own experiences and values as well as his comprehension of the story.

On page 124, have S. read the directions for the set of four questions. Then have him write the answers. Let him refer to the story if he needs to. Check his work, and have him correct any errors.

Oral reading. Have S. read aloud pages 11-12 of story 2, starting with *Day after day* on page 11. Make notes on his progress in oral reading.

II. Skills Practice

PRACTICE 1: Noun Ending *-er*

Write *teach, write, work, read* in a column. Have S. read each word, and tell what it would be with the ending *-er*. As he answers, write *teacher, writer, worker, reader* in a second column.

T: The words in the first column are verbs. They tell what a person *does.* The words in the second column are nouns. They mean *the person* who does that thing.

T: I'll say a sentence using one of these verbs. Then I'll say another sentence with a word missing at the end. Finish the sentence with the noun ending *-er.*

1. Carlos *works* hard. He is a hard ________.
2. Mrs. Smith *teaches* Carlos. She is a good ________.
3. Carlos *reads* well now. He has become a good ______.
4. Maria *writes* letters to Carlos. She is a good letter ________.

PRACTICE 2: Adjective Endings *-er* and *-est*

Write *hard, hot, large, dark, nice, sad, near, bright,* in a column. Next to *hard,* write *harder* and *hardest*. Have S. read *hard, harder, hardest.*

T: Here, the ending *-er* has another meaning. These words all describe something. When we add *-er* to a word that describes something, *-er* means *more*. We can also add the ending *-est* to words that describe; *-est* means *most.*

Have S. read each root word, tell what it would be with *-er* and *-est*, and tell how to spell those forms. Write the *-er* and *-est* forms. Have S. explain when to double the final consonant and when to add just *-r* and *-st*.

PRACTICE 3: Ending *-ly*

Write *sadly, slowly, quickly, lovely, freely, gladly,* in a column. Have S. read each word and tell what the root word is. Write the root words in a second column.

PRACTICE 4: Two Ways to Pronounce *read*

Write these two sentences: *I read the paper every day. I read the paper yesterday.* Read each sentence aloud, and have S. read it after you. Underline *read* in each sentence.

T: The same spelling *r-e-a-d*, stands for /rēd/, as in the first sentence, and for /red/, as in the second sentence. The way the word is used in the sentence or paragraph tells us whether it is /rēd/ or /red/.

Have S. read aloud the last two paragraphs on page 13 of *Changes* and the first paragraph on page 14, observing how *read* is pronounced. Give help if needed.

III. Writing

HOMEWORK: Page 124

Turn to page 124 in the skill book. Go over both sets of directions with S. Ask him to do both exercises for homework and to reread the first two stories in *Changes*.

CURSIVE WRITING WORKBOOK: Lesson 3

If S. is learning cursive writing, check his homework from Lesson 2 in the *Cursive Writing* workbook and do Lesson 3. At the end of the period, remind him that he has homework both in Lesson 3 of the *Cursive Writing* workbook and on page 124 of *Skill Book 3*.

ALTERNATIVE WRITING LESSON (In Notebook)

If S. has already mastered cursive writing, check the list of words you asked him to alphabetize as homework. The words should be in this order: *afford, agree, anyway, baby-sit, born, can't, everything, herself, Jay, kind, Mary, matter, parents, paycheck. share, spend, stay, upset, we're, wonder.*

Help S. correct any errors in his list. Then give him the following word dictation and letter-writing exercises.

Words. Have S. write the titles *Story 2* and *Words* and then number from 1 to 12 in two columns. Give him a chance to study the new words in story 2. Then dictate the words below for him to write. Check his work, and have him correct any errors.

1. crop	4. sadly	7. peach	10. enough
2. free	5. lovely	8. migrant	11. handsome
3. own	6. cotton	9. worker	12. training

Letter writing. Ask S. to pretend that he is Pablo and to write a letter to Maria for Carlos. Have S. look at the top of page 15 in *Changes* to remember the things Carlos wanted to say. S. can use the letter on page 14 as a model letter. He can look in the skill book or in *Changes* for any words he needs. Let him start the letter in class and finish it as part of his homework.

Write a short answer to each question.

1. What was one crop that Maria picked? ______________
2. Who was the farmer's son? ______________
3. Who helped Carlos find a teacher? ______________
4. Which man did Maria love? ______________

Homework

Read the word. Write the two words that it comes from.

1. we're ________ ________
2. what's ________ ________
3. you're ________ ________
4. don't ________ ________
5. won't ________ ________
6. can't ________ ________

Fill in the right word: *we're, can't, won't, what's, don't, you're.*

1. "____________ the matter?" asked Jason.
2. "____________ going to be parents," said Gail.
3. "We ____________ afford a baby-sitter," said Jason.
4. "I ____________ be upset," said Gail to herself.
5. "____________ nice, Carlos," said Maria.
6. "Please, Maria, ____________ let Ed come near you," said Carlos.

124 Lesson 23

CHECKING PROGRESS

Note your student's ability in these skills when he is reading stories in *Changes*:

1. Recognizes most of the words.
2. Understands main ideas.
3. Locates specific detail by scanning page.
4. Understands cause and effect.
5. Interprets feelings of characters.
6. Relates story to own experience.
7. Reads smoothly, in phrases, when reading aloud.
8. Observes punctuation marks.

MEETING INDIVIDUAL NEEDS

If time remains in the lesson period, let S. finish reading story 2 aloud. If it took him much longer to read the story silently than the time that was suggested here, you may want to read the story aloud *with* him, using the duet reading method described in Lesson 15.

If S. is unable to recognize many words, plan extra practice for those words. Use any of the exercises or games suggested in earlier lessons.

In the *Workbook for Skill Book 3*, the exercises for Lesson 23 may be used at this time.

LESSON 24-A

Changes, Story 3

Skill Book 3, Page 125

Cursive Writing, Lesson 4

OBJECTIVES

To help your student:

- use a table of contents.
- read story 3 in *Changes* independently, understanding the main ideas of this factual article.
- increase the speed of silent reading.
- recognize cause and effect.
- predict outcomes.
- understand figurative language in the story.
- interpret feelings of persons in the story.
- distinguish between fact and fiction.
- relate the story to personal experience and values.
- scan the story to locate specific details.
- review words learned in *Skill Book 3* by recognizing them in a new book.
- apply phonics skills in reading new words independently.
- distinguish the vowel sounds /ā/, /ē/, /ī/, /ō/, /ū/ and /or/.
- recognize the new compound words *overcome* and *understand* and review other compound words.
- recognize the suffix *-ness* as in *sickness*.
- study Lesson 4 in the *Cursive Writing* workbook, or if S. has already mastered this skill, write words from dictation and write sentences about story 3.

INTRODUCTION

T: Today you will read another story in *Changes* and discuss the study questions in the skill book. Look at the table of contents in *Changes*. Find the page number for story 3, and then turn to that page.

I. Reading in *Changes*

STORY 3: Helen Keller

Silent reading (pages 17-22 in *Changes*). Have S. read the story title and new words on page 17. Explain that this is a true story about a real person.

1. Ask S. to read page 17 to himself and be ready to tell the main facts it tells about Helen's early life. When S. has finished, have him summarize those facts.

2. Have S. read the new words on pages 18-19. Then ask him to read those two pages silently to find out how Helen's life changed.

Time your student's reading. He should be able to finish the two pages in about three minutes. Record the time, but do not comment on it. When S. has finished, have him tell briefly how Helen's life changed.

3. Have S. read the new words on pages 20-22. Then ask him to finish the story to find out what other things Helen was able to do in her lifetime.

Time his reading, and record the time. When S. has finished, have him give a brief answer to the question you asked, but do not go into detail at this time.

Study helps (page 125 in *Skill Book 3*). Have S. read the titles *Lesson 24* and *Study Helps for Changes.*

Have S. read the heading *Helen Keller* and the directions for the first set of questions. Have him read each question silently and then aloud. Then have him give his answer. Let him look back at the story if he needs to. (The answers to questions 2 and 4 will depend on the student's own opinions.)

Let S. do the second exercise by himself. Let him refer to the story if he needs to. Check the answers he wrote, and have him correct any errors.

Oral reading and discussion. Have S. read pages 18-19 aloud. When he comes to the sentence *A light came on in her dark world* on page 19, ask him to tell in his own words what this means.

Make notes on his progress in phrasing, intonation, and expression in oral reading. Do not comment on your evaluation except to praise S. for some improvement that you have noticed in his reading.

Have S. look at the photo on page 18 and read the caption under it. Help him figure out Helen's age in this picture, taken in 1890, by referring to her birth date (1880) at the beginning of the story. Also, have S. read the caption under the photo on page 21. Help him figure out what year this photo was taken if Helen was 70.

Ask S. to compare this story to the first two stories. What are some ways a person can tell that story 3 is fact, not fiction? S. might mention the photos, the use of actual dates and place names in the story, and the fact that Helen Keller is a well-known person.

II. Skills Practice

PRACTICE 1: Recognizing Long Vowel Sounds

Write *ā, ē, ī, ō, ū, or.* Have S. say the sound for each vowel.

T: (Point to *ā*.) I will say two words. Tell which word has the sound /ā/:

stay, can't	*raise, matter*	*hear, train*
Anne, able	*Braille, sadly*	*great, began*

Follow the same procedure for each of the sounds, using the words listed below.

/ē/	*free, deaf* *lip, peach*	*agree, Helen* *Keller, teacher*
/ī/	*kind, sick* *ear, wild*	*right, Jay* *finish, blind*
/ō/	*own, dot* *write, wrote*	*alone, agree* *throat, thrust*
/ū/	*music, Mary* *use, us*	*touches, beauty* *enough, menu*
/or/	*born, crop* *short, throat*	*afford, world* *water, before*

PRACTICE 2: Recognizing Compound Words

Write *overcome*. Ask S. to read this compound word and tell the two words it is made from. As he answers, write *over* and *come*. Follow the same procedure with *understand, sometimes, anyway, everything, himself, yourself.*

PRACTICE 3: The Ending *-ness*

T: (Write *sick, blind, dark, sad* in a column.) These words all describe something. (Write *sickness* next to *sick*.) We can add the ending *-ness* to some words that describe to change them into nouns.

Have S. read *sick* and *sickness*. Then have him read each of the other root words and tell what it would be with the ending *-ness* added. As he answers, write *blindness, darkness, sadness* in the second column.

Write out the exercise below for S. to do. Go over number 1 with S. as an example. Ask him to fill in the blank with the noun ending in *-ness*. Let S. complete the exercise by himself. Then have him read all the sentences aloud.

1. Helen was very sick.
   The sickness hurt her eyes.
2. Helen was blind.
   Her ________ was a handicap.
3. Helen's world was dark.
   Helen was alone in the________.
4. Helen's parents were sad.
   They were filled with ________.

III. Writing

CHECK HOMEWORK: Page 124

Check the student's homework on page 124 of *Skill Book 3*. Have him correct any errors.

CURSIVE WRITING WORKBOOK: Lesson 4

If S. is learning cursive writing, check his homework from Lesson 3 in the *Cursive Writing* workbook and do Lesson 4. His only homework for this time will be the homework for Lesson 4 in the *Cursive Writing* workbook.

Lesson 24 **Study Helps for *Changes***

Helen Keller

Tell your answer to each question.

1. What three handicaps did Helen Keller overcome?
2. Do you think that Anne Sullivan was a good teacher? Why or why not?
3. In what ways did Helen Keller help other handicapped people?
4. Do you like this story? Why or why not?

Write a short answer to each question.

1. When was Helen Keller born? ________
2. Was she blind and deaf from birth? ________
3. What was the first word that Helen was able to understand? ________
4. What kind of writing can many blind people read? ________

Martin Luther King Jr.

Tell your answer to each question.

1. Why did Dr. King and the others start a bus boycott?
   What change did the boycott make for blacks in Montgomery?
2. Why did blacks in Birmingham have sit-ins?
3. What big changes came from civil rights protests in the 1960s?
4. What do you think of Dr. King's way of fighting for civil rights?

Write a short answer to each question.

1. Who led blacks in their fight for civil rights?
   ____
2. What prize did he win? ________
3. What was Dr. King's age when he was killed? ________

Lesson 24 125

ALTERNATIVE WRITING LESSON (In Notebook)

If S. has already mastered cursive writing, give the following word dictation and sentence-writing exercises.

Words. Have S. write the titles *Lesson 24, Story 3*, and *Words*. Have him number from 1 to 20 in two columns. Give S. a chance to study the new words in story 3. Then dictate the words below for him to write. Check his work, and have him correct any errors.

1. blind	6. lips	11. trust	16. overcome
2. deaf	7. throat	12. touch	17. understand
3. hear	8. great	13. beauty	18. sickness
4. idea	9. wild	14. college	19. remember
5. ears	10. wrote	15. courage	20. possible

Sentences. Ask S. to write four sentences about Helen Keller. When he has finished, check his work, and have him correct any errors. Have him write the title *Study* and any words he missed in the word dictation and sentences. For homework, ask S. to write six more sentences about Helen Keller in his notebook.

MEETING INDIVIDUAL NEEDS

If time remains in the lesson period, let S. finish reading story 3 aloud. If it took him a very long time to read the story silently, read aloud with him using the duet reading method described in Lesson 15.

LESSON 24-B

Changes, Story 4

Skill Book 3, Page 125

Cursive Writing, Lesson 5

OBJECTIVES

To help your student:
- use a table of contents.
- read story 4 in *Changes* independently, understanding the main ideas of this factual article.
- increase the speed of reading.
- recognize cause and effect.
- predict outcomes.
- understand figurative language in the story.
- interpret feelings of persons in the story.
- distinguish between fact and fiction.
- relate the story to personal experience and values.
- scan the story to locate specific details.
- review words learned in *Skill Book 3* by recognizing them in a new book.
- apply phonics skills in reading new words independently.
- review adding the endings *-ing*, *-s*, or *-es*, and *-ed* to verbs and the rules to remember in regard to changes in the root word.
- review the noun ending *-er*.
- know when to change *y* to *i* before the adjective endings *-er* and *-est*.
- recognize two prefixes that mean *not*: *in-* in the word *injustice* and *non-* in the word *non-violent*.
- locate words in an alphabetical list.
- study Lesson 5 in the *Cursive Writing* workbook, or if S. has already mastered this skill, write words from dictation and write sentences about story 4.

INTRODUCTION

T: Today you will read the last story in *Changes* and discuss the study questions in the skill book. Look at the table of contents in *Changes*. Find the page number for story 4, and then turn to that page.

I. Reading in *Changes*

STORY 4: Martin Luther King Jr.

Silent reading (pages 23-30 in *Changes*). Ask S. to read the story title to himself. Tell him to look at the word list if he needs help in pronouncing some of the words in the title. Then have him read the title aloud.

Have S. read the new words on pages 23-24 first silently and then aloud. Point out that *Jr.* is an abbreviation that is used after a man's name. It is used by a man who has the same name as his father.

1. Ask S. to read pages 23-24 silently to find out what kind of boycott started in Montgomery, Alabama, and what caused it. When he has finished, have him answer these questions.

2. Have S. read the new words on page 25, first silently and then aloud. Point out that the word *act* will be used in two ways in this story; sometimes it will mean *behave* and sometimes it will mean a *law* passed by Congress. Also, point out that *non-* in *non-violent* means *not.*

Ask S. to read page 25 silently to find out the result of the bus boycott. When he has finished, have him tell the result.

3. Have S. read the words on page 26, first silently and then aloud. Point out that when *in-* is added to the beginning of *justice, in-* means *not*, so that *injustice* means *not having justice*. Also, write the number 250,000. Tell S. that it is read as two hundred fifty thousand.

Ask S. to read page 26 to find out why Dr. King thought blacks needed to protest. When he has finished, have him give his answer.

4. Have S. read all of the new words in the rest of the story, first silently and then aloud. Also, write the number $54,000. Tell S. this is read as fifty-four thousand dollars.

Ask S. to finish the story to find out more about Dr. King's life. Time his reading. Have him summarize some of the facts that are told about Dr. King.

Study helps (page 125 in *Skill Book 3*). Have S. read the heading *Martin Luther King Jr.* and the directions for the first set of questions. Have him read each question silently and then aloud. Then have him give his answer. The answer to question 4 will depend on his own experience and values as well as his comprehension of the story.

Oral reading and discussion. Have S read the last paragraph on page 26, page 28, and the first three paragraphs on page 29. Ask S. what Dr. King was referring to when he said, "The road ahead will be hard."

Point out that Dr. King's "I have a dream" speech was one of his most famous speeches. Ask S. what kind of dream Dr. King was talking about.

Have S. read the caption under the photo on page 28. Point out that Dr. King is the third from the right in the front row. His wife, Coretta Scott King, is the woman in dark glasses in the front row. Read some of the signs people are carrying to S. since they include several words that he is not yet able to sound out.

You may want to bring a map to class, and help S. find places mentioned in the story.

II. Skills Practice

PRACTICE 1: Endings *-ing, -s* or *-es,* and *-ed*

Write these words in column 1: *march, bomb, plan, stop, vote, change, dream, stay, try, carry.* Write these headings at the top of columns 2, 3, and 4: *-ing, -s* or *-es, -ed.*

Have S. read each root word, and tell what it would be with each of the endings, and tell how to spell each of these forms. Write the words with the endings in the appropriate columns as he answers. Review the rules for doubling the final consonant, dropping final silent *e*, and changing *y* to *i*.

PRACTICE 2: Noun Ending *-er*

Write these words in a column: *worker, driver, marcher, leader, protester.* Have S. read each word and tell what the root word is. Write the root word as he answers.

PRACTICE 3: Changing *y* to *i* before *-er* and *-est*

Write these words in a column: *happy, funny, pretty, windy, heavy, angry, lovely.* Write *happier* and *happiest* next to *happy.*

Have S. read *happy, happier, happiest.* Point out that when a consonant comes before the final *y*, we change *y* to *i* before the endings *-er* and *-est.*

Have S. read each root word, tell what it would be with *-er* and *-est*, and tell how to spell those forms. Write the words with *-er* and *-est* in the appropriate columns as he answers. Finally, have him read all three forms of each word.

PRACTICE 4: Alphabetical Order

Have S. look at the word list at the end of *Changes.* Explain that all the new words in the book are listed here in alphabetical order. Say each word below. Have S. find it in the list and tell the number of the page where the word is first used.

bomb	[25]	great	[22]	violent	[25]
world	[17]	raise	[19]	courage	[22]

Also, have S. look at the word list at the end of *Skill Book 3.* Ask him to go over both lists at home and see how many of the words he can read. If he needs help with a word, the list will tell him where the word was first used.

III. Writing

CURSIVE WRITING WORKBOOK: Lesson 5

If S. is learning cursive writing, check his homework from Lesson 4 in the *Cursive Writing* workbook and do Lesson 5. As this lesson is somewhat longer and more difficult than previous lessons, you may not be able to complete it during this lesson period. If that is the case, follow the directions in the *Cursive Writing Teacher's Guide* for dividing Lesson 5 and its homework into two parts. You may be able to complete the second part after S. does the *Checkups for Skill Book 3* in your next lesson period.

ALTERNATIVE WRITING LESSON (In Notebook)

If S. has already mastered cursive writing, give the following word dictation and sentence writing exercises.

Words. Have S. write the title *Story 4* and *Words.* Have him number from 1 to 24 in two columns. Give S. a chance to study the new words in story 4. Then dictate these words for him to write. For number 6, give a sentence using *won.* When he has finished, check his work, and have him correct any errors.

1. led	7. march	13. lead	19. protect
2. sat	8. bomb	14. dream	20. protest
3. act	9. court	15. peace	21. arrest
4. met	10. jail	16. even	22. empty
5. God	11. fight	17. vote	23. equal
6. won	12. prize	18. spoke	24. freedom

Sentences. Write the following dates in a column: 1955, 1963, 1964, 1965, 1968. Ask S. to write a sentence or two about something that happened in Dr. King's life in each of these years. Let S. refer to story 4. Check his work, and help him correct any errors. If S. needs extra time, let him finish the sentences as homework. If he finishes them in class, for homework, ask him to write a summary of the story in *Changes* that he liked best.

CHECKING PROGRESS

Comprehension skills. Your student's responses to the questions in the Study Helps for stories 3-4 will help you to evaluate his progress in comprehension skills. You may refer to the list of skills given at the end of Lesson 23-B or to the list given in the Introduction to Skill Book 3 in this manual.

Word recognition skills. The homework on page 124 of *Skill Book 3* and the Skills Practice sections of Lessons 24-A and 24-B will help you evaluate your student's progress in recognizing contractions, compound words, and words with various endings. Also, you will have noted his ability to read the new words listed in the stories and to recall old words that he should know by sight.

MEETING INDIVIDUAL NEEDS

If S. is having difficulty with word recognition skills, you may want to plan one or two review sessions before giving the *Checkups for Skill Book 3.* You may use any exercises or games suggested in this manual. You may also want to have S. complete oral reading of story 4, either by himself or in duet reading with you.

In the *Workbook for Skill Book 3*, the exercises for Lesson 24 may be used after story 4 is completed.

CHECKUPS for Skill Book 3

To evaluate the student's progress in reading and writing skills, use the separate booklet *Checkups for Skill Book 3*, available from New Readers Press.

OBJECTIVES

The objectives of the evaluation are:

- to measure the student's progress in relation to the learning objectives of *Skill Book 3*.
- to diagnose the student's strengths and weaknesses in phonics, reading comprehension, and writing.
- to develop the student's confidence in taking a test.

ADMINISTERING THE CHECKUPS

Checkups for Skill Book 3 consists of 10 parts. You may give the *Checkups* in two sessions if you feel that would be desirable for your student. In that case, it is suggested that the first six checkups can be given in one session and the other four in another session.

Simple written directions are given for each part, and most parts have one or two sample questions. Go over the directions and samples with S. before he does each part. Help him correct any errors he makes in the samples, but do *not* correct his errors in the actual test items.

INTRODUCTION

T: Today you will do some checkups on *Skill Book 3*. They will help you find out if there are any sounds or words you need to study more. Some of the checkups will show how well you understand what you read. You will also write some words and sentences.

T: There are no new words in the checkups. And most of the checkups are like exercises you have done in your skill book. There is no certain score that you need to make in order to go on to *Skill Book 4*. But the checkups will help us know what things to give more attention to when you are studying that book.

Give S. his booklet. Have S. read the title *Checkups for Skill Book 3.* Have him read the word *Name* and write his name. Have him read the word *Date* and write today's date.

Checkup 1: Sound-letter relationships (page 1)

S. circles words that have the vowel sound designated at the beginning of the line. The sounds and their regular spellings are those taught in *Skill Book 3*:

1. The sound /ā/ as in *paper*, written with *a-e, ai, ay,* and *a* at the end of a stressed syllable.
2. The sound /ē/ as in *we*, written with *e-e, ea, ee, ey.*
3. The sound /ī/ as in *I*, written with *i-e, ie, igh, i* followed by *ld*, and *y* at the end of a one-syllable word.
4. The sound /ō/ as in *go*, written with *o-e, oa, ow,* and *o* followed by *ld.*
5. The sound /ū/ as in *music*, written with *u* at the end of a stressed syllable.
6. The sound /or/ written with *or* as in *York* or with *ore* as in *store.*

Each of the six sounds is followed by seven words, from which S. chooses the correct ones to circle. There are 28 correct answers in all. There is one sample exercise.

What to do. Have S. read the title *Checkup 1* aloud. Have him read the directions first silently and then aloud. Point to *ē* at the beginning of the sample line, and have S. give the sound. Have him read each word across the line aloud. Ask him to tell which words have the sound /ē/ [*me, see, eaten*]. If he gives a correct answer, have him circle the word. If he indicates a word that does not have the sound /ē/, say the word and have him listen for the vowel sound.

Let S. do the rest of page 1 by himself. Give help only if he does not understand what to do, but do not tell him any of the sounds or words.

Checkup 2: Number of syllables (page 2)

S. reads a word to himself and writes the number of syllables it has. There are eight items and two samples.

What to do. Have S. read *Checkup 2* aloud and read the directions first silently and then aloud. Have him read aloud the first sample word, *alone*, and tell the number of syllables [2]. If his answer is correct, have him write the number. If it is not correct, have him read the word again and tell the number of vowel sounds—or beats—he hears. Then have him write the correct answer. Go over *department* [3] the same way.

Then have S. read each of the words in the checkup to himself and write the number of syllables it has. Do not give any help.

Checkup 3: Compound words (page 2)

S. reads a compound word and writes the two words from which it is made. There are eight items and one sample.

What to do. Have S. read the title *Checkup 3* aloud and read the directions first silently and then aloud. Ask him to read the sample word, *anything*, aloud and tell the two words it is made from. Have him write the words, *any* and *thing*.

Let S. complete the checkup by himself. Do not give any help. If he doesn't know a word, tell him to skip it and do the ones he knows.

Checkup 4: Contractions (page 3)

S. reads a contraction and writes the two words it comes from. There are ten items and two samples.

What to do. Have S. read the title *Checkup 4* aloud and read the directions first silently and then aloud. Ask him to read the sample word, *what's*, and tell the two words that it is made from. Have him write the words, *what is.* Go over the second sample word, *don't*, in the same way.

Let S. complete the checkup by himself. Encourage him to do as many as he can, but do not tell him any words.

Checkup 5: Endings (pages 3-4)

This checkup has four parts, each of which has one or two sample items:

1. Drop the ending, and write the root word.
2. Add *-s* or *-es.*
3. Add *-d* or *-ed.*
4. Write the missing ending.

What to do. Have S. read the title *Checkup 5* aloud. Tell him that there are four parts to this checkup.

Have S. read the directions for the first part silently and then aloud. Go over the sample items with him. Then let him complete the first part by himself. Do not give any help. If he doesn't understand what to do, go over the sample items again.

Follow the same procedure for the other three parts.

Checkup 6: Word recognition (page 5)

S. circles one of three words to complete a sentence. There are 20 items and one sample.

What to do. Have S. read the title *Checkup 6* aloud and read the sample sentence to himself, circle the right word, *table*, and then read the completed sentence aloud. Then let S. complete the page by himself. (It may help him keep his place if he uses a strip of paper as a marker under the sentence he is working on.)

Checkup 7: Listen and write (Page 6)

S. writes 10 words and five sentences from dictation. Sentences include the use of capital letters, period, question mark, apostrophe, prices, street addresses, dates and time of day.

What to do. Have S. read the title *Checkup 7* aloud and read the first set of directions silently and then aloud. Tell him you will say the words for him to write. Dictate the following words:

1. table	6. snow
2. music	7. cold
3. three	8. milk
4. cry	9. sport
5. meat	10. nineteen

Have S. read the second set of directions silently and then aloud. Tell him you will say the sentences for him to write. Remind him to use capital letters where needed and to put in the right punctuation marks. Also, explain that he should write any numbers as numbers instead of spelling out the number words. Give the following two examples for S. to observe as you say and write them:

Example 1: She died at the age of 87.
Example 2: Tony lives at 118 Valley Drive.

Dictate the following sentences for S. to write:

1. Joan lives at 1346 York Street.
2. They paid $14.50 for the gray paint.
3. Is Lee 16 years old?
4. I don't like to drive at night.
5. Jane's wedding will be May 12 at 2:30 p.m.

Checkup 8: Reading comprehension (page 7)

S. reads a short paragraph and then answers five questions by writing short answers. There are two paragraphs with a total of 10 questions. There is no sample.

What to do. Have S. read the title *Checkup 8* aloud and read the directions first silently and then aloud. Ask him to read story 1 to himself and answer the questions.

Follow the same procedure for story 2. Give encouragement, but do not tell S. any words.

Checkup 9: Reading an ad (page 8)

S. reads a grocery ad similar to the one he had in *Skill Book 3.* He answers five questions about the ad.

What to do. Have S. read the title *Checkup 9* aloud and read the directions first silently and then aloud. Then have him do this checkup by himself.

Checkup 10: Filling in an application (page 8)

S. fills in an application similar to the ones he had in *Skill Book 3.*

What to do. Have S. read the title *Checkup 10* aloud and read the directions first silently and then aloud. Explain that this application is like ones he had in the skill book and that applications for many things ask the same questions. Ask S. to fill in this application talking about himself.

Concluding the lesson

Collect the student's booklet when he has completed all he can. Praise him for his effort and concentration. Tell him that you will go over the checkups together at the next lesson. If there is time, have him read aloud from *Changes*, or complete Lesson 5 in the *Cursive Writing* workbook if you have not done so.

SCORING AND EVALUATING THE CHECKUPS

On the student's booklet, mark his *correct* answers rather than his wrong answers. Answer keys are included in the Teacher's Evaluation Form on the next two pages. Use this to record his scores. Do not count the answers to the sample questions. The suggested satisfactory score is about 75% of the perfect score for each part. If you want to translate the student's score into a percentage, divide his score by the perfect score and multiply by 100. The student's scores are for *your* use. The numbers would be of little use to the student.

The scores for each part of the *Checkups* will give you an informal diagnosis of the student's strengths and weaknesses. If he made less than the suggested satisfactory score for a particular checkup, analyze the type of errors he made. List the items that he needs to review the most.

REVIEWING THE CHECKUPS WITH THE STUDENT

At your next session, go over the *Checkups* with S. Be sure to point out his correct answers so that he receives some encouraging news about his work. Help him correct his wrong answers, as you have done with skill book exercises, so that he has a chance to learn from the *Checkups*.

Be sure to give S. some encouraging report about his progress. Also, assure him that the *Checkups* are only one way to measure progress. What he does in class and the use he makes of reading and writing in his daily life are even more important.

CHECKUPS FOR SKILL BOOK 3: Teacher's Evaluation Form

Student's Name ______________________________

Date of Enrollment ____________________ Date Checkups Given ____________________

Section	Perfect Score	Satisfactory Score	Student's Score
1. Sound-Letter Relationships Count 1 point for each correct word circled. Subtract 1 point for each incorrect word circled. 1. ā pan (pay) (cake) back (nail) (baby) key 2. ē (key) (need) (Pete) pet (tea) ten (we) 3. ī (by) (time) did (die) (high) hit (child) 4. ō got (go) (cold) (snow) (road) rock (robe) 5. ū must (music) (menu) (Hugo) Hunt (union) uncle 6. or (for) from (more) (short) (floor) word (born)	28	21	
2. Number of Syllables Each correct answer counts 1 point. 1. before [2] 3. cheese [1] 5. application [4] 7. university [5] 2. slowly [2] 4. radio [3] 6. yesterday [3] 8. salesperson [3]	8	6	
3. Compound Words Each correct answer counts 1 point. Both little words must be written correctly. 1. land lady 5. some times 2. under line 6. every one 3. your self 7. week end 4. time table 8. pay day	8	6	
4. Contractions Each correct answer counts 1 point. Both words that make up the contraction must be written correctly. 1. I am 6. did not 2. it is 7. you are 3. can not 8. we will 4. will not 9. was not 5. I will 10. let us	10	7	
5. Endings Each correct answer counts 1 point. **Drop the ending:** 1. wind 2. tie 3. fly 4. try 5. bake 6. start 7. bright 8. slow 9. big 10. city **Add *-s* or *-es*:** 1. parties 2. keys 3. boys 4. families **Add *-d* or *-ed*:** 1. played 2. cried 3. died 4. painted 5. saved 6. dried **Missing ending:** 1. -ly 2. -er 3. -y 4. -est	24	18	

	Perfect Score	Satisfactory Score	Student's Score
6. Word Recognition Each correct answer counts 1 point. 1. milk 5. plate 9. hockey 13. toast 17. floor 2. April 6. dollars 10. license 14. clothes 18. boat 3. rent 7. eaten 11. China 15. snow 19. menu 4. stairs 8. teacher 12. smoke 16. store 20. future	20	15	
7. Listen and Write Count one point for each *word* spelled correctly. 1. table 3. three 5. meat 7. cold 9. sport 2. music 4. cry 6. snow 8. milk 10. nineteen Count 3 points for each *sentence* written correctly, as follows: — 1 point if a capital letter is used at the beginning of the sentence. — 1 point for correct spelling of all words, including the correct use of capital letters on names; correct placement of apostrophe, colon, decimal point, periods for abbreviations; correct writing of dollar signs and numerals. — 1 point for correct end punctuation—period or question mark. 1. Joan lives at 1346 York Street. 2. They paid $14.50 for the gray paint. 3. Is Lee 16 years old? 4. I don't like to drive at night. 5. Jane's wedding will be May 12 at 2:30 p.m.	25	19	
8. Reading Comprehension Each correct answer counts 1 point. **Story 1:** 1. Carla's class 2. In the park 3. Jason 4. Ham 5. Iced tea **Story 2:** 1. In a coffee shop 2. The menu 3. Breakfast 4. Tony 5. Jane	10	7	
9. Reading an Ad Each correct answer counts 1 point. 1. Ham hamburger 2. 55¢ 3. $2.25 4. $1.10 5. $1.00	6	4	
10. Filling in an Application For each part filled in correctly, count 1 point as follows: **Name** Last–1 First–1 **Date of birth** Month–1 Day–1 Year–1 **Sex** 1 point if correct box is marked **Address** Number and street–1 City–1 State–1 Zip code–1 **Signature** 1 point if signed	11	8	
Total Score	**150**	**111**	

The publisher hereby grants permission to reproduce this Teacher's Evaluation for the purpose of evaluating student performance.

Completing Level 3

Cursive Writing

If your student is learning cursive writing, spend the next few lesson periods completing the first nine lessons in the *Laubach Way to Cursive Writing* workbook before going on to *Skill Book 4.*

When a student has completed Lessons 1-9 in *Cursive Writing*, he will know all the small and capital letters and he will have practiced writing sentences in cursive enough so that he should be able to do the written exercises in *Skill Book 4* in cursive writing. (Lesson 10 in the *Cursive Writing* workbook, which covers some examples of practical everyday writing, may be done at any time after the student has started *Skill Book 4.*)

Review

Part of each lesson period should be spent reviewing reading skills that need reinforcement, as revealed by the student's performance in the *Checkups for Skill Book 3.*

If your student missed many items in the *Checkups*, you may want to spend one or two periods reviewing before going on to *Skill Book 4*, even if he already knows cursive writing.

Reading Practice

For reading practice, use any of the following suggestions that seem most suitable for your student:

1. Oral reading from *Changes*.

2. Silent reading, followed by oral reading, of other material written in familiar vocabulary. You can get a list of local literacy councils that publish material correlated to the Laubach Way to Reading by writing to LLA, Laubach Literacy International, Box 131, Syracuse, NY 13210.

3. Duet reading of material written at the 2nd or 3rd grade level, but not in controlled vocabulary. (See Lesson 15 for a description of the duet reading method.) By reading such material aloud *with* the student, you will help him with any sight words containing spellings that he has not yet learned how to sound out. Try to select material that does not include a very heavy burden of such vocabulary.

The New Readers Press catalog includes several books written at the 2nd and 3rd grade levels, including Sundown Books, which are easy short novels. Suitable materials from other publishers for adults and teenagers with limited reading skills are described in these bibliographies:

- *Reader Development Bibliography,* by the Reader Development Program of The Free Library of Philadelphia, published by New Readers Press.
- *Bibliography of Basic Materials: Reading, English as a Second Language, and the Humanities*, published by Literacy Volunteers of America, 404 Oak St., Syracuse, NY 13203.
- *Books for Adult New Readers*, published by Project: LEARN, 2238 Euclid Ave., Cleveland, Ohio 44115.

4. Language experience stories, which are dictated by the student in his own language. To develop a language experience story, follow these steps:

a. Engage the student in discussion about a topic of interest to him.
b. Ask the student to dictate a summary of the ideas he expressed for you to write down. Sit next to the student, and make sure he watches as you write. If the student is hesitant, you may prompt him or ask questions to guide him, but try to let him give as much of the wording as possible. Write exactly what the student says. Don't try to improve his grammar, but do spell and punctuate correctly.
c. Student and teacher both say each word as it is written. When each sentence is completed, have the student reread it with you, as you point to each word. When the student has completed his dictation (which should be no longer than about five to eight sentences), have him read it aloud with you. Move your hand along under the sentence being read. Finally, you may ask the student to read the selection aloud by himself.
d. Items that occur in the student's language experience story can then be used for a variety of exercises on word recognition, adding or subtracting endings, sequence of events, and the like.

For more ideas on how to use language experience activities, you may be interested in the book *Using Language Experience with Adults*, published by New Readers Press.

Word Recognition Practice

For practice in word recognition skills, you may use any of the exercises or games suggested in this manual. You may also use *Focus on Phonics-3: Long Vowel Sounds* and the Laubach Way to English *Workbook for Skill Book 3* if you have not already done so. (They are described more fully at the end of Lesson 1.)

Review Practices for Lessons 6, 10, 15, and 21

The exercise called Review Practice in Lessons 6, 10, 15, and 21 are given here in a form suitable for photocopying. The publisher hereby grants permission to reproduce these Review Practices for non-profit instructional purposes.

If you are not able to copy these exercises by photocopying or by hand, have S. read them aloud and give oral answers.

Review Practice for Lesson 6

Write the missing word in the sentence.

back	bake	1. Gail will __________ a cake for the party.
hat	hate	2. Kay will pay for the __________.
at	ate	3. Jason __________ a ham sandwich.
man	Main	4. My friend lives on __________ Street.
ran	rain	5. Gail __________ up the stairs.
back	bake	6. When are you coming __________?
tack	take	7. I put up the picture with a __________.
pan	pain	8. Ray has a __________ in his neck.
car	care	9. I am taking __________ of my friend's cat.

Review Practice for Lesson 10

Read each sentence. Circle the words with the sound ē

1. Mrs. Green lives on Second Street.
2. Lee will eat a cheese sandwich.
3. Will you have coffee or tea with your meal?
4. Turkey is cheaper than beef.
5. Steve worked three evenings this week.

Write the missing word in each sentence.

weeds	seeds	1. The farmer will plant some ________________.
peas	fleas	2. Mrs. Green brings a can of ________________.
jeep	deep	3. That river is very ________________.
cream	steam	4. Ed puts ________________ in his coffee.
bees	beach	5. Let's look for shells on the ________________.
chair	cheer	6. I'll ________________ for Pete's hockey team.

Review Practice for Lesson 15

Write the missing word in each sentence.

kit	kite	1. Sam likes to fly a ____________.
fit	fight	2. The two men started to ____________.
but	buy	3. Gail did not ____________ the white dress.
sad	same	4. Ellen Roberts was feeling very ____________.
pin	pie	5. Mike baked an apple ____________.

Read the word. Write the two words it comes from.

it's	_______	_______	that's	_______	_______
I'll	_______	_______	didn't	_______	_______
I'm	_______	_______	wasn't	_______	_______

Each word in List 1 will make a big word with a word in List 2. Write the big word.

List 1	***List 2***	
pay	line	1. payday
under	day	2. ____________________
some	table	3. ____________________
my	thing	4. ____________________
time	self	5. ____________________

Review Practice for Lesson 21

Circle the right word.

1. Bob's car was stuck in the	show	slow	snow
2. The police didn't find Tony's	sale	sofa	smoke
3. Last night it was five below	zero	zip	York
4. Steve tore his brother's	short	shore	shirt
5. I'll wear my old	cold	coat	boat

Read the story. Write short answers to the questions.

Joan and her mother went to Porter's Department Store. They looked at the store directory to find camping things. The sports department was on the fourth floor. The salesperson helped them find a sleeping bag. Joan's mother paid for it.

1. What was the name of the store? ______________________

2. On what floor were the camping things? ______________________

3. What did Joan and her mother buy? ______________________

4. Who paid for it? ______________________

Word List

Skill Book 3 and its correlated reader *Changes* introduce the 543 words and 3 symbols listed below. Variants with *-s, -es, -'s, -s', -ed, -ing,* and *-er* (comparative) are not listed except when *y* is changed to *i* before an ending. New words are listed in their root form when they are used with these previously taught endings. Variants are indented under their root word. Italics indicate a variant of a known word or a word taught earlier as a sight word which is reintroduced and taught phonetically at this level.

Words introduced in titles and directions are starred. The number indicates the lesson in which the word is introduced. The abbreviation *cr* stands for the correlated reader, and the number following it refers to the story number in the correlated reader.

cr. 3 able
cr. 4 act
8 ad
cr. 1 afford
7 again
12 age
15 ago
cr. 1 agree
19 ahead
13 air
cr. 3 Alabama
17 alone
13 a.m.
22 America
20 & (and)
7 angry
cr. 3 Anne
2 * answer
16 anyone
17 anything
cr. 1 anyway
2 apartment
11 application
2 April
cr. 4 arrest
14 arrive
15 as
5 ate
3 away
2 baby
cr. 1 baby-sit
2 baby-sitter
5 bake
8 baker
22 band
3 bank
7 be
8 beans
cr. 3 beauty
22 became
12 been
7 beer
20 before
cr. 3 began
14 behind
19 below
8 best
11 bicycle
22 *–biggest*
1 bill
cr. 4 Birmingham
11 birth
cr. 3 blind
19 blow
18 boat
cr. 4 bomb
cr. 1 born
16 both
cr. 4 boycott
cr. 3 Braille
12 breakfast
14 bright
21 broke
16 broken
12 bus
15 buy
13 by
5 cake
5 came
18 camp
10 Canada
cr. 1 can't
cr. 4 capital
3 card
4 care
1 Carla
cr. 2 Carlos
1 ¢ (cent)
4 chair
13 * change
8 cheap
20 –cheapest
3 check
8 cheese
14 child
14 China
5 church
17 cigarette
14 *–cities*
22 citizen
cr. 4 civil
1 class
9 clean
20 close (cloze)
18 clothes
18 coat
1 coffee
17 cold
cr. 3 college
20 corner
1 cost
cr. 2 cotton
22 country
22 –countries
cr. 3 courage
cr. 4 court
cr. 2 crop
13 cry
13 –cried
13 –cries
22 Cuba
22 Cuban
11 Dallas
5 date
1 David
3 day
cr. 3 deaf
5 dear
14 depart
17 department
7 didn't
13 die
20 directory
1 $ (dollar)
17 don't
16 door
cr. 3 dot
cr. 4 dream
1 drink
11 drive
11 driver
13 dry
13 –dried
8 each
cr. 3 ear
8 eat
8 eaten
7 eight
7 eighteen
7 eighty
7 eleven
cr. 4 empty
18 end
15 English
cr. 3 enough
cr. 4 equal
cr. 4 even
9 evening
4 ever
12 every
17 everyone
cr. 1 everything
11 eye
7 face
13 feel
cr. 3 felt
7 fifteen
7 fifty
cr. 4 fight
14 find
15 fine
15 finish
17 fire
14 flight
20 floor
22 Florida
13 fly
19 follow
21 forget
7 forty
22 forward
7 fourteen
20 fourth
5 frame
cr. 2 free
cr. 4 freedom
13 Friday
22 future
4 Gail
4 gallon
22 Garcia
14 gate
5 gave
17 glad
1 go
cr. 4 God
16 gold
cr. 2 Gomez
cr. 4 grave
4 gray
cr. 3 great
7 Green
3 had
4 hair
1 ham
1 hamburger
cr. 3 handicap
cr. 2 handsome
cr. 2 hard-working
7 *he*
cr. 3 hear
18 heavy
cr. 3 Helen
9 here
cr. 1 herself
14 high
14 * himself
10 hockey
17 home
17 hope
22 Hugo
3 hundred
12 husband
1 *I*
19 ice
19 icy
15 I.D.
cr. 3 idea
11 if
1 I'll
14 I'm
cr. 4 injustice
2 instant
21 instead
7 it's
cr. 4 jail
5 Jane
1 Jason
cr. 1 Jay
18 Joan
17 Joe
21 Jones
cr. 4 Jr.
cr. 4 justice
3 Kay
9 keep
cr. 3 Keller
9 key
cr. 1 kind
19 know
9 labor
2 lady
18 lake
4 landlady
3 last
7 late